# NEW MEXICO FAMILY OUTDOOR ADVENTURE

# New Mexico Family Outdoor Adventure

**An All-Ages Guide to Hiking, Camping, and Getting Outside**

## CHRISTINA M. SELBY

University of New Mexico Press • Albuquerque

ISBN 978-0-8263-6292-6 (paper)
ISBN 978-0-8263-6293-3 (e-book)

Library of Congress Control Number:
2021937743

Founded in 1889, the University of
New Mexico sits on the traditional homelands
of the Pueblo of Sandia. The original peoples
of New Mexico—Pueblo, Navajo, and Apache—
since time immemorial have deep connections
to the land and have made significant
contributions to the broader community
statewide. We honor the land itself and those
who remain stewards of this land throughout
the generations and also acknowledge our
committed relationship to Indigenous peoples.
We gratefully recognize our history.

Cover illustration: Canoeing on the Rio Chama
    in summer, courtesy of the author.
Maps by Mindy Basinger Hill
Composed in Minion Pro and Gotham
All photographs by Christina M. Selby
    unless otherwise noted.

**TO TAYLOR**, my husband and incredible partner in life
who wholeheartedly supports my passion projects,
I couldn't have done this without you.

And my two free-range sons and daily inspiration,
**OSCAR AND CLAYTON**. I look forward
to many more years of adventures with you all!

# Contents

# Hikes

# New Mexico Family Adventure Sites

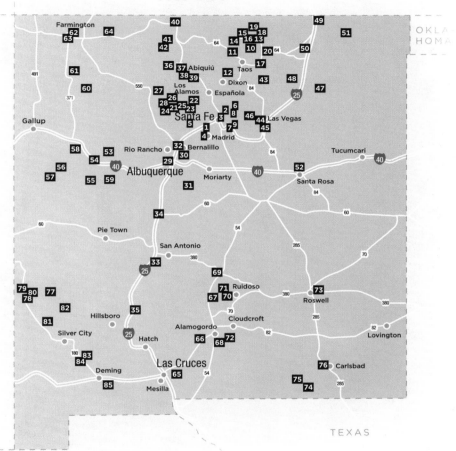

# Preface

The first time I went camping as the mother of a new family, my first son was about 6 months old. I spent most of the time in the tent nursing him and playing on the air mattress. We ventured out in the afternoon for a short hike along the creek, where we splashed around and ogled the colorful wildflowers. Other than that, we barely left the campsite. And yet, that was adventure enough at that moment of our lives.

Today, my two boys are 8 and 13 and variety is the name of the game. Now when we head out for an outdoor adventure, we choose a basecamp with easy access to hiking, biking, fishing, climbing, nature, and more to pique their interest. We still have those leisurely trips where we mostly sit around the campsite and play in the nearby creek, but we make sure to have options if the inspiration strikes (or to distract from digital device withdrawal).

We parents hope that our children will find beauty, health, and truth in the same things we have in our lives. My husband and I agree that spending time in nature is a good thing. And, just as we have the responsibility to feed our kids healthy meals and limit their screen time, we also have the responsibility to take them outside to keep their bodies healthy with recreation and to experience the wonder and awe of nature. We can only have faith that through the introduction we provide, they too will fall in love with nature and grow up working to live in harmony with it.

My husband is a gearhead, so he makes sure we have all the fun outdoor toys with us (bikes, fishing poles, campers, kayaks, etc.). I'm a naturalist, so I choose spots where we are likely to see the kind of flora and fauna whose beauty will bring us all to our knees. When we can find a place that brings those two things together, we know we've found family adventure gold. And there's plenty of gold to be found in New Mexico.

That's what I'm sharing with you here: the best of our adventures. This guide is not a comprehensive list of everything there is to do outside with a family in New Mexico. Instead, it is a curated guide to adventures, each with plenty of options for fun and opportunities to deepen your family's relationship to the natural world. We hope you enjoy time together in nature as much as we do!

Taking in the view of the Florida Mountains in southeast New Mexico

# Introduction

**N**ew Mexico Family Outdoor Adventure Guide describes adventures in nature across the state. Activities include both DIY adventures and those best led by an experienced outfitter. The guide is designed to appeal to parents traveling with children, families traveling with grandparents, and grandparents traveling with grandchildren.

Activities for families in New Mexico abound and include a mix of enjoying nature, learning about natural history, and adventure sports. Hiking, biking, paddling, horseback riding, water play, camping, skiing, sledding, rockhounding, wildlife watching, fishing, climbing, and outdoor cultural activities are all included.

All kids are different. Some kids like the outdoors, some kids don't. Some kids spend their time outdoors observing colors, sounds, and smells, interested by everything around them. Other kids stay in the car or tent playing with their phone and rarely notice their surroundings. So, if you want to enjoy family outdoor adventures, plan for the kids first. Family trips are about them first and only then about you. The key to a great trip is a healthy respect for the needs and interests of your children when exploring the outdoors. Below are some basic rules of thumb to make your trip fun and rewarding.

## Choosing the Right Trip

Choosing an adventure that is too difficult for your children (or yourselves) is an exercise in frustration for everyone. Read descriptions carefully and make sure they are a match for your family's ability. If you are uncertain how far children, grandparents, or you, for that matter, can go or how long they will last, better to choose something short and easy, or take a small bite out of a bigger adventure to start. Better to linger and enjoy each other's company rather than listen to complaining and whimpering. Try also to match your children's interests with an outing's particular attractions, whether they like more active adventures such as rock climbing or swimming or prefer a quiet walk through a field of wildflowers.

## Bring Cool Trail Gear

All you really need for any nature expedition is interest and enthusiasm. However, bringing along an adventure pack filled with fun trail gear will help keep your children engaged along the way. Creating an adventure pack with your children before you head out can be part of the joy of outdoor adventures. Packing materials for simple projects like bark or stone rubbings brings a welcome diversion for kids who need a break. Consider including:

binoculars (7 × 35 power is good for watching birds)

a camera

a penknife, multitool, or scissors

a magnifying glass

small field guides

a notebook

pens, pencils, colored pencils, and an eraser

walking sticks

For siblings, make sure each has their own adventure pack (with exactly the same stuff) and hiking sticks.

## Relax

Enjoying outdoor adventures with children is about enjoying the process, the small achievements, the discoveries you'll share, and being outside together. Save the peak bagging and rushing rapids for special occasions (or for when they are teenagers). The rewards of sharing positive experiences with your children in nature will last a lifetime and build a foundation for your next trip.

## Wilderness Ethics

Over millennia, every ecosystem works toward a balance where every species has its role or niche in the place. Missteps that lead to the loss of species can tip that balance into a swift decline. No matter how much we love the wild places we visit, our way of being in the wilderness can contribute to that decline if we are not careful.

The practice of wilderness ethics and Leave No Trace can help us to leave a place better than when we found it and teach our kids to do the same. Everyone should have access to our rivers, mountains, and deserts and be able to find peace and even healing in those places. But in order for future visitors to experience the same beauty that we do, and for wildlife and wildflowers to continue to thrive, it's important for us to minimize our impact and leave the wilderness intact.

The basic principles are as follows:

Take only pictures.

Carry out your trash and others'.

Don't leave anything permanent.

If you build it, take it down.

Obey rules of parks, monuments, preserves, etc.

Do not feed the animals.

Know how to protect and respect wildlife.

Let wildflowers flourish.

Stay on the trail.

Prepare for the weather and elements.

To learn more, visit www.lnt.org.

## Resources for Equity in the Outdoors

Access to the outdoors is a basic human right, yet historically, many communities of color were excluded from outdoor spaces and recreation. Even today, many still face discrimination and underrepresentation in the outdoors, as well as higher barriers to getting outside. For example, low-income communities (which are often communities of color) tend to be situated in areas devoid of safe parks and green spaces, and many don't have access to transportation to get away, the luxury of being able to take time off to get outside, or the disposable income to buy hiking, camping, and other outdoor gear. We can collectively work to change this and to make the outdoors a more diverse place that is welcoming, inclusive, and accessible to all—a place that better reflects the diversity of our state and our country.

NEW MEXICO OUTDOOR EQUITY FUND helps fund outdoor recreation and education programs for low-income youth, allowing them to engage with their cultural traditions and learn about climate and the environment. Small grants help local governments, Native American communities, and nonprofits run their own outdoor recreation and education programs. *www.nmoutside.com*

**OUTDOOR AFRO** helps people, particularly Black people, equitably reconnect with the natural world through outdoor recreation. Their national network includes groups in nearly 30 states, where trained volunteer leaders facilitate activities such as hiking, biking, camping, environmental education, conservation stewardship, and more. *www.outdoorafro.com*

**LATINO OUTDOORS** is a Latinx-led organization that is breaking down real and perceived barriers to the outdoors by inspiring, connecting, and engaging Latino communities while ensuring their history, heritage, and leadership are valued and represented. *www.latinooutdoors.org*

**MELANIN BASECAMP** is ground zero for promoting diversity in outdoor adventure sports. As a relatively new organization founded in 2016, they are already doing amazing work to raise the visibility of Black, Brown, Asian, Indigenous, and queer people of color in the outdoors. *www.melaninbasecamp.com*

**NATIVE WOMEN'S WILDERNESS** is a nonprofit that is inspiring and raising the voices of Native women in the outdoors. They provide education about the beauty and heritage of their ancestral lands. *www.nativewomenswilderness.org*

**DIVERSIFY OUTDOORS** is a coalition of social media influencers sharing information and promoting diversity in outdoor spaces. They promote equity and access to the outdoors for all bodies, skills, and ages. *www.diversifyoutdoors.com*

## How to Use This Guide

This guide is geared toward families: parents and grandparents traveling with kids of all ages that want to make spending time in the outdoors the central focus of their vacations together. The book is organized around weekend adventures in all seasons. You won't find reviews of resorts or restaurants or ski areas, however. You will find suggestions for great hikes, wildlife viewing areas, floating trips, rock climbing, camping, backpacking, and the occasional RV park (I acknowledge that sleeping on the ground gets harder the older you get). Locations that are accessible to people with disabilities are marked with this symbol: &.

As the fifth largest state in the union, New Mexico is a state of just over 2 million people on 121,590 square miles of land. That's to say, there is a lot of

Bisti/De-Na-Zin Wilderness

open space here to be enjoyed. Almost 23 million acres are public land. The Bureau of Land Management is the major land manager, followed by the National Forest, National Parks, State Parks, etc.

Outdoor recreation is a 9-billion-dollar industry in New Mexico, providing nearly unlimited options for how to spend your time in the outdoors. And still, New Mexico is a down-home state. Some of our facilities are state of the art, but many are intimate, casual, and a little quirky. Not everything is handed to you in New Mexico; it can take a bit of planning to enjoy the enormous wide-open spaces, but that's the unique charm of New Mexico. My family likes it that way, and we hope you will too.

Providing children with rich and repeated experiences in nature throughout their childhood will help them develop a lifelong love and appreciation for the natural world. © Sean Fitzgerald

Natural wonders abound in New Mexico, encouraging kids to discover and explore nature throughout the state. All we really need to do as parents is open the doors and let them walk through.

However, doing some research before you go to find out what wildflowers will likely be blooming, what wildlife you might see, or what minerals you might find can add a sense of discovery when you actually encounter them. Also, finding out ahead of time what hikes, biking trails, climbing routes, or paddling opportunities are appropriate for their skill levels will increase the likelihood that your time together outdoors will be a positive one. In this guide, I recommend many opportunities to both discover and play in nature.

## Discover Nature

The world our children face is different from the one we as parents grew up in. The next several generations will confront the dire environmental and climate challenges that have become front and center in today's world. One of the best ways to counter the despair and overwhelm that may come with the knowledge that our world is threatened is to spend time basking in the beauty of nature. In my experience, taking in the magic of a sunset, riding a bike on a dirt path, listening to an elk bugle in the woods, or finding an intricately decorated wildflower tucked into a forest inspires, refreshes, and calms my kids (and myself).

According to Richard Louv, author of *Last Child in the Woods*, the desire to connect with animals and plants is an innate need for kids. Providing children with rich and repeated experiences in nature throughout their childhood will help them develop a lifelong love and appreciation for the natural world.

How can parents cultivate a love for nature in their kids? Start with sharing your enthusiasm for being in nature, organizing your vacations around experiences in the outdoors, giving them some fun tools like binoculars and butterfly nets, playing outside, and discovering together what is right in front of us.

## Birdwatching with Kids

There are a lot of good reasons for sharing the world of birds with children. First of all, a love of birds gets kids outdoors, and that's a good place for kids (and all of us) to be. An interest in birds can be a child's first step to falling in love with biology and the other sciences. Also, a love of birds may spill over into a desire to protect the wild spaces in which birds live. Keep it fun. Children are active and like to involve all their senses. See if your kids can mimic the honk of a Canada goose or the dance of a sandhill crane. If you find a feather, enjoy the tactile experience of it. If you find an old, abandoned nest, let them touch it, but leave it where you found it, as some birds reuse their nests.

Really engage with a child's questions: How do birds fly? (Bernoulli's principle.) What do crows eat? (A surprisingly large menu of things.) Are those robins fighting or playing? (Let's ask them!) Don't be afraid to say you don't know, but show them how to find the answers to their questions in books, on the internet, or by observing. To study up on birds' unique behavior before you head out with your kids, visit Cornell's All About Birds website (www.allaboutbirds .org) or pick up a laminated pocket guide like *Birds of the Southwest* by Stan Tekiela. A field guide will help you learn the birds' names. It's like having an expert by your side so you'll know what you're seeing.

## Sit Spot

The idea is simple: find a place outside and simply sit down, relax, and just observe. Try getting out of your head and dropping into your senses and consciously look/listen/observe what's happening around you. Notice the squirrels. Watch the birds feeding in the brush and wonder about why they suddenly fly up to a higher branch. What are they doing? What plants and trees are blooming right now? How are these patterns affecting an insect's life? There's a whole world to discover out there, and each new observation is stimulation for your mind. A sit spot can help us recalibrate our minds and develop our natural intelligence.

It's also the simplest way to cultivate naturalist skills like animal tracking, bird language, knowledge of plants, and wilderness survival. Throughout human history, almost all of our sensory stimulation came from cultivating a deep knowledge of birds, plants, trees, animal tracking, wilderness survival skills, and the stories of our elders. Humans are able to tap into their intelligence, emotional openness, and creativity when we are sensorily connected to nature.

Often, sit spots are places you return to regularly over the course of the seasons, so you become aware of the changes and movements of nature. Sit spots can also be a relaxing and interesting activity during family outdoor adventures. Make it part of your family experience each time you plan a trip.

Really little kids like seeing birds that are numerous and easy to find, such as gulls at the beach, pigeons at your local city monument, or chickadees in parks. Ducks are another easy-to-spot option for small children. For parents who want to show their small children more unusual or elusive species, visit a zoo or humane wildlife park. We took our owl-obsessed son to our local wildlife rehabilitation center so he wouldn't think owls only exist in magical movies.

Older kids enjoy more challenging "bird hunts." When you go birdwatching with kids, show them that it's like being a detective or a ninja. To not scare away the birds, you have to move through the forest or meadow stealthily. So, how quiet can you be? Can you creep across the forest floor? Can you use gestures to communicate with each other silently? It's also helpful if you wear clothes that camouflage you. You get to use binoculars or a spotting scope. Bird-watching is an exciting adventure!

Binoculars can be very hard for young children to learn how to use. Kids also have trouble looking through spotting scopes. If your child is advanced enough to use binoculars, show them how to use them by asking kids to read signs at varying distances. Start with the closest and move farther away until they can hold the barrels steady and turn the focus wheel. Once those basics are down, play I Spy to have them find smaller objects.

### RESOURCES FOR BIRDWATCHING IN NEW MEXICO

Tekiela, Stan. *Birds of New Mexico*. Adventure Publications, 2003.

Tekiela, Stan. *Birds of the Southwest*. Adventure Quick Guides, 2014.

New Mexico Game and Fish's Southwest New Mexico Birding Trail: www.wildlife.state.nm.us/recreation/birding

New Mexico Ornithological Society Bird Finding Guide: www.nmbirds.org

New Mexico Tourism Department's Northeast Region Interactive Birding Map: www.newmexico.org

Randall Davey Audubon Center and Sanctuary (Santa Fe): (505) 983-4609, randalldavey.audubon.org

Sangre de Cristo Audubon Society: (505) 988-1708, www.audubonsantafe.org

Visit Albuquerque's "Birding at Three Elevations in Albuquerque": www.visit albuquerque.org

**BEST BIRDWATCHING SITES FOR KIDS**

## Wildlife Viewing and Tracking

"The earth is a manuscript, being written and unwritten every day," wrote John Stokes, master wildlife tracker who offers outdoor tracking courses through the Tracking Project in New Mexico (thetrackingproject.org). Learning to distinguish the tracks of different animals is like learning the letters of the alphabet. A word comes together by reading the movement of the animal from its tracks: Which way was it headed? How fast was it moving? With time and practice, tracks combine with signs on the landscape like scat, animal trails, rubs on a tree, and chewed branches to make paragraphs and then complete books. Tracking allows us to enter the world of animals, to be able to read the books of their lives on the landscape, and to be able to know an animal without disturbing it. Kids, and adults alike, can become enchanted with nature in the process of learning to spot animal signs and understand what they mean.

One of the first things a tracker learns is where to look for animals. Throughout this book, I've included mention of the wildlife you might expect to see at any given location. Wildlife can be notoriously elusive, however. As any experienced guide will tell you, seeing them depends on the weather, the season, and the luck of each person. The best times to view wildlife are typically early in the morning and late in the afternoon/evening when they are on the move.

**RESOURCES FOR WILDLIFE TRACKING**

These field guides will help you get started learning to recognize animal signs on the landscape.

Dinets, Vladimir. *Peterson Field Guide to Finding Mammals in North America.* Houghton Mifflin, 2015.

Halfpenny, James C. *Scats and Tracks of the Rocky Mountains.* Falcon Guide, 2001.

Murie, Olaus J., and Mark Elbroch. *Peterson Field Guide to Animal Tracks.* Houghton Mifflin, 2005.

Stall, Chris. *Animal Tracks of the Southwest.* Mountaineers Books, 1990.

**BEST WILDLIFE VIEWING SITES FOR KIDS**

## Play in Nature

Studies show that spending time in nature is beneficial to our physical and mental health. Among other things, it improves blood pressure, helps lift depression, reduces stress, and boosts short-term memory. Ample, unstructured time outdoors provides kids with the opportunity to experiment with activities such as climbing trees and jumping over streams, and this gives them increased confidence, creative problem-solving skills, gross motor skills, and flexibility. A "wild child" has a greater ability to concentrate and develops an academic edge. Introducing your kids to outdoor adventure sports early can have positive results, and maybe you'll find a new hobby too.

### Hiking

Choose hikes that will appeal to children. Adults enjoy scenery, but often kids need something more to keep them going. Waterfalls, creeks, climbing rocks and boulders, caves, insects, signs of wildlife, wildflowers, signs of ancient peoples—these are the things that appeal to children on the trails. For older kids, the challenge of a summit might do it. The recommended hikes in this book were selected with these things in mind—that something extra for the kiddos.

#### MOTIVATION

There are numerous ways to motivate children. For some, regular stops to enjoy their favorite snacks or drinks is enough. For others, it's the promise of a waterfall or picnic at your destination. For others, encouraging good-natured competition with siblings or peers can do the trick. When a child's motivation wears thin, distraction can be the best solution. Songs, scavenger hunts along the trail, and stories can energize a sluggish child.

#### POSITIVE REINFORCEMENT

I learned the hard way while hiking with my first child that getting upset when they are too tired or unmotivated to continue ruins the experience for everyone. Scolding him didn't improve his performance; it only made us both unhappy and turned him off from anything remotely resembling hiking for years to come. I've been undoing that hike for years. Praise your children for all their achievements in the outdoors. Refrain from criticism if children disappoint you. Positive reinforcement is essential to building a base of good feelings about outdoor adventures.

#### ESSENTIAL GEAR

Bring along what you need to keep kids safe and happy. Make sure your clothing, including shoes, fits the weather.

bug repellent
sunscreen
extra clothing
water (1 quart for each two hours
    on an expedition)
appropriate footwear
walking sticks
a windbreaker or rain jacket
a fleece or sweater
food
first aid kit and medications
lip balm
a hat

### Fishing with Kids

Nick Streit, long-time New Mexico fishing guide and father of two, says action is the name of the game when it comes to fishing with kids. "You really want to think about

In New Mexico, opportunities to fish in freshwater lakes, ponds, small streams, and rivers abound. © Monkey Business/Shutterstock

places to take kids that are going to be productive. I find that kids rarely care about the size of fish, it's more about the quantity over quality."

In New Mexico, opportunities to fish in freshwater lakes, ponds, small streams, and rivers abound. The New Mexico Department of Game and Fish regularly stocks a variety of nonnative species, including rainbow, brown, brook, and lake trout, as well as kokanee salmon (landlocked Pacific sockeye salmon), in lakes throughout the state. Native, though less plentiful, species include the Rio Grande cutthroat trout and the Gila trout. Combine those with bass, catfish, northern pike, and walleye, and you have one of the best places to fish in the country. Some lakes and sections of streams are designated Special Trout Waters, where only artificial flies and lures with single, barbless hooks can be used. Many Indian pueblos and reservations stock ponds or lakes for public fishing. All have restrictions on bag and possession limits.

### FLY VS. REEL AND ROD

When I asked Nick Streit whether it's better to start kids fly fishing or with a reel and rod, his response surprised me. I, like most people, had the perception that fly fishing is a complicated thing. "Really at its root, it's not, especially when you're talking about a single dry fly on a small rod, in a mountain stream. I see it click with kids really quickly. For the young kids, I've always found that fly fishing just comes more naturally." The process of fly fishing can hold a kid's interest. "You're typically continuously moving up a stream, you're casting into different spots, and you're casting a lot more often." All that means action.

### GETTING STARTED

First, choose a location that's going to provide a lot of action. For fly fishing, Streit recommends looking for high mountain streams that have "lots of small, dumb fish." For example, brook trout tend to overpopulate and thrive in New Mexico's high mountain streams. They typically don't grow over 7 or 8", but you can catch lots of them. "That's always a good, safe bet for kids," he says.

Another option is New Mexico's stocked ponds designated for kids under 12 where a fishing license is not required. Try to find one that isn't very crowded. Kids can get enthusiastic with their casting, and we want to catch fish, not people.

There are also a nearly infinite number of man-made lakes throughout the state that are regularly stocked with fish. To increase your chances of catching fish, check out the New Mexico Department of Game and Fish's weekly fishing and stocking report (wildlife.state.nm.us) and go soon after the ponds and lakes are stocked.

### BEST FISHING SPOTS WITH KIDS

8. Cowles Ponds Fishing Site (page 32)
18. Valle Vidal Wildlife Management Unit, Shuree Children's Pond (page 47)
27. San Pedro Parks Wilderness, San Gregorio Reservoir (page 60)
52. Santa Rosa Lake State Park, Blue Hole Fishing Ponds (page 103)

### OUTFITTERS

If fishing is something you want to get into as a family, but parents are not well-versed in casting or fly fishing, think about hiring a guide for a day. "A guide can impart some knowledge on mom and dad that will help them be able to teach the kids on future excursions," says Streit.

If you want some guidance, fishing outfitters are numerous across the state. Nick Streit's personal experience growing up fishing with his angler father and as a member of the US Junior Fly Fishing Team, and now instilling a love of fishing in his own kids, recommends him as a great guide for families. Set up a half- or full-day adventure through one of his shops:

*The Reel Life*
(505) 995-8114
www.thereellife.com

*Taos Fly Shop*
(575) 751-1312
www.taosflyshop.com

### GEAR

If you don't want to spend more time untangling knots than fishing, buy high-quality fly fishing equipment. Forget the cute, cheap fishing rods that are sold for kids. They are usually too difficult to cast, and the line is usually cheap.

### RESOURCES FOR FISHING

New Mexico fishing license: www.wildlife .state.nm.us/fishing/licenses-permits
New Mexico Trout Youth Program: www.newmexicotrout.org/youth/
Trout Unlimited Stream Explorers: www.streamexplorers.org/go-fishing
Weekly fishing and stocking report: www.wildlife.state.nm.us/fishing /weekly-report

## Climbing: Learning the Ropes

Rock climbing has skyrocketed in popularity across the country in the past decade and along with it, New Mexico's climbing locales have gotten much more user- and beginner-friendly. Rock climbing as a family can be a fun and rewarding experience. It builds trust and confidence in kids and adults alike. And if done with safety in mind and encouragement from parents, it can be a great bonding experience.

Make no mistake, climbing outdoors is a risky sport. Once you leave the ground and enter the vertical world, accidents can and do happen. New climbers nurtured in a

Rock climbing at La Cueva
in the Organ Mountains

climbing gym are especially vulnerable to making mistakes. Outdoors, it's best to learn under the supervision of experienced climbers. If you are not yet a climbing family but think it would be fun to learn, there are many options to get started in New Mexico.

## CLIMBING GYMS

Several indoor climbing gyms in New Mexico can teach you the ropes. All of these gyms offer indoor climbing classes and instruction, gear rentals, and instruction on becoming belay certified, which parents will need if they intend to climb outside with kids someday. Summer and after-school youth programs can help build kids' skills for future family adventures.

*Los Alamos Family YMCA Climbing Gym*
(505) 662-3100
climbingwall@laymca.org
https://laymca.org

The Family YMCA offers a variety of rock climbing courses for adults and children, from basic skills to advanced technique. Private instruction and group rates are also available upon request. The gym is open to climbers ages 3+. Climbing equipment is available for rent and includes a helmet, harness, and shoes.

If you are going to be in the area for a while, also check out the Los Alamos Mountaineers Club (www.lamountaineers .org), which hosts monthly presentations from expert climbers and field trips to outdoor rock climbing locations in New Mexico, as well as the occasional class.

*Santa Fe Climbing Center*
(505) 986-8944
climbsantafe@qwestoffice.net
www.climbsantafe.com

Owner Andre Wiltenburg's lively climbing gym provides a great introduction to novices and a place for experts to practice advanced skills. Families can spend a few hours or a day at the gym and, after basic instructions, get on the wall using auto-belay routes. For families who want a deeper dive, sign up for Intro to Climbing classes together or plan a guided adventure with one of their expert staff to a scenic climbing destination.

*Stone Age Climbing Gym*
(505) 341-2016
climb@stoneagegym.com
www.climbstoneage.com

Stone Age Climbing Gym is New Mexico's largest indoor rock climbing gym. Their climbing wall, located in Albuquerque, provides plenty of climbing terrain for climbers of any experience level. No matter what your vertical goals are, they have something to offer, including memberships, a climbing school, group activities, birthday parties, team building, climbing guide services, summer camps, and youth programs.

*Clovis Rock Gym*
(575) 218-3420
clovisrockgym@gmail.com
https://chrisrgym.wixsite.com/clovisrockgym

Located in eastern New Mexico on the border of Texas, Clovis is not the first place you'd expect to find a climbing gym. But for owner Chris Robertson, that's just the point of opening the gym here. He established the gym to provide an entrée to rock climbing to the growing Clovis community, where outdoor recreation opportunities are limited. He offers a safe and family-friendly climbing experience and is working to create a strong climbing community.

## OUTDOOR CLIMBING

A truly safe way to start climbing with your family outdoors is to find an experienced climber to guide you and head to a climbing area with enough beginner options to fill a day or a weekend adventure. Beginner climbs require someone who can set up top rope for you. If you don't already know experienced climbers, chose a guide from one of New Mexico's many outfitters.

*Mountain Skills Rock Climbing Adventures*
    (575) 776-2222
    climb@climbingschoolusa.com
    www.climbingschoolusa.com

This well-established outfitter based in Taos has been guiding novice and experienced climbers alike to some of northern New Mexico's top locations for over 20 years. That's given them plenty of time to dial in a great day adventure for families. Combo rock and rafting trips are also available. You can sign up for an existing trip or hire a private guide to lead your family up rock faces with stunning views at the top.

*The Santa Fe Climbing Center*
    (505) 986-8944
    climbsantafe@qwestoffice.net
    www.climbsantafe.com

Book a half- or full-day adventure with a guide from Santa Fe Climbing Center. Their tours to the beautiful basalt cliffs high above the Rio Grande make a perfect destination for first-timer families. All guided adventures are custom built with two weeks' notice.

### BEST FAMILY CLIMBING AREAS

Once you've sharpened your skills at the gym and are ready to head out for some outdoor family climbs, there's no shortage of great beginner routes. Many of these are in scenic locations in northern New Mexico, but climbing and bouldering locales can be found throughout the state.

12. *Rafting the Rio Grande*, Tres Piedras, Tusas Mountains, Tierra Amarilla (page 37)

*El Rito Sport Area*, Carson National Forest, Taos (page 38)
*Dead Cholla Wall*, Rio Grande Gorge, Taos (page 39)
22. *Pajarito Environmental Education Center*, Gallows Edge, White Rock Canyon, White Rock (page 52)
21. *Santa Fe National Forest/Jemez Mountains (page 51)*
65. *Organ Mountains-Desert Peaks National Monument*, La Cueva, Organ Mountains, Las Cruces (page 127)

### ROCK CLIMBING ORGANIZATIONS

Rock climbing has traditionally been a white man's sport, and much of the opportunity in climbing is geared toward them. But in reality, rock climbing is done by everyone and is for everyone. Today, there is a growing number of resources and programs for kids, women, and people of color who want to rock this sport.

*Elevate*
    www.elevatesantafe.com

Elevate is a Santa Fe–based NGO that creates climbing opportunities for those who have not traditionally been able to take advantage of such activities. Their programs give participants the opportunity to experience the thrills of rock climbing, as well as the physical, mental, and emotional benefits, which they can apply in all areas of their lives. Afterschool programs for kids are run at the Santa Fe Climbing Center.

*Brown Girls Climb*
    www.browngirlsclimb.com

Brown Girls Climb is a small, national, women of color-owned and -operated company created to increase visibility of diversity in climbing by establishing a community of climbers of color, encouraging leadership opportunities for self-identified women climbers of color, and creating

# Climbing Lingo

Rock climbers are generally a friendly and welcoming bunch. However, there is a lot of lingo that can be intimidating and feel exclusive for beginners. Here's some basic climbing jargon to get you started:

**Belay:** The person on the ground is "belaying" the rope, pulling it tightly as the climber moves up the wall and "catching" them when they fall. Belay systems ensure safety for the climber, as well as the belayer.

**Beta:** Beta is information about a climb that you gather before heading out into the field. This may include information about a climb's difficulty, style, length, quality of rock, ease to protect, required equipment, and specific information about hand or foot holds.

**Bouldering:** Bouldering is a style of rock climbing undertaken without a rope and normally limited to very short climbs over a crash pad (a.k.a. bouldering mat) so that a fall will not result in serious injury. It is typically practiced on large natural boulders or artificial boulders in gyms and outdoor urban areas.

**Crag:** A cliff or group of cliffs in any location suitable for climbing.

**Free solo:** Free solo climbing, also known as free soloing, is a form of free climbing where the climber (the free soloist) forgoes ropes, harnesses, and other protective gear while ascending and relies only on his or her physical strength, climbing ability, and psychological fortitude to avoid a fatal fall.

**Grades:** A rating system that informs the difficulty level of climbs. Grades start at 5.1 and currently go up to 5.15c for the most difficult. The grades differ depending on the quality of rock you are climbing and the type of climb (trad, sport, etc.). Don't assume that a 5.9 in a gym will feel the same as a 5.9 outside on real rock. Most beginners can tackle a 5.6–5.8 on their first time out.

**Mountaineering:** Alpine climbing is the oldest, most adventurous, and most dangerous type of climbing. It requires a lot of skills in order to safely climb up a mountain and get back down. A mountaineer must be good at climbing on rock, snow, and ice and be aware of all natural hazards.

**Sport:** Sport climbing relies on permanent anchors fixed to the rock, and possibly bolts, for protection. Since the need to place protection is virtually eliminated, sport climbing places an emphasis on gymnastic-like ability, strength, and endurance—as opposed to the adventure, risk, and self-sufficiency that characterize traditional climbing.

**Top rope:** Top rope climbing is considered the safest way for beginners to learn. In top roping, you will ascend a wall with a rope fixed to an anchor at the top of the route. The rope runs from a belay person on the ground, through the anchor at the top, and back down to the climber.

**Trad:** Traditional climbing, or trad climbing, is when a climber places all gear required to protect against falls (pitons, etc.) and removes it when a passage is complete.

inclusive opportunities to climb and explore for underrepresented communities.

## Brothers of Climbing
www.facebook.com/official.boccrew/

Brothers of Climbing tackles diversity in rock climbing by working toward inclusion, better representation of BIPOC in adventure sports media, and building a tighter community.

## Mountain Project
www.mountainproject.com
(available on the App Store and Google Play)

Mountain Project is the first place most climbers now look for beta about a climb. The advantage of apps is that they are able to be updated with frequency that books are not. Mountain Project is a digital guidebook loaded with 110,000 routes around the world. The database lets you download your chosen crags for offline use. You can browse routes, photos, comments, and ratings from other users. And it's free. Made by Adventure Projects Inc.

### ROCK CLIMBING GUIDEBOOKS

An area guidebook can be a main resource of information on a crag or a specific climb. Guidebooks typically contain a list of all the climbs in a specific area organized by location, along with descriptions, maps, and images. These are available for purchase online or at most climbing gyms. Some guidebooks cover the entire crag, while others are bouldering- or rope climbing-specific. Often, climbing gyms have a library so you don't have to buy all the books yourself.

Beverly, J. Marc. *Jemez Rock & Pecos Area.* Sharp End Publishing, 2006.
Foley, Jay. *Taos Rock Climbs and Boulders of Northern New Mexico.* Sharp End Publishing, 2005.

Jackson, Dennis. *Rock Climbing New Mexico.* Falcon Guide, 2006.
Moore, K. J. *Rock Climbing for the Absolute Beginner: A Complete Guide to Bouldering, Mountaineering, Top-Rope and Trad Climbing.* Independently Published, 2019.

## Paddling

Imagine gliding across a glassy stretch of water reflecting puffy white clouds on a clear day, or tumbling through a narrow river canyon, your adrenaline racing from heart-pumping rapids. Paddling can be a fun, family-bonding activity, and with plenty of flat water and whitewater, New Mexico has something for all skill and adventure levels.

### GETTING STARTED WITH KIDS

For your first paddling adventures, choose a small, calm body of water, such as lakes or ponds with little or no powerboat traffic. Also find a gently sloping sandy beach to launch as steep, mucky, and rocky shorelines will be more challenging to approach the water. The ideal day is sunny and windless, but if it's breezy, start out by paddling into the wind. When you're tired on your way back, paddling into a headwind is a struggle; paddling with a tailwind is a breeze.

Your first time out, plan on an outing, not an expedition. By keeping your paddling time under two hours, you'll avoid fatigue overshadowing the fun. Many outfitters offer kayaks and canoes for rent so you don't have to buy when trying out the sport. To hone your skills and boost your confidence, sign up for a tour, class, or private lessons with an outfitter.

To find out more about where and when to go paddling in and around New Mexico State Parks, visit the website www.emnrd .state.nm.us/SPD/.

Canoeing on the Rio Chama in summer

## OUTFITTERS

*Kokopelli Rafting Adventures, Santa Fe*
(505) 983-3734
www.kokopelliraft.com

Offering guided rafting adventures on the Rio Grande and Rio Chama, gear rentals, and kayaking and stand up paddleboard (SUP) instructional classes.

*Santa Fe Rafting Company, Santa Fe*
(888) 988-4914
www.santaferafting.com

Offering guided rafting adventures on Rio Grande and Rio Chama.

*New Mexico River Adventures, Taos*
(800) 983-7756
www.newmexicoriveradventures.com

Offering a variety of climbing, biking, paddling, and hiking adventures throughout northern New Mexico. They also offer two-day whitewater kayaking clinics for an introduction to the sport. Private and custom instruction also available for those wanting to improve their skills.

*Far Flung Adventures, Taos*
(575) 758-2628
www.farflung.com

Offers combo adventures of rafting, climbing, fishing, and horseback riding trips, including a three-day adventure through the whole of the Rio Grande Gorge down 40 miles of river. Gear rentals available for those who want to venture out without a guide.

*Los Rios River Runners, Taos*
(575) 776-8854
www.losriosriverrunners.com

From half-day to multiday and multisport trips, these guides dish up adventure throughout northern New Mexico. Founded by legendary Rio Grande guide and story-teller Cisco Guevara in the 1970s, they run experienced and extensive guide services.

## Mountain Biking

Mountain biking is a great activity to boost confidence, connect with the great outdoors, and deepen your relationship with your child. It often works best to let the kids set the pace, so let them go first. That way, you know they are riding in their comfort zone. Weather, energy levels, or mood can change a good family ride into an awful one. Having endured too-difficult rides with accompanying complaints, it is usually better to call it off early than prolong the suffering. To start, look for a dirt road, doubletrack, or well-groomed singletrack trails rated as "easy"—flat or gently rolling with no prolonged climbs.

Mountain biking in the badlands of northwest New Mexico

## GEAR

Proper kids' mountain bike gear is essential to helping your young rider build confidence and ride happy. Get them a bike that works well, is properly sized, and is not too heavy. Bike fit matters a lot when mountain biking. For kids, err on the smaller size so they can comfortably put their feet down in a tough spot. Kids' bikes tend to be heavy, but pushing a heavy bike up a hill can ruin a ride. Go lighter when possible. Larger wheels are easier on the bumps. Look for a bike with the biggest wheels available on a frame that fits.

Make sure you have appropriate clothing for the weather. Cover those elbows and knees with pads and riding gloves for hands! A helmet that fits properly and is comfortable to wear is essential.

### BEST MOUNTAIN BIKING AREAS FOR BEGINNERS

### RESOURCES FOR MOUNTAIN BIKING

Included in each region of this book are one to a few beginner trails to get out mountain biking. If you want to go further or are looking for more challenging trails, today's user-updated apps provide a wealth of up-to-date information on mountain biking trails and options for riding.

### Trailforks
www.trailforks.com

Trailforks is available as a mobile app and desktop platform for mountain bike trails, routes, parking areas, shops, and land-ownership with trailhead information and photos and videos of rides.

### MTB Project
www.mtbproject.com

MTB Project is available as a mobile app or in a web browser. These user-created trail maps and information about rides will show you how to get out on the trails wherever you are.

## Cross-Country Skiing

Cross-country skiing is easy to learn, a great workout, and a fun way to continue outdoor adventures into the winter. It's a very accessible outdoor activity and can be enjoyed by family members of all ages.

To make sure cross-country skiing is fun for children, avoid strenuous hills and scary out-of-control downhill runs. The key is for your child to have a positive experience on the first few cross-country ski outings. Bring some chocolate treats, talk about animal tracks, and encourage your child. Remember, as with any outdoor activity, it's more about spending time together in nature than clocking miles or reaching a destination.

It may be easier (and a good decision) to have your child begin with a qualified instructor in a class with other kids. After the lesson, join them for an easy, family cross-country ski at a nearby destination.

*New Mexico Cross-Country Ski Club*
instruction@nmccskiclub.org
www.nmccskiclub.org/instruction/beginner
-instruction

Based in Albuquerque, each winter the ski club offers free lessons for beginning cross-country skiers and trips to Cumbres Pass above Chama or the Enchanted Forest Trails near Red River.

## BEST BEGINNER CROSS-COUNTRY SKI TRAILS

## SNOWSHOEING

Snowshoeing is another fun and accessible winter activity. Even easier than cross-country skiing, all you need to do is strap snowshoes on your boots and grab a couple of poles. No training is necessary, and if you can hike, you can snowshoe.

A few essential pieces of equipment include a pair of snowshoes and waterproof boots. Poles are helpful for maintaining balance but optional. Often, kids are better without poles. Waterproof pants or gaiters help keep you warm and dry. You can snowshoe anywhere you like to hike in the summer, as long as you avoid steep slopes that can pose an avalanche hazard. Always bring a map or GPS device, as trails can be harder to follow in deep snow.

## DRESSING FOR WINTER ACTIVITIES

Even if it is cold outside, if you're snowshoeing or cross-country skiing, you can expect to heat up fast and perspire. If the sweat you produce during this workout is trapped next to your skin, you will eventually feel chilled. Not only is this cold, clammy feeling uncomfortable, it can be dangerous, especially as you start to cool down. Protect yourself and your kids by dressing in lightweight layers that you can remove quickly and stow away as you warm up. Start with a lightweight, synthetic base layer of long underwear, then a lightweight, stretchy insulator, such as a breathable fleece sweater or vest, then top it off with a lightweight and versatile shell jacket. Look for underarm zippers, as well as venting pockets and back flaps.

Depending on the activity and weather, a lightweight, wicking layer and stretch fleece pant are often all you'll need on the bottom. In deeper snow, you can wear gaiters to protect your feet and ankles, but carry lightweight shell pants with side zips just in case the weather gets nasty. Always bring a light hat and gloves made for movement (not alpine gloves), regardless of the weather or your activity level. As with the rest of your clothing, synthetic materials work best for protecting you against the extremes—plus they don't itch!

You may be tempted to outfit your kids with all hand-me-downs. But improper equipment may be too heavy, cause blisters, and expose kids to frostbite. Poorly equipped kids won't be able to glide, turn, or stop as quickly when cross-country skiing, which quickly takes the fun out of it for them. Get properly fitted equipment and clothing for children, whether it's brand new or previously used. Some shops have buy-back, trade-in, or long-term rental plans for children's gear, so check with ski shops in your area.

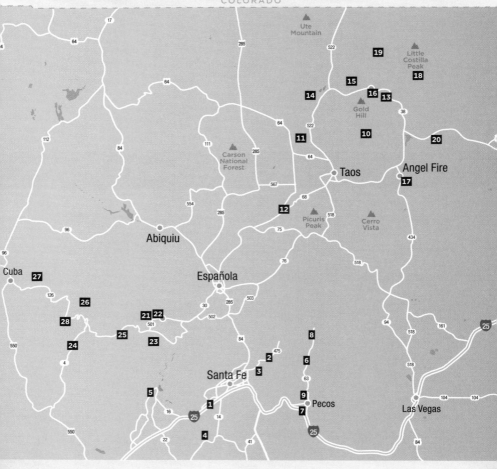

| 1 | Leonora Curtin Wetland Preserve | 15 | Cabresto Reservoir |
| 2 | Sangre de Cristo Mountains | 16 | Red River |
| 3 | Randall Davey Audubon Center and Sanctuary | 17 | Angel Fire Bike Park |
| 4 | Cerrillos Hills State Park | 18 | Valle Vidal Wildlife Management Unit |
| 5 | Kasha-Katuwe Tent Rocks National Monument | 19 | Rio Costilla Park |
| 6 | Pecos Canyon State Park | 20 | Cimarron Canyon State Park |
| 7 | Pecos National Historical Park | 21 | Santa Fe National Forest/Jemez Mountains |
| 8 | Cowles Ponds Fishing Site | 22 | Pajarito Environmental Education Center |
| 9 | Monastery Lake | 23 | Bandelier National Monument |
| 10 | Carson National Forest | 24 | Jemez Historic Site |
| 11 | Natural Hot Springs | 25 | Valles Caldera National Preserve |
| 12 | Rafting the Rio Grande | 26 | Natural Hot Springs |
| 13 | Enchanted Forest Cross-Country Ski Area | 27 | San Pedro Parks Wilderness |
| 14 | Rio Grande del Norte National Monument | 28 | Fenton Lake State Park |

The Sangre de Cristos and Jemez are the main mountain ranges of northern New Mexico. Spanish for "blood of Christ," *Sangre de Cristo* refers to the phenomenon of alpenglow, when snow-covered mountains turn pink in the evening light. The range, which starts in Colorado and ends at Santa Fe, is the southernmost subrange of the Rocky Mountains.

Wheeler Peak (elevation 13,161') is located in the Wheeler Peak Wilderness, between Taos and Angel Fire. To the north of Wheeler Peak, the range continues at high elevation through the Latir Peak Wilderness and on into Colorado.

Hermit's Peak rises above Las Vegas (NM) on the southeastern flank, marking the very southern edge of the Pecos Wilderness. Santa Fe, an art mecca of the Southwest, sits at the southwestern edge of the Pecos Wilderness, where Santa Fe Baldy towers above.

Another group of high peaks is located in between Taos and Santa Fe—the Truchas Peaks (*truchas* is Spanish for "trout"), topping out at 13,102' (South Truchas Peak).

In the summer, cattle and sheep graze in the mountains, where forests provide firewood for the nearby villages. The traditional lifestyles of the original Native American inhabitants and Spanish colonizers are very intertwined with these mountains.

The mountains have also become a hot spot for outdoor recreation and adventure and as a place to connect with nature. The range contains a number of ski areas: Taos Ski Valley, Angel Fire, Sipapu, Pajarito, and Santa Fe. Because of its southerly location, the skiing climate in the Sangre de Cristos and Jemez is warmer and sunnier than in states to the north. Hiking trails are found throughout the ranges, providing endless possibilities for exploration.

Elk, deer, bighorn sheep, black bear, and other montane species are readily encountered. Trout inhabit the streams and lakes, including the rare and brilliantly colored Rio Grande cutthroat trout, found only in the headwaters of mountain streams. Rainbow and brown trout are found at the lower elevations. Wildflowers are abundant throughout the summer, while golden and orange aspen enliven autumn.

## Santa Fe and Surrounds

Although Santa Fe is famous for its culture and art, the natural beauty surrounding the high desert city is a destination in its own right. The Sangre de Cristo Mountains frame the eastern edge of the city, where hikers, backpackers, mountain bikers, and equestrians access a network of trails that crisscross the Santa Fe National Forest and take visitors into the magnificent Pecos Wilderness. Nature preserves and state parks afford the opportunity to experience the unique wetlands and ancient volcanoes in the foothills and desert. Summer brings an abundance of wildflowers to the mountains, autumn paints aspen forests gold, and winter finds ample snow for snowshoeing and cross-country skiing. Day trips and overnight camping are both possible within the natural abundance found here.

## 1. Leonora Curtin Wetland Preserve

(505) 471-9103

www.santafebotanicalgarden.org

**Nearest Town:** Santa Fe

**Best Season to Visit:** Spring–fall

**Visitor Information:** The preserve is open only on weekends from May to October.

**Getting There:** From Santa Fe, take I-25 south to Exit 276 for NM 599. Turn left onto Frontage Road at the stoplight. Follow I-25 along Frontage Road for about 3 miles. Watch for the sign for the preserve and the parking area on the right at a large metal gate.

Spend a fall afternoon sitting under ancient cottonwood trees, listening to their golden leaves rustle in the wind while the kids climb their enormous branches. In summer, admire the fields of yerba mansa and learn about these ancient medicinal wildflowers from the docents. Find a tiny hummingbird nest in the cottonwood branches or willows.

Managed by the Santa Fe Botanical Garden, this 35-acre preserve protects a rare ciénega habitat that is quickly disappearing throughout the Southwest. Ciénegas, spring-fed wet meadows in otherwise arid lands, are often home to rare species found nowhere else in the world.

A trail circles the property under huge cottonwood trees, around a pond with a boardwalk, and through the high desert landscape. Bring a field guide and work with your kids to identify dragonflies abundant around the pond. Color and wing shape are the main clues. Songbirds are found throughout the preserve. This is a wonderful place to have a picnic and spend

Fall colors in the aspen groves of the Sangre de Cristo Mountains outside of Santa Fe

a leisurely afternoon admiring nature together.

## 2. Sangre de Cristo Mountains

In Santa Fe's backyard, the Sangre de Cristo Mountains are a well-loved and well-used recreational and natural area. The piñon-juniper scrublands at the base give way to cool conifer forests and alpine tundra at the summits. Santa Fe Baldy is the highest peak near Santa Fe, rising to 12,631'. A network of trails, from the Dale Ball Trails in the foothills to the Skyline Trail at the top, crisscross the Santa Fe National Forest and take hikers into the Pecos Wilderness. Ski Santa Fe hosts events throughout the year. Hyde Memorial State Park's interpretive trails inform visitors about the flora and fauna of the area. Mountain bikers, equestrians, hikers, cross-country skiers, and snowshoers share and enjoy the trails and campgrounds.

### WILDLIFE

Watch for signs of elk, mule deer, mountain lions, bobcats, and black bears. Marmots and pika hang out at high elevation.

### BIRDWATCHING

In the Black Canyon Campground and surrounds, watch for Williamson's sapsuckers, Hammond's flycatchers, western tanagers, red-breasted nuthatches, white-breasted nuthatches, pygmy nuthatches, mountain chickadees, Steller's jays, and western warblers. At higher elevations, starting at the Ski Santa Fe basin, find blue grouse, hermit thrushes, house wrens, juncos, cordilleran flycatchers, Lincoln's sparrows, gray jays, and Clark's nutcrackers.

### HIKE | BORREGO/BEAR WALLOW LOOP

**Distance:** 4.3 miles lollipop
**Difficulty:** Easy
**Getting There:** From Santa Fe, take Artist Road to the Santa Fe Ski Basin. At 8.5 miles from the start of Artist Road, turn into the small gravel parking area on the left.

A year-round stream and enchanting forest make this a great route with kids. The trail starts at the far-left corner of the parking area. Hop on the Borrego Trail, an old route along which sheepherders brought their flocks to market in Santa Fe. Along the trail, ask kids to search out the old livestock corral (now covered in weeds) and a faded sign from a historic mica mine. Pass through sublime montane forest with abundant seasonal wildflowers to a mountain stream near the junction with the Winsor Trail. Those hiking with smaller children may want to linger by the water and return the way you came for a shorter hike. Otherwise, turn left onto the Winsor Trail heading downhill to the junction with Bear Wallow Trail, which climbs up following a stream for a while and returns you to the

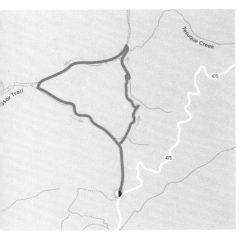

**BORREGO/BEAR WALLOW LOOP**
4.3 miles lollipop

parking area. This is an excellent trail for cross-country skiing and snowshoeing in the winter. Stay alert for fast-moving mountain bikers on the Winsor Trail.

### MOUNTAIN BIKING

Santa Fe and Los Alamos have lively mountain biking scenes with well-maintained trails. The most well-known is the Winsor Trail, which cuts a steep decline from the Santa Fe Ski Basin to downtown Santa Fe. Most of this trail is for expert riders, though portions can be tackled by beginners. Good beginner trails in the area include Bayo Point Trail and Aspen Ridge in the mountains and Rail Trail and La Tierra Trails on the desert floor.

### SANTA FE SKI LIFT RIDES IN FALL

(505) 982-4429
www.skisantafe.com

For a popular family adventure, hop on the ski lifts at Ski Santa Fe to enjoy the expanse of golden aspens blanketing the mountain in September and early October. The 20-minute ride up the mountain affords treetop views of the changing colors and a long view of Santa Fe in the valley below. Once up at the top, hike or ride back down the mountain. Small kids and seniors ride for free. Check their website for days and times.

### CAMPING

Tent camping is available (from the top of the mountain down) at Aspen Basin, Big Tesuque, and Black Canyon Campgrounds. There are also group camping and RV sites near the Hyde Memorial State Park lodge.

### YURTS

Yurts for overnight stays are a more recent addition to Hyde Memorial State Park. Each yurt sleeps six and has a small kitchen and outdoor fire ring. Just a short walk from parking and nestled into the alpine ponderosa pine forests, they offer an enjoyable way to spend a night in the outdoors for those needing a bit more comfort than tents afford. Yurts originate on the Mongolian steppes. The traditional portable, round tents were used as dwellings by nomadic cultures that moved across Central Asian steppes several times a year. It's fun to imagine with your kids what life was like for the Mongolian nomadic groups and how they would deconstruct and reconstruct their round homes in a matter of hours.

### CROSS-COUNTRY SKIING/SNOWSHOEING

(505) 983-7175
www.emnrd.state.nm.us

Several trails in the Hyde Memorial State Park area accumulate deep snow for great cross-country skiing or snowshoeing adventures in winter: Big Tesuque Campground, Borrego/Bear Wallow Loop, Norski Trail 255, and Black Canyon Campground are a few favorites.

## 3. Randall Davey Audubon Center and Sanctuary

**Nearest Town:** Santa Fe

**Best Season to Visit:** Year-round; call ahead in winter about closures due to weather.

**Visitor Information:** Center is open daily Monday–Saturday, the Nature Store is open Monday–Saturday. Docent-led tours of the Randall Davey House weekly.

**Getting There:** From St. Francis Drive (US 84/285), take Alameda east. At the four-way intersection with Upper Canyon Road, turn left. Follow this road until it ends at the parking lot.

The center offers summer camps and events for kids and youth, but families are welcome to visit anytime. The Audubon's 135 acres are nestled in the foothills of the Sangre de Cristo Mountains up against

Cattails fill the wetland ponds at Santa Fe Canyon Preserve

National Forest and Santa Fe River watershed. Several public access trails branch out from the gardens and Nature Store into piñon-juniper, ponderosa pine forest, and meadows.

### BIRDWATCHING

Guided birdwatching tours are held every Saturday by local experts.

### HIKE | SANTA FE CANYON PRESERVE

**Distance:** 1.5 mile loop

**Difficulty:** Easy

**Getting There:** From St. Francis Drive (US 84/285), take Alameda east (toward the mountains). At the four-way intersection with Upper Canyon Road, turn left. Turn left at the junction with Cerro Gordo Road. The parking area is just off the junction on the right.

Adjacent to the Audubon Center is the Nature Conservancy's Santa Fe Canyon Preserve, protecting 575 acres of riparian area. In this lush, watery canyon in the desert foothills, point out to children that the presence of water along the trail makes good habitat for trees like willows, box elders, and cottonwoods, different than in the mountains above, where fir, spruce, and pine dominate. Children will enjoy searching for leopard frogs and salamanders in the ponds. Pass the remains of Old Stone and Two-Mile Dams that used to supply Santa Fe with its drinking water. The area has been restored for resident beavers, wildflowers, red-winged blackbirds, and other wildlife. Cottonwoods and willows provide ample shade along this riparian trail. Kids will ask what the metal cages around the base of cottonwoods are for. Point out the beaver chews and talk about the diet and habits of beavers and the need to sometimes protect trees from their zealous dam building. Stop at the interpretive signs to learn more about the unique life in this place. Stand on the edge of the extensive cattail wetlands and ask your kids if they can distinguish the unique call of the red-winged blackbirds.

## 4. Cerrillos Hills State Park

(505) 474-0196

www.cerrilloshills.org

**Nearest Town:** Cerrillos/Madrid

**Best Season to Visit:** Year-round

**Visitor Information:** Open year-round, day-use only. Visitor center open limited days and times; call ahead for details.

**Getting There:** From Santa Fe, take NM 14 and turn right onto Main Street in Cerrillos. Turn right onto 1st Street/County Road 59 and follow this to the park.

Cerrillos Hills State Park is located in the historic Cerrillos Mining District, one of the oldest mining areas in North America. Mining dates back to 1000 AD, when Native Americans plied underground veins for turquoise. The Spanish mines of the 17th century followed, and mining still takes place today on a small scale. Five miles of hiking trails through the park lead to mining ruins. Spend some time with children searching around the mines for different colored minerals. Discuss with kids what it would be like to work underground.

The state park was formed by millennia of eruptions and intrusions of two ancient volcanoes; today only the highly eroded remains of those volcanoes rise up from the flat desert surrounds. Riparian areas fed by natural springs enliven this unique desert environment. Hike here in spring and early summer to see brilliant cactus flower in bloom.

After spending some time in the park, stop in the historic town of Cerrillos at the Casa Grande Trading Post, which includes a petting zoo, turquoise mining museum, and rock shop run by a local gem and mineral prospector. Kids will be amazed by the variety and abundance of gems and minerals in the shop and thrilled to feed the animals in the free petting zoo. (505) 438-3008, www.casagrandetradingpost.com.

HORSEBACK RIDING

Kids 10+ can take part in a family horseback riding adventure through the park. The riding trail climbs through the high desert to 360-degree scenic overlooks for spectacular views of the Sandia, Ortiz, Jemez, and Sangre de Cristo Mountains. The sunset tour is especially beautiful. Broken Saddle Riding Company is the exclusive and official concessionaire for the park. Their horses live on a ranch just outside park boundaries and are well trained and experienced on these trails. (505) 424-7774, www.brokensaddle.com.

## 5. Kasha-Katuwe Tent Rocks National Monument

(505) 761-8700

www.blm.gov/visit/kktr

**Nearest Town:** Cochiti

**Best Season to Visit:** Year-round

**Visitor Information:** Open daily but hours change through the year. Closed on most major holidays and occasionally for tribal ceremonies; check website for details. Fees apply. This is a day-use-only area. No dogs allowed in the monument.

**Getting There:** From Santa Fe, take I-25 south to NM 16. Exit and follow the road through Cochiti to Indian Service Route 85. Head northwest on Indian Service Route 92 to the national monument.

Slot canyons, fairytale-like rock formations, colorful walls, and new discoveries around every corner make this a place even easily bored kids will enjoy. On the edge of the Pajarito Plateau, the cone-shaped tent rocks are the result of volcanic eruptions that occurred six to seven million years ago. Over 1,000'-thick deposits of pumice, ash, and tuff are punctuated by rock fragments that exploded out of the massive Jemez volcano. Over time, water and wind eroded the landscape, forming uniformly shaped tapering hoodoos up to 90' tall. Some of the hoodoos retain their hard caprocks and form, while others have lost their protective barrier and are disintegrating.

The monument has two hiking trails. The longer, 3.1-mile Canyon Trail enters the Utah-like slot canyons and climbs the ridge to an aerial view of the tent city below. Keep kids close at the top around the steep cliffs. Even though this is a popular location, and in summer months there may be a wait to enter, it is worth making the trip.

### LOCAL ATTRACTIONS, BUSINESSES

*Broken Spoke*: Santa Fe's dedicated bike shop. (505) 992-3102, www.brokenspoke santafe.com

*Santa Fe Children's Museum*: Dynamic, hands-on indoor and outdoor exploration and play. (505) 989-8359, www.santafechildrensmuseum.org

*Santa Fe Mountain Adventures*: Private guided hikes, mountain bike tours, and family adventures. (505) 988-4000, www.santafemountainadventures.com

*Meow Wolf*: Interactive art you have to experience at least once in your life. (505) 395-6369, www.meowwolf.com

The Nambe River tumbles from the mountain surrounded by wildflowers in midsummer

## Pecos

Snow-topped mountain peaks, alpine meadows that explode with wildflowers in July and August, rushing mountain streams carving deep canyons, shady conifer forests, and lush aspen groves that turn liquid gold in the fall make up the scenic Pecos Wilderness in the Sangre de Cristo Mountain Range. Alpine lakes offer first-rate fishing, as do 150+ miles of sparkling streams, where rainbow trout, brown trout, and the native Rio Grande cutthroat trout can all be found. On the western side of the Pecos Wilderness, steep canyons drain toward the Rio Grande. The rest of this large area lies in Santa Fe National Forest, with easy access from Santa Fe, Pecos, and surrounding towns. The small town of Pecos, with a few art studios and restaurants, sits at the mouth of the Pecos River Canyon. The relatively gentle upper Pecos River Valley boasts broad, flat mesas and grassy meadows. Twenty miles of the Pecos River from its headwaters are designated Wild and Scenic and remain free-flowing. Most hikers come during the summer months to explore the extensive system of trails. Several campgrounds and vacation rentals in the valley make stellar basecamps.

### WILDLIFE

Elk, deer, bears, turkeys, and one of America's healthiest herds of Rocky Mountain bighorn sheep are found here.

### BIRDWATCHING

White-tailed ptarmigans inhabit alpine tundra and timberline habitats. Find boreal owls and blue grouse in spruce-fir forests. The endangered Mexican owl is partial to Douglas-fir. Also look for Clark's nutcrackers, warbling vireos, mountain bluebirds, northern goshawks, hairy woodpeckers, wild turkeys, piñon jays, and several species of hummingbirds, especially at the small store in Tererro that puts up feeders.

Going for a fall hike along the trail
to Mora Flats in Pecos Canyon

## 6. Pecos Canyon State Park

**Nearest Town:** Pecos

**Best Season to Visit:** Late spring–fall

**Visitor Information:** This newly created state
park doesn't yet have a visitor's center or
developed facilities outside campgrounds
and recreation areas.

**Getting There:** From Santa Fe, take I-25 north
to Exit 299. Take NM 50 about 6 miles into
Pecos. At the four-way stop, turn left onto
NM 63 and head into the Pecos River
Canyon.

This high-elevation, forested park is New
Mexico's newest state park in a well-loved
and often-visited section of the Santa Fe
National Forest that bustles with campers
and hikers on summer weekends. Hike a
couple miles on a trail and you will enter
the solitude and peace that wilderness areas
are made to protect. Hiking, camping, fishing, and horseback riding, or just sitting on
the shores of a river during the day and
cozying up to a campfire in the evening,
provide an ideal family getaway.

**Distance:** 2.5 miles one-way

**Difficulty:** Easy

**Getting There:** Trailhead located in the
Panchuela Campground.

Cave Creek enters a set of limestone caves
perfect for exploring with kids. Along the
way, the trail is painted with beautiful wildflowers in aspen meadows and conifer forests. Cascading creeks along the length of
the trail make this a perfect summer destination. Moss and lichen grow plentiful on
the rocks around the caves. Have children
feel the difference between the two, without
removing them, and discuss their differ-
ences. Moss forms soft, dense, green
clumps or mats and likes shade, and lichen
is crusty and leaflike, preferring sunshine.
Lichens are fascinatingly two plants—fungi
and algae—living symbiotically together.

**CAVE CREEK TRAIL** 2.5 miles one-way

**Distance:** 7.8 miles out and back

**Difficulty:** Moderate (the hike is uphill on the way back)

**Getting There:** From Pecos, take NM 63 east into the Pecos River Canyon. At 18.6 miles, turn off onto FR 223 to Iron Gate Campground. Continue 4.4 miles on rough road (high-clearance vehicle is recommended) to the trailhead in the campground.

The hike starts on the Hamilton Mesa Trail, ascending to a ridge and then descending on Rociada Trail 250 to Rio Mora and Mora Flats—a large, open meadow in the river valley. The trail oscillates between conifer and aspen forests that are magnificent in the fall.

Aspen is a successional species, meaning it comes in after a fire or other disturbance. Aspen groves tend to be open and sunny, making them a favorite of almost everyone. They also have the unique ability to produce genetically identical offspring from their roots. One aspen grove in Utah, named Pando, consists of 47,000 aspens that originated from a single male tree. It's thought to be the oldest living land organism in the world. The pale green bark is very soft, making it easy for people to carve them. Tell children this would be like giving someone an unwanted tattoo.

Mora Flats is an excellent place for a kid's first overnight backpack trip. The meadows and banks of the river overflow with colorful wildflowers in the summer months and trout are plentiful in the river.

The Rio Mora runs through the Mora Flats, providing great fishing opportunities

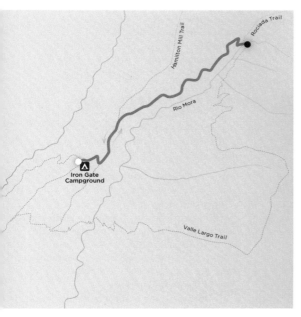

**MORA FLATS** 7.8 miles out and back

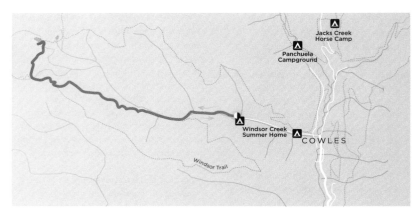

**STEWART LAKE** 8.4 miles out and back

## HIKE | STEWART LAKE

**Distance:** 8.4 miles out and back

**Difficulty:** Moderate

**Getting There:** From Pecos, take NM 63 east into the Pecos River Canyon. Drive 20.2 miles to Cowles. Make a left over the Pecos River and drive 1 mile to the Winsor Creek Trailhead.

This lovely hike passes through serene meadows and aspen groves and up into the montane forest to two lakes with Santa Fe Baldy towering overhead. This is a popular backcountry camping and fishing spot for families with older children. Take time to explore the wildflowers growing in the marshes around the lake and ask children to notice how they are different species than those in the dry forests. Take the Winsor Trail 254 to Skyline Trail 251 and bear right for Stewart Lake.

## 7. Pecos National Historical Park

(505) 757-7241

www.nps.gov/peco

**Nearest Town:** Pecos

**Best Season to Visit:** Year-round

**Visitor Information:** Hours vary through the year; check website for details. The visitor center closes one hour before the park. Entrance is free.

**Getting There:** From Santa Fe, take I-25 north to Exit 299 near Glorieta and take NM 50 to Pecos village. Then head south for 2 miles on NM 63. The park will be on the right.

&#9855; accessible

An interesting short historical detour on your way to the wilderness. Take a walk through the history of the Pecos people, the Spanish conquerors, and the enduring natural beauty of this place. Located between the Sangre de Cristo Mountains and the flat-topped Glorieta Mesa, for centuries this strategic location attracted settlers and became the site of historic battles.

Talk to your children about how the Pueblo people, fed up with ill treatment at the hands of the Spaniards, banded together on August 10, 1680, to expel the Spanish government and Franciscan friars from the Southwest. The successful revolt, led by Po'pay from Ohkay Owingeh (San Juan Pueblo), represented the only time that European invaders were successfully expelled from the Americas. Subsequently, the Pueblo people were weakened by disease spread by Europeans, and when the Spanish returned in 1692, they met with little resistance from the people of Pecos Pueblo. In the 1830s, the last remaining Pecos people migrated permanently to the Pueblo of Jemez, where the Pecos traditions live on. This is a good opportunity to talk with your children about whose land you are on. The park preserves the history of their lives, and of those who followed, recorded on the land, in the ruins, and shared in ranger-guided tours of this place.

## CAMPING

(505) 757-7241

www.nps.gov/peco/index.htm

This is a day-use-only park.

## HORSEBACK RIDING

### Cloud Nine Trails

(505) 310-8527

www.cloudninetrailsnm.com

Allen and Colleen offer horseback rides into some of the most scenic country in the Pecos Wilderness. From a couple hours to multiple-day rides, these experienced back-country riders and their horses traverse the Pecos Wilderness like it's their backyard. Most of their rides originate from Jacks Creek Campground, already in the high country of the Sangre de Cristo Mountains, and continue into the aspen groves, meadows, and alpine areas. Kids 10+ can ride.

## VISION QUEST

(505) 469-8130

www.visionquesthorsebackrides.com

This Native American–owned and –operated business is led by Joaquin Gonzales, a professional horseman and actor, who has been riding horses since he was 3 years old,

The ruins of old Spanish mission at Pecos National Historical Park; courtesy of NPS

and his wife, Marcia. They invite riders of all levels to share in their enthusiasm and love of horses with horseback rides into the Sangre de Cristo Mountains and western riding lessons through the year. Kids under 7 can also take a pony ride.

## 8. Cowles Ponds Fishing Site

(505) 757-6360

www.wildlife.state.nm.us/fishing/weekly
-report/

**Nearest Town:** Pecos

**Best Season to Visit:** Summer

**Visitor Information:** Fishing allowed from shore only. Children 12 and under fish without a license.

**Getting There:** 20 miles north of Pecos on NM 63 and Forest Road 121.

Situated in the Pecos Canyon, these two good-sized ponds butt up against the Pecos River, surrounded by coniferous forests and grassy meadows. The larger one is available

to all anglers with a current NM fishing license, and a smaller pond is open only to those 12 years of age and under and persons with disabilities. Both ponds are stocked periodically with brown and rainbow trout. To find out when the ponds were last stocked, or when the next stocking might be, contact the New Mexico Department of Game and Fish.

### FISHING THE PECOS RIVER

**Getting There:** Access along NM 63 in the Pecos River Canyon.

The Pecos River originates high up in the Sangre de Cristo Mountains just north of Santa Fe. A handful of tiny streams loaded with small brown and cutthroat trout flow into the Pecos above Cowles. Below Cowles, the stream becomes a small to medium river ranging 10–25' wide. Sections of the Pecos River cross through private property. The best river fishing for families

Cowles Fishing Ponds in the Pecos River Canyon

Glacier, the family dog, enjoys the wildflowers in the Pecos Wilderness

and kids are at several fishing access and picnic areas off NM 63: Dalton, Field Tract, and Windy Bridge, and at the Bert Clancy Campground. For more experienced anglers, the 20 miles of the Pecos River above Cowles has been designated a National Wild and Scenic River, and access to this portion of the river and its tributaries is gained only by trail.

## 9. Monastery Lake

**Nearest Town:** Pecos
**Best Season to Visit:** Summer–fall
**Visitor Information:** Open year-round from 30 minutes before sunrise to sunset. Fishing allowed from shore only. Children 11 and under fish without a license.
**Getting There:** From the four-way stop in Pecos, turn onto NM 63 heading into the Pecos River Canyon. After 1.8 miles, turn left onto Monastery Lake Road.

Only a few miles from the town of Pecos, and just inside the Santa Fe National Forest, northern New Mexico's Monastery Lake is a favorite for many trout anglers. Stocked frequently by the New Mexico Department of Game and Fish with rainbow trout, this small lake is easily accessible, ideal for families and kids. According to experienced anglers, you can spend an evening here catching your five fish limit with salmon eggs and fixed float set up on a spincast rod.

### MOUNTAIN BIKING

Mountain biking is not allowed in designated wilderness areas and because the trails here quickly cross the wilderness boundary, this is not an ideal place for mountain biking. However, if you are staying at Jacks Creek or Holy Ghost Campgrounds, bring the kids' bikes as the roads there make a great, scenic ride for little ones.

### CAMPING

Several developed public campgrounds line the Pecos River Canyon: Field Tract, Bert Clancy, Tererro, Davis-Willow, Mora, Willow Creek, Holy Ghost Campground, Panchuela Campground, Iron Gate, and Jacks Creek Campground. On summer weekends and holidays these fill up fast.

The Taos Mountains rise up from the sage flats in northern New Mexico

## Taos and Surrounds

Taos is a world-famous destination on the sagebrush flats of northern New Mexico, bounded by the rugged Sangre de Cristo Mountains. Wheeler Peak, the highest mountain in New Mexico at 13,161', and the Rio Grande Gorge, carving an 800'-deep canyon, provide the backdrop for epic outdoor adventures. Historic and cultural sites such as Taos Pueblo and San Francisco de Assisi Mission Church will fascinate older family members. The art and quirky mountain town scene in Taos and Taos Ski Valley provide all amenities needed for outdoor adventures. There are plentiful outfitters to show you to the best spots.

POINT OF INTEREST | **RIO GRANDE GORGE BRIDGE**

**Getting There:** Follow US 64/NM 522 north for approximately 3.5 miles to the last four-way intersection of town. Turn left to get onto US 64 West. Travel about 8 miles. Cross the bridge and the parking area is on the left.

The bridge is an engineering wonder, with steel trusses and a cement deck spanning the width of the Rio Grande Gorge. Kids will find it thrilling to stand 650' above the Rio Grande, on the fifth highest bridge in the United States. Overlooks along the bridge and parking area provide stunning scenic views of the Rio Grande Gorge and the mountains to the east. This is a great quick stop to stretch your legs and take in the scene.

## 10. Carson National Forest

(575) 758-6200

www.fs.usda.gov/carson

**Nearest Town:** Taos, Red River, Questa

**Best Season to Visit:** Year-round

**Visitor Information:** Questa and Taos have ranger stations open daily during the week.

**Getting There:** The Carson National Forest stretches from north of Taos to north of Mora.

This national forest's 1.5 million acres in the southern Rocky Mountains, with five wilderness areas, afford visitors some of the finest mountain scenery in the Southwest. Enjoy views from high peaks and adventure in lush, forested mountains.

### WILDLIFE

Watch for mule deer, elk, pronghorn, black bears, coyotes, bobcats, mountain lions, foxes, bighorn sheep, and many species of smaller mammals that make their home in the forests and mesas.

### LLAMA TREKKING

*Wild Earth Llama Adventures*

(800) 758-5262

www.llamaadventures.com

Wild Earth Llama Adventures offers educational eco adventures supported by gear-packing llamas. For families who love to backpack, or want to try it for the first time, this is a great way to get you and your little ones into the wilderness with a bit more ease. Why llamas? Kids love trekking with a woolly hiking buddy who caries their heavy gear for them.

Leah and Stuart Wilde, who started Wild Earth Llama Adventures, say llamas have been helping people carry their wares for thousands of years in the South American

Sunset at the Rio Grande Gorge Bridge

Andes. Their gentle and well-trained llamas eagerly follow adults and children alike and walk at a comfortable pace for their human companions. They are low-impact animals that move with ease in the high country, important to the conservation and stewardship mission of their company. The llamas pack you into seldom-visited wilderness areas of New Mexico's Sangre de Cristo Mountains and Rio Grande Gorge, near Taos and Santa Fe.

Wild Earth Llama Adventures designs customized family trips that vary from multiday overnights to day hikes with gourmet lunch. On multiday treks, families can choose to summit peaks, explore ancient forests, or discover hidden alpine lakes and meadows.

Along the way, their experienced naturalist guides share their extensive knowledge of local ecology, native plants and wildlife, edible and medicinal plants, natural and cultural history, and wilderness living skills. The guides entertain with educational nature games, teach animal tracking, and tell stories around evening campfires. You can even customize your menu choices to keep all family members happy and well-fed on the trip.

### HIKE | WILLIAMS LAKE TRAIL

**Distance:** 2 miles one-way
**Difficulty:** Moderate
**Getting There:** In Taos at the intersection of US 64 and NM 150, take NM 150 north for 18.6 miles. Turn left onto Twining Road and continue for 2.1 miles to Kachina Road. Follow the signs for Williams Lake through the ski area to arrive at the trailhead parking lot.

As far as alpine lake hikes go, this short hike is doable for all fitness levels and ages. The scenery changes from dark forests, to open meadows flanked by rock walls, to boulder fields where kids can climb and explore. The lake and nearby waterfall at the end motivate young ones to continue up the sometimes steep trail!

From the parking lot, follow the signs on the road through two large boulders. The first mile of this trail passes through development and near constant construction of the Taos ski area. Follow the road along Lake Fork Creek. Dive into a dense forest of Engelmann spruce. The trail veers left, away from the creek into a little meadow filled with beautiful wildflowers during the height of summer. After the meadow, the road narrows to a dirt path—Williams Lake Trail 62. Arrive at the Wheeler Peak Wilderness boundary sign. Dive back into the conifer trees, crossing several avalanche slopes.

The trail now climbs up several rocky switchbacks and passes to the left of huge boulder fields. Kids will enjoy a stop to watch the whistling pikas, overly friendly chipmunks, and golden-mantled ground squirrels dodge in and out of view as they navigate their tiny tunnel trails through the rocks carrying plants to their dens. Help them tell the difference between the three. Arrive at a second boulder field and admire the towering peaks of the Taos Mountains now in view. Gain a ridge with views of Williams Lake and Wheeler Peak, the tallest mountain in New Mexico at 13,161'. A sign indicates an elevation of 11,040' on the ridge. The lake sits in a beautiful alpine bowl surrounded by Lake Fork Peak and other mountains. Boulder fields are dotted with colorful wildflowers. The lake is an extremely popular destination; camping and campfires are not allowed on the shores to preserve the fragile alpine environment. The lake is too shallow to support fish, but look for gilled tiger salamanders in the waters. When you've had your fill of this cool alpine lake, retrace your steps back to the ridge and descend through the forest to return to the trailhead.

## 11. Natural Hot Springs

*Black Rock Hot Springs*
**Nearest Town:** Taos
**Best Season to Visit:** Year-round
**Visitor Information:** Clothing is optional. Black Rock is fairly well known and easy to reach, so expect company.
**Getting There:** Black Rock Hot Springs is located north of Taos, west of the town of Arroyo Hondo. From NM 522 North, at mile 5.3 turn west onto CR B007. After about 2.5 miles, the road turns hard to the right. Continue on, staying to the left and downhill until you reach a narrow one-lane bridge that takes you across the Hondo River, then cross the John Dunn Bridge over the Rio Grande. Go left uphill and park at the first switchback.

Kids will enjoy this short, scenic hike to hot water pools along the cool river. On our visit, we swam across the river to a private beach on the opposite shore and returned to the hot pools to warm up. When my kids had enough of soaking, they were entertained by climbing around on the huge boulders above the hot springs and looking for petroglyphs.

The hot springs are about a 5–10-minute walk on the trail downstream to two mud-bottomed rock pools on the west bank of the Rio Grande. Pool temperatures are usually about 97°F, depending on how high the river is.

*Manby Hot Springs*
**Nearest Town:** Taos
**Best Season to Visit:** Year-round
**Visitor Information:** Clothing optional. Slightly harder to get to than Black Rock Hot Springs, but still expect company.
**Getting There:** Located north of Taos and southwest of the town of Arroyo Hondo. From NM 522 North, at mile 5.3 turn west onto CR B007. Go about 2.5 miles and turn left onto another dirt road just before B007 makes a hard turn to the right (see Black Rock Hot Springs, above). This stretch of road to the Manby Hot Springs parking lot needs to be taken slowly and is best negotiated with a high-clearance vehicle. Continue past the Dobson House sign and take the next left fork. Continue staying to your right until you reach the large parking lots for the Manby Hot Springs.

At the left side of the parking area, take a dirt and rock path to the river, about a 15–20 minute walk. Two sand-bottomed rock pools are located in the ruins of an old stagecoach stop on the east bank of the Rio Grande. Water temperatures are usually about 97°F, depending on how high the river is.

## 12. Rafting the Rio Grande

The Rio Grande provides a variety of trips, from easy floats to hard-core whitewater.

*Float—OVRA:* A scenic float trip through the Orilla Verde Recreation Area (OVRA), in a 700'-deep, cliff-rimmed canyon, with an occasional easy rapid. This float trip is great for families with grandparents and children as young as 4. This trip floats down a section of the Rio Grande designated as Wild and Scenic, allowing time to slow down and connect with nature. Along the river, you may encounter beavers, muskrats, deer, river otters, songbirds, herons, golden eagles, and various falcons and see trout rising to catch a variety of insect life. Talk to kids about the presence or absence of river otters (see the sidebar).

*Whitewater—Racecourse:* Starting below the Orilla Verde area, the next 5-mile section of the Rio Grande, known as the Racecourse, has moderate to difficult (in high water), adrenaline-pumping rapids. In this section, the river runs along the base of the reddish Pilar cliffs. Rockfall from these cliffs and from the bordering

basalt mesas to the north create the
rapids of the Racecourse.

*Whitewater—Taos Box:* The Rio Grande's
most challenging whitewater adventure.
This difficult one-day wilderness trip,
one of the most famous in the country,
travels through the wild section of the
Rio Grande Wild and Scenic river,
ending at the upper end of OVRA, at the
Taos Junction bridge. Not for the faint of
heart; you are guaranteed to get wet.

Raft guiding companies offer full-day experiences for families on both the flat water
and whitewater. Some conveniently split
the day with the morning spent on flat
water. At lunch, younger and sensitive
members of the family can choose to hop
out of the boat and watch the rest brave the
whitewater waves from the road.

### OUTFITTERS

*New Mexico River Adventures*
(800) 983-7756
www.newmexicoriveradventures.com

Offering a variety of climbing, biking, paddling, and hiking adventures throughout
northern New Mexico. They also offer two-
day whitewater kayaking clinics for an
introduction to the sport. Private and custom instruction also available for those
wanting to improve their skills.

*Far Flung Adventures*
(575) 758-2628
www.farflung.com

Offers combo adventures of rafting, climbing, fishing, and horseback riding trips,
including a three-day adventure through
the whole of the Rio Grande Gorge down
40 miles of river. Gear rentals available for
those who want to venture out without a
guide.

*Los Rios River Runners*
(575) 776-8854
www.losriosriverrunners.com

From half-day to multiday and multisport
trips, these guides dish up adventure
throughout northern New Mexico.
Founded by legendary Rio Grande guide
and storyteller Cisco Guevara in the 1970s,
they run experienced and extensive guide
services.

### CLIMBING

The Taos area has many options for climbing adventures due to the diverse topogra-
phy spanning from the basalt crags of the
Rio Grande Gorge to the pristine granite of
Tres Piedras or Questa Dome, the meta-
morphic rocks of Comales Canyon, and the
cobble conglomerate of El Rito, all within a
reasonable drive of historic Taos.

*Tres Piedras, Tusas Mountains*
**Getting There:** From the junction of US 285 and
US 64, go west on US 64 for 0.7 miles (past
the ranger station) to an unmarked dirt road
on the right. Follow this dirt road for a half
mile to the parking area (left at the "T," left at
the "Y").

Thirty miles northeast of Taos, outside of
the sleepy town of Tres Piedras, is one of
New Mexico's best climbing destinations.
The area also offers great scrambling and
hiking for those in the family who don't
want to scale walls. The Tres Piedras Crags
are found on the extreme southeastern
fringe of the Tusas Mountains, where the
range gradually subsides into the Rio
Grande Valley. All of the major rocks boast
several established routes with difficulty
ranging from 5.4 to 5.13.

*El Rito Sport Area, Carson National Forest*
**Getting There:** Situated north of the village of
El Rito in the Carson National Forest, a short
jaunt from Abiquiu. From the east end of the

village, turn north on FR 44 (dirt). Drive 3.75 miles from the pavement and park to the left just after the sign for Cañada del Potrero. Camping is available at several locations up this spur road, which ends in about a half-mile. Now walk across the road to a trail paralleling it headed south. The trail crosses a bridge, then turns south up the sidehill to the crags.

The rock here is cobblestone with large holds for grabbing onto, making El Rito a great spot for beginners. There are 120 total climbs at the sport area, with over 30 routes ranging up to 5.9. Some of the easier climbing routes exist along the Schoolhouse Slab, all of which are 5.7.

*Dead Cholla Wall, Rio Grande Gorge*

**Getting There:** From Taos, drive south on US 68 to Pilar. Turn northwest at Pilar, toward the campgrounds of Orilla Verde Recreation Area, and drive over the bridge across the Rio Grande and up the other side of the gorge. Once you hit the paved road, take your first right; that will take you over to the trailhead to park. Then hike down about 300 yards and you will be over the top of the crag.

This Taos-based crag is arguably one of the most gorgeous climbing spots in the state. Propped along the Rio Grande Gorge, you'll have 360-degree views hiking in, as well as while you're belaying and climbing. There are only 25 total climbs on this wall—just two 5.7s and three 5.9s for easier options. The crag sits high above the gorge, so you'll feel more exposed than you actually are, which may make it more challenging for families.

*Mountain Skills Rock Climbing Adventures*
　(575) 776-2222
　www.climbingschoolusa.com
Owned by Jay Foley, who literally wrote the book on climbing in northern New Mexico.

Mountain Skills' guides specialize in one-on-one or group teaching that helps families get started in outdoor climbing. They offer guided trips to some of the best spots around Taos.

## 13. Enchanted Forest Cross-Country Ski Area
　(575) 754-6112
　www.enchantedforestxc.com

Enchanted Forest is best known as a cross-country skiing and snowshoeing area in the winter, but the stunning vistas and meandering forest trails are also wonderful for yurt camping, hiking, and mountain biking in the warm season. The yurts offer a soft adventure for families—a bit like backcountry camping with the convenience of car camping. The ski area offers group and private lessons for people of all ages to get started in cross-country skiing.

*Yurt Camping–Southwest Nordic Center*
　(575) 758-4761
　www.southwestnordiccenter.com

Families will enjoy the relatively short ski or hike to comfort in the backcountry. The Southwest Nordic Center operates yurts in the San Juan Mountains, Colorado, and one yurt above Taos Ski Valley in New Mexico. The Bull of the Woods Yurt is 2 miles from Taos Ski Valley and provides a backcountry camping experience for hikers and backcountry skiers. The yurt lies at 10,800' along the ridge between Wheeler Peak and Gold Hill. Day hikes or skis along this ridge take you into the high alpine terrain and spectacular scenery. Spring skiing is excellent from this yurt. In fall, listen for bugling elk in the surrounding meadows and talk with kids about their impressive annual rutting ritual.

## 14. Rio Grande del Norte National Monument

*Bureau of Land Management,
Taos Field Office*

Wild Rivers Visitor Center

(575) 758-8851

https://www.blm.gov/visit/wild-rivers
-recreation-area

**Nearest Town:** Questa, Pilar

**Best Season to Visit:** Year-round

**Visitor Information:** The national monument begins on the border of Colorado and ends where the river passes the village of Pilar, on NM 68. US 285 runs through the western edge of the monument and NM 522 just outside the eastern border. The monument has two distinct areas: Wild Rivers Area in the northern portion of the monument and Orilla Verde Recreation Area at the southern edge.

**Getting There:** To access the Wild Rivers Visitor Center from Questa, drive north on NM 522 for 2.6 miles. Turn left onto NM 378. The road takes you through the sagebrush flats, follows the rim of the Rio Grande Gorge, and loops around to the visitor center.

♿ some areas accessible

When we visited the northern section of this monument, my kids were most excited by the bighorn sheep that walked through our campground each morning and the ladybugs converging by the hundreds on the juniper trees at the edges of the canyons. They also delighted in riding bikes along the miles of paved roads that meander through the wide open sage flats with views of the mountains. The Rio Grande del Norte National Monument protects rugged, wide-open plains and big sagebrush flats cut through by steep canyons of the Rio Grande and Red River.

The Rio Grande's 800' gorge displays layers of volcanic basalt flows and ash. Surrounded by volcanic cones, the highest is Ute Mountain, rising to 10,093'. The area is rich with petroglyphs, prehistoric dwelling sites, and other archaeological sites left behind by ancient Southwestern cultures. The monument provides excellent opportunities for viewing Rocky Mountain bighorn sheep, which often graze in the campgrounds and are seen on the canyon rims and trails. Recreational opportunities such as hiking, rafting, biking, and camping abound. The monument blooms with abundant wildflowers in spring and fall.

Rangers offer guided tours throughout the summer on weekends. The monument has two visitor centers: Wild Rivers Visitor Center near Questa and Rio Grande Gorge Visitor Center near Pilar. Both have interpretive displays, small bookstores, and information about the area.

### WILDLIFE

Watch for bighorn sheep along the canyon rim. Good viewing of mule deer and elk

### River Otters

The North American river otter, a lovable and social member of the weasel family, is a native species in New Mexico. Along with beavers, they once held the spot at the top of the food chain on the Rio Grande. By 1953, their populations were wiped out due to overhunting, trapping, pollution, and deforestation.

Nearly 60 years later, starting in 2008, 33 otters were released back into the Upper Rio Grande. Captured in the estuaries of the Pacific Northwest, they were labeled "problem otters" for rudely leaving shells and scat on local boats and boat docks. Now they leave their scat and leftovers among the basalt boulders of the wild and scenic Rio Grande, to the delight of rafters and hikers. Spot them swimming in the river or sunning on the shores.

The Rio Grande runs fast and deep through the Rio Grande del Norte National Monument

year-round but best in predawn hours of late winter. During the summer, watch for coyotes. Look for Gunnison's prairie dog village at La Junta Overlook in the Wild Rivers section. Watch for the elusive ringtails at the bottom of the gorge near shelters.

## BIRDWATCHING

Good year-round viewing of raptors. Golden eagles are spotted in the river corridors in winter; ducks and geese use the rivers in summer. Western tanagers, violet-green swallows, Clark's nutcrackers, and white-throated swifts are present spring through fall. An abundance of broad-tailed hummingbirds nest here in May and stay through October. Mountain bluebirds are also plentiful.

## FISHING

The Rio Grande has over 50 miles of pristine trout water that runs throughout a gorgeous and lightly fished canyon. The lower river near Pilar and the Orilla Verde

Recreation Area can be easily accessed by vehicle and short trails for easy family fishing adventures.

### Wild Rivers

The Wild Rivers area on the Rio Grande, west of Questa, provides camping along the rim and hiking access into the Red River and Rio Grande Gorges, with campsites at riverside. Primitive trails are found elsewhere in the upper gorge.

## HIKE | BIG ARSENIC SPRINGS TRAIL

**Distance:** 2 miles

**Difficulty:** Moderate

**Getting There:** North of Questa, look for the Wild Rivers turnoff and turn left onto NM 378. Follow this road 3.5 miles to the entrance of Wild Rivers. Go south another 8 miles. Head right at the split to reach the trailhead.

My boys delighted in the descent to the valley floor, where we found petroglyphs in animal shapes alongside the roaring June

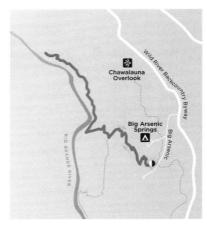

**BIG ARSENIC SPRINGS TRAIL** 2 miles

**Distance:** 2.5 miles round trip

**Difficulty:** Easy

**Getting There:** From Taos, take NM 68 south for 16 miles to Pilar. Turn right onto NM 570 and follow the Rio Grande for 6 miles to the trailhead and parking on the right.

This short excursion drops down a few rocky steps into high-desert meadows with cacti, tall grass, and piñon and juniper trees. Ask kids to find ancient pictographs and petroglyphs, some reportedly 5,000 years old. Admire them but ask kids not to touch, as the oil on your fingers can cause this ancient art to fade. Arrive at a bench with fantastic views of the Rio Grande. Fly fishing on this section of the river is quite good.

### CAMPING

In the southern portion of the monument, FR 570 meanders through the beautiful Rio Grande river valley between the Taos

**LA VISTA VERDE TRAIL** 2.5 miles round trip

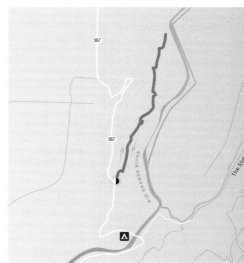

river on our hike. We sat to watch its power from the shade of trees by a bubbling, cool, natural spring with green and orange dragonflies buzzing around our heads. The visitor center has a dragonfly field guide where we later identified what we saw. This trail leads from the ridge of the Rio Grande Gorge down to the river and Big Arsenic Springs, a cold spring surrounded by lush, green vegetation. The trail has interpretive signage; look for petroglyphs on the flat section in the bottom of the gorge. Backcountry camping shelters have been set up in the gorge and make for a relatively easy overnight for families.

*Orilla Verde Recreation Area*

The Orilla Verde Recreation Area is a very scenic 700'-deep canyon rimmed by black basalt cliffs. The area includes campgrounds on the river's edge and boat launches. The Rio Grande Gorge Visitor Center with interpretive displays sits at the entrance to this area.

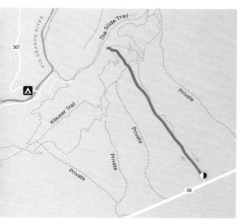

This family-favorite hike follows a rolling trail out and back through the sage and juniper to the rim of the Rio Pueblo. A bench at the end of the trail provides views to the confluence of the Rio Pueblo and Rio Grande. The often-snow-capped mountains above Taos make a stunning backdrop for this trek. Trader's Trail is part of an extensive system of trails that is open for hiking, mountain biking, and horseback riding. Connect up with the Slide Trail to the north or Picuris Trail to the south to descend toward the rivers below. Watch for bighorn sheep and bald eagles during the winter months. This is also an easy mountain biking trail.

**TRADERS TRAIL AT TAOS VALLEY OVERLOOK** 3 miles round trip

Junction Bridge and the town of Pilar. Seven campgrounds, picnic areas, and boat launches line the river here and are heavily used by river paddlers and guiding companies as launching points. All but two sites are on a nonreservation, first come, first served basis. The group sites at the Rio Bravo and Taos Junction Campgrounds must be reserved in advance by calling the BLM at (575) 758-8851.

*Taos Valley Overlook*
This 2,581-acre area off NM 68 preserves the sweeping views of the Sangre de Cristo Mountains and the Rio Grande Gorge with trails for hiking and mountain biking.

HIKE | **TRADERS TRAIL AT TAOS VALLEY OVERLOOK**

**Distance:** 3 miles round trip
**Difficulty:** Easy
**Getting There:** North of Pilar on the east side of NM 68 between mile markers 35 and 36. This is the trailhead for a system of interconnecting trails offering 20 miles of hiking, mountain biking, and horseback riding trails.

## Questa

Founded in 1842, Questa is a small, remote, historic village surrounded by beautiful scenery and outdoor recreation. The town is an access point to the Rio Grande del Norte National Monument, Sangre de Cristo Mountains, several wilderness areas, and fishing hot spots.

### 15. Cabresto Reservoir

**Nearest Town:** Questa
**Best Season to Visit:** Summer
**Visitor Information:** The sides of the lake are steep and inaccessible for boating.
**Getting There:** Follow Cabresto Road/FR 134 east 6 miles, then FR 134A north 2 miles. FR 134A is closed in winter.

This man-made mountain lake sits at 9,150' and offers excellent fishing for several species of trout. Dispersed camping, picnic sites, and a trailhead into the Latir Peak Wilderness can be found off the parking lot. After a short stint at fishing, what my kids enjoyed most on our visit was skipping rocks from the lakeshores near the creek at the far end of the lake. We also took some time to identify animal tracks in the mud-flats.

*Carson National Forest, Questa Ranger District*
> (575) 586-1150
> www.fs.usda.gov/detail/carson

## HIKE | HEART LAKE

**Distance:** 5 miles one-way
**Difficulty:** Moderate
**Getting There:** The hike begins to the left of Cabresto Lake.

This hike is a great two- to three-day back-pack trip for families with older kids. Once you reach the lake, adventure awaits on additional hikes to Latir and Venado Peaks above. For smaller kids, adventure is found even in the first mile of the trail where you can descend to mudflats on the lakeshore to look for animal tracks and skip rocks or, further down the trail, find easy access to play along the creek.

From the parking lot, the trail skirts the west side of Cabresto Lake, passing through conifer forest. At the far end of the lake where Cabresto Creek enters the reservoir, the trail follows along the creek, passing hillsides of yellow and red flowers. Pass the Latir Peak Wilderness boundary sign. A few side trails lead down to the water's edge. Tell kids to watch out for stinging nettles, but also mention their traditional medicinal use to treat muscle and joint pain.

Reach a trail junction where Bull Creek Trail 85 continues to the left and Lake Fork Trail veers to the right. Cross the creek over a log bridge to continue right to Heart Lake. The trail climbs moderately but steadily. At a sign marked Lake Fork Trail, follow the arrow to the left for Heart Lake. The final push to the lake ascends a rocky path following a creek layered with cobble-stones and flanked by hordes of

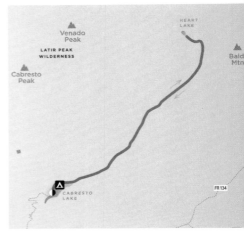

**HEART LAKE** 5 miles one-way

water-loving wildflowers. A final ascent through an alpine meadow ends at Heart Lake. Towering above, spy the treeless Venado Peak, Cabresto Peak, and the long ridge of Latir Mesa that connects them. The east shores of the lake are perfect for a lunch break, with dispersed camping spots available for those wanting to stay a while.

## HORSEBACK RIDING

*Rio Grande Stables*
> (575) 776-5913
> www.riograndestables.net

From his perch on Hormiga the mule, my then 7-year-old announced, "This is fun," after the first five minutes of the ride. He also let us know he would now like to be a cowboy when he grows up. Our guide indulged his enthusiasm, telling him stories about her horseback-riding days as a child and letting him take the reins to coach his mule to stop eating the grass. Needless to say, he really enjoyed this horse ride.

Headquartered in Texas but seasonally

based outside of Questa, the Rio Grande Stables have been offering rides for more than 30 years in the mountains and forests of northern New Mexico. Their rides take you to Bull of the Woods Trail in Taos Ski Valley and through sagebrush flats of Cebolla Mesa overlooking the Red River and Rio Grande Gorge. Kids as young as 6 can ride. I highly recommend the Bull of the Woods ride through the lush forest and meadows.

### CAMPING

Between Questa and Red River, several campgrounds line NM 38.

Columbine Campground, located between the towns of Questa and Red River, makes a great basecamp for further exploration and adventure in the area. The Red River flows past the spacious campground tucked into pine and spruce forest at 7,900'. At the south end of the

**MIDDLE FORK LAKE** 4.3 miles out and back

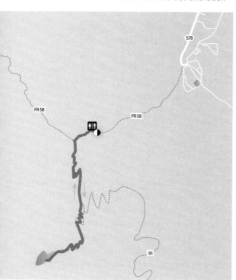

campground, the trailhead for Columbine Canyon Trail leads into the Columbine-Hondo Wilderness and connects to 14 miles of hiking trails. My boys especially enjoyed setting up makeshift traps intended to catch small fish in the creek and exploring the beaver ponds just beyond the trailhead. From the shores, you can even peer into an old beaver lodge. Two campground loops provide ample space for bike riding. Spacious sites along the river are private enough.

Three other campgrounds are located along the Red River on the way to the town of Red River: Elephant Rock Campground, Fawn Lakes Campground, and Junebug Campground.

## 16. Red River

If the kids get bored hanging around camp, head into town and indulge in some high-energy activities at the ski area. Zip-lining, high ropes obstacle courses, and tubing really spice up a weekend. Red River, a town that describes itself as a "big mountain hug," sits in a charming valley surrounded by cool, forested mountains punctuated with alpine lakes and rushing creeks. Just over the mountains from the Taos Ski Valley, this town caters to outdoor adventurers.

The Red River Nature Trail, at 3.2 miles round trip, begins in the town of Red River and follows the water into the high country.

### HIKE | MIDDLE FORK LAKE

**Distance:** 4.3 miles out and back

**Difficulty:** Moderate

**Getting There:** From Red River, take NM 38 to NM 578 to FR 58 to the trailhead. High-clearance vehicle needed on FR 58. Access to FR 58 usually begins in June. When the gate is closed, add another 1.5 miles to the hike to reach the trailhead.

Kids will love this heavily trafficked, family-friendly, shaded trail that comes to a rushing waterfall at the halfway point and ends at a stunning high alpine lake nestled among conifer forest in the mountains of the Wheeler Peak Wilderness. Enjoy a picnic and bring some fishing gear—the lake is stocked with trout. Summer wildflowers are abundant around the lake. This is one of the easier trails to an alpine lake in New Mexico.

### SUMMER AT RED RIVER SKI AREA

(575) 754-2223

www.redriverskiarea.com

The ski area opens their lift chairs to intermediate and advanced downhill mountain bikers in the summer. Bike passes are available and allow you to load your bike on the lift and ride up with it. Hikers can also ride the scenic chairlift on a relaxing climb up 1,600' to the summit. Stunning views from the top accompany activities such as a 21-hole disc golf course, hiking trails, summer mountain tubing with kid-friendly tracks, a unique aerial obstacle course with a seated zip line, and music at the mountaintop restaurant on Saturdays.

### HORSEBACK RIDING

(575) 754-1700

www.redriverstables.com

In business for over 30 years, Red River Stables offers horseback rides into the forest and mountains around Red River. Several guided trips depart throughout the day, from easy beginner trails to all-day adventures to Wheeler Peak for advanced riders.

### SNOWSHOEING

You can snowshoe in almost any area you can hike in the Carson National Forest. Good, short trails for snowshoeing around Red River are the Red River Nature Trail and Pioneer Canyon. Bighorn Sports and Rental and Sitzmark Sports and Lodging both offer snowshoe rentals.

### LOCAL BUSINESSES

*Red River Angler and Sport*

(575) 754-5086

www.redriveranglerandsport.com

Gear and books for outdoor adventures.

## 17. Angle Fire Bike Park

Rental reservations: (575) 377-4331

Lessons: (800) 633-7463

www.angelfireresort.com

**Nearest Town:** Angel Fire

**Best Season to Visit:** Summer

**Visitor Information:** Open March–October. Rentals and repairs are offered at Angel Peak and in high demand; make reservations a day ahead. Mountain biking lessons are also offered in small groups.

**Getting There:** At Angel Fire Resort. From Taos, take US 64 for 21 miles east. Turn right onto Mountain View Boulevard. Turn left onto N. Angel Fire to arrive.

Your high-intensity teenagers will love a day at this bike park! Angel Fire Ski Area boasts the best downhill mountain biking in the Southwest and the largest in the Rocky Mountains. Over 60 miles of purpose-built, lift-served terrain featuring skinnies, jump lines, manicured flow, and super chunk trails. If you know what that means, then you are ready to hit these trails. The bike park is open seven days a week in the summer with lift tickets to give you and your bike a ride up the mountain.

### MOUNTAIN BIKING

For athletic youth, the 23-mile South Boundary Trail will burn off all that preteen or teen angst built up while camping with the parents. The trail traverses the mountains from Angel Fire to Taos. It's a jewel of an all-day excursion in a setting of stunning mountain scenery, but this ride requires (at a minimum) an intermediate level of ability and stamina. It's physically demanding with a hard 4-mile climb at the start near Black Lake, south of Angel Fire. Once you finish the climb, it is an up-and-down trail with a long final descent back toward Taos. Following Carson National Forest Trail 164, the route starts at an elevation of 8,700', topping out at 10,800'. It rolls on as single-track through spruce and aspen forests, winds through Garcia Park and Paradise Park, and offers sweeping views from the Paradise overlook. The trail finally leads to El Nogal Campground at 7,200' on US 64, just east of Taos. This ride requires plenty of food, water, tools, and good equipment.

## 18. Valle Vidal Wildlife Management Unit

**Nearest Town:** Cimarron (southeast entrance), Amalia (northwest entrance)

**Best Season to Visit:** Summer and fall

**Visitor Information:** The east side of the unit, east of the Taos/Colfax county line, is closed January 1–March 31 for elk calving. The area west of the county line is closed May 1–June 31 for elk calving. The area opens each year on July 1 to hiking and mountain biking. There are no services or amenities in the unit; bring all your own water and provisions.

**Getting There:** From Cimarron, take US 64 east. Turn left after 4.7 miles at the Valle Vidal Unit sign. The long gravel road that meanders through the area can be rough in areas. From Taos, go north on NM 522 to Costilla. Turn right on NM 196 to a viewing area.

To settle in and enjoy a bit of quiet in nature, the Valle Vidal is the spot to take the family. On a trip in early fall, my kids were awed by the sound of elk bugling. If you're lucky, you'll get to witness a pair of males knocking their antlers together in a battle for mates. Since there are no official trails in the area, we also enjoyed wandering in the meadows and practicing our orienteering and GPS skills to get us safely back to camp. Between Costilla and

Cimarron on US 64 is 100,000 acres of prime elk habitat in the Valle Vidal. A herd of about 2,000 elk make their home among high, rolling meadows, forested hills, and meandering streams. Black bears are also common, although rarely spotted here.

### FISHING

Located at the edge of a large meadow bordered by thick woods at 9,500' the Shuree Ponds are open July 1–December 31 and are stocked with 15" or larger rainbow trout. One pond is reserved for anglers under 11. Open daylight hours from 30 minutes before sunrise until sunset. The daily bag is two fish 15" or longer, and only artificial flies or lures with single, barbless hooks may be used. Fall is an ideal time to fish here. The half-mile trail to the ponds is located in the back of Cimarron Campground. The streams throughout the Valle Vidal are catch-and-release and are good for Rio Grande cutthroat trout.

### CAMPING

Two campgrounds are located in Valle Vidal—McCrystal Creek Campground and Cimarron Campground.

## 19. Rio Costilla Park

(505) RIO-PARK

www.riocostilla.com

**Nearest Town:** Costilla

**Best Season to Visit:** Late spring–early fall

**Visitor Information:** Open from May 15 to Labor Day Weekend. Latir Lakes are closed until July 1 to allow native trout to spawn undisturbed. Entrance and camping fees apply.

**Getting There:** From Taos, take NM 522 north to the town of Costilla. Turn east on NM 196 and continue for 15 miles into a box canyon and to the park visitor center. To reach the Little Blue Lake or the bottom lake in the series of nine alpine lakes, you'll need a 4×4 high-clearance vehicle.

The gem of this location is the 1.5-mile hike from the lower Latir Lake to the ninth Latir Lake above the tree line. The hike is steep but short enough to keep kids enjoying it. Add frequent stops to enjoy the waterfalls and colorful wildflowers, inspect animal tracks and scat, and spot songbirds that will accompany you the entire way. Each lake has its own special beauty.

A second trip to Little Blue Lake is worth it just to see the turquoise color of the small alpine lake and skip rocks on its shores. Camping in the high country at the lower lake is a unique experience.

The lower camping areas in the meadows along Rio Costilla are also kid-friendly, with bikeable roads and streams and meadows to explore.

This private park on the edge of Valle Vidal in the Latir Mountain range is owned and operated by the Rio Costilla Cooperative Livestock Association. They manage over 80,000 acres of land; 10,000 of these are open to the public for camping, fishing,

hiking, and mountain biking. The spectacular high peaks of Latir, Mount Blanca, and Ortiz Mountain can be seen from most areas of the park. Inside the park, Big Costilla Peak, Ventero Peak, and adjacent peaks range in elevation from 12,700' to 12,900'. The park has designated campsites on the Rio Costilla and at the lowest of a series of high alpine Latir Lakes that reach an altitude of 11,930'.

### WILDLIFE

Deer, elk, wild turkeys, and bighorn sheep are abundant in the park. Black bears and mountain lions are elusive but present. Watch for an occasional golden eagle.

### FISHING

Fishing for Rio Grande cutthroat trout is excellent on the Rio Costilla and at Latir Lakes.

Waterfalls and high alpine lakes are among the gems of Rio Costilla Park

The Palisades Picnic Area's impressive monoliths in Cimarron Canyon State Park

## 20. Cimarron Canyon State Park

(575) 377-6271

www.emnrd.state.nm.us/SPD/cimarron
canyonstatepark

**Nearest Town:** Eagle Nest

**Best Season to Visit:** Year-round

**Visitor Information:** Open all year; check
website for details.

**Getting There:** From Eagle Nest, travel 3 miles
on US 64 to the park signs. Continue east 4
miles to the Palisades Picnic Area and 4
more miles to the end of the canyon.

♿ picnic areas and some campgrounds
accessible

For climbers or naturalists, this park has a
lot to offer families. Set in New Mexico's
high country, the swiftly flowing Cimarron
River runs through this narrow, forested
canyon. The Palisades Picnic Area features
rugged cliffs that tower 800' over the road.
The park's beautiful views, interesting
geology, quiet camping, fly fishing, and hiking and equestrian trails sit at the center of
the Colin Neblett Wildlife Management
Area, the largest in the state.

### WILDLIFE

Wildlife viewing is plentiful, especially if
hiking to more remote areas on surrounding mesas and mountains. Early morning
and late evening are best to view the elk,
deer, bears, turkeys, grouse, and an occasional black bear that call the park home.
Abert's squirrels, golden-mantled ground
squirrels, and Colorado and least chipmunks are abundant year-round.

### BIRDWATCHING

Downy woodpeckers, Steller's and Canada
jays, Clark's nutcrackers, mountain chickadees, pygmy nuthatches, and Townsend's
solitaires are year-round residents in the

park. Summer brings violet-green swallows, house wrens, and western tanagers in the riparian and mountain forests.

### FISHING

The cool, high mountain park offers excellent trout fishing. Anglers can fish 8 miles of premier brown trout waters for stocked browns or rainbows. Small trout and solitude can be found in the Cimarron River's tributaries—Clear Creek and Tolby Creek.

### CLIMBING

Cimarron Canyon has short sport routes on two 50'-high metamorphosed sandstone cliffs. Maverick Cliff has routes from 5.4 to 5.11. Fred's Friendly Face, at 5.4, is an excellent beginner wall. The crag is located 0.3 miles east of Maverick Campground at a small dirt pullout off US 64.

### CAMPING

Campgrounds along US 64 include Maverick, Toby, Ponderosa, and Blackjack Campgrounds. Most have room for RVs. Maverick offers quiet walk-in tent campsites along the Cimarron River.

## Jemez Mountains

The Jemez Mountains are a volcanic group of mountains in northcentral New Mexico. Much of the range is federal land, including the Santa Fe National Forest, Bandelier National Monument, and the Valles Caldera National Preserve. State lands include camping facilities at Fenton Lake State Park. Private and Santa Clara Pueblo lands are closed to public use. Los Alamos and the Los Alamos National Laboratory occupy the eastern portion of the range, with Jemez Springs on the west and Cuba on the western foothills.

Elevations range from about 5,600' at the Rio Grande to 11,561' at the summit of Chicoma Mountain. The mountains are a popular destination for hiking, mountain biking, and rock climbing. Due to constraints of geography and land ownership, the towns of Los Alamos and White Rock are compact, populated places. Outside of these, the mountains are sparsely populated, and wildlife is abundant and diverse.

Numerous Puebloan Indian tribes have lived in the Jemez Mountains since before the Spanish arrived in New Mexico. The Pueblo Indians of this region are the Jemez people for which this mountain range is named, the Keresan Indians, and the Tewa Indians. The Jemez Mountains play a significant role in the culture of the Pueblo people, as well as for the Hispanic and Anglo settlers who followed.

The Jemez are one of the most easily accessible mountain ranges in northern New Mexico. Forest roads created over nearly a century of logging and mining activity provide multiple vehicle routes into the mountains. But the patchwork of public, tribal, and private lands limit

The Rio Grande cuts a 900' deep valley at White Rock Canyon

Waterfalls and swimming holes of Jemez Falls area

long-distance hiking, except in the Bandelier National Monument area.

### WILDLIFE

The Jemez Mountains harbor elk, deer, black bears, coyotes, beavers, and a small but stable population of mountain lions, which typically flee from humans. Smaller mammals such as raccoons, skunks, golden-mantled ground squirrels, Gunnison's prairie dogs, and gophers are common. White Rock Canyon is notorious for rattlesnakes.

### BIRDWATCHING

The high elevation Jemez Mountains laced with creeks and rivers provide excellent habitat for birds. Watch for American dippers, American kestrels, barn owls, grosbeaks, orioles, Cooper's hawks, warblers, woodpeckers, and many more. The Rio Grande supports a significant migratory flyway that brings many birds (notably,

sandhill cranes) to the Pajarito Plateau during migration seasons (spring and fall). Three species of hummingbirds are abundant during summer and can be seen at the Pajarito Environmental Education Center.

## 21. Santa Fe National Forest/ Jemez Mountains

HIKE | JEMEZ FALLS

**Distance:** 0.5 miles one-way
**Difficulty:** Easy
**Getting There:** Located in the Jemez Falls Campground off NM 4.

This heavily used trail is a favorite mountain excursion for families, so if you don't love crowds, it's best to visit on a weekday. My kids loved playing in the pools at the bottom of the upper falls and quickly made new friends with other visiting kids. A trail from the campground leads to the highest waterfall in the Jemez Mountains on the East Fork of the Jemez River. The short trail is great for hikers of all levels and ends at an overlook of the 70' falls. It is also accessible from Battleship Rock to the west or East Fork Trailhead from the east, if you want to lengthen your walk through the woods. From the overlook, hiking upstream will take you to a smaller waterfall with a large natural pool for cooling off or having lunch at the sandy edge.

## HIKE | LAS CONCHAS TRAIL

**Distance:** 4 miles out and back

**Difficulty:** Easy

**Getting There:** From Los Alamos, take Diamond Drive to West Road. Turn right onto W. Jemez Road/NM 501. At the junction with NM 4, turn right again. Take NM 4 to Las Conchas Trailhead, which will be on the right.

This stroll along the East Fork of the Jemez River is an easy, relaxing hike with kids. The rock walls with crevices to explore, several crossings on interesting bridges, and stopping to play in the water keep it fun for kids. Although it is heavily trafficked, the stunning scenery and wet meadows—perfect for finding wildflowers from June to September—make it worth the extra company. The trail follows a stream flowing in through a rocky canyon in a deep conifer forest and then meanders through a series of open meadows. The trail goes for nearly 2 miles before climbing out of the canyon in a series of switchbacks, a good point to retrace your steps back to the trailhead.

## CLIMBING

*Las Conchas, Jemez Mountains*
At the same location as the Las Conchas Trail. With cool summer temperatures and more than 150 climbs, this crag is accessible year-round and one of the more popular summer sport climbing areas in northern New Mexico. While there are fewer beginner routes, the easier stuff is top-notch.

Shorter 20–30' climbs take you to winning views of the Jemez. Some classics include the 5.7+ Johnny Can't Lead and a 5.8 called Crucible.

### CROSS-COUNTRY SKIING/SNOWSHOEING

Easy-rated ski trails in the Jemez include the 3-mile-long Pajarito Nordic Ski Trail, beginning at the Guaje Canyon Trailhead at the Pajarito Mountain Ski Area; the Las Conchas Trail; the Calzada Trail in the Peralta Canyon Trails on the west side of NM 4 just past Valles Caldera; FR 376 to San Antonio Hot Springs, FR 144/Fenton Hill Road; and St. Peter's Dome Road and Upper Frijoles Ski Trails in Bandelier.

## 22. Pajarito Environmental Education Center

(505) 662-0460

www.peecnature.org

**Nearest Town:** Los Alamos

**Best Season to Visit:** Year-round

**Visitor Information:** A good two-hour stop. Open daily except Thursdays; call ahead or check website for special programs and events.

**Getting There:** In Los Alamos, take Central Avenue to Canyon Road. PEEC is next door to the Aquatic Center.

♿ accessible

The Pajarito Plateau, for which the nature center is named, is part of the Jemez Mountains bounded on the east by the White Rock Canyon of the Rio Grande and on the west by the Valles Caldera, a 13.7-mile-wide volcanic caldera. Hot springs, streams, fumaroles, natural gas seeps, and volcanic domes dot the caldera floor.

Families with elementary-aged kids will enjoy the displays and terrariums full of critters on the way to other adventures in the Jemez Mountains. The center sits on the bluffs of Los Alamos with spectacular views

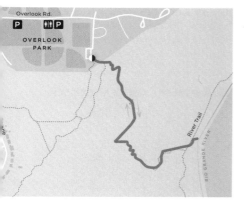

### BLUE DOT TRAIL
2 miles to the mini badlands

of the mesa country and surrounding peaks. The center has several indoor and outdoor interpretive exhibits, live small animal displays, a full-dome planetarium, wildlife viewing areas, penstemon wildflower gardens, a kids' play area, a bookstore and gift shop, and knowledgeable interpretive staff.

### HIKE | BLUE DOT TRAIL

**Distance:** 2 miles to the mini badlands
**Difficulty:** Strenuous because it's steep
**Getting There:** From White Rock, turn onto Rover Boulevard from NM 4. Follow the signs for Overlook Park. Take the first left onto Meadow Lane and continue 0.7 miles to the entrance of Overlook Park. Turn left and continue past the baseball diamonds and soccer fields on the paved road to the parking area and trailhead.

This is one of the most scenic trails in New Mexico, dropping from the White Rock Canyon rim to the Rio Grande. Springtime wildflowers can be abundant, adding splashes of color against the sheer, black basalt cliffs. Before you begin the 900' descent into the canyon, take in the stunning view of the gorge carved by the south-flowing Rio Grande. The Sangre de Cristo Mountains fill the eastern horizon at the mouth of the canyon. Tell kids to watch for petroglyphs on the black volcanic rocks tumbled throughout the canyon. Make a game out of deciding what stories the ancient art tells. Descend two benches with big sagebrush to a natural spring near the river. Reach a junction with the River Trail and turn right to continue on through a mini badlands and find a large beach on the river. Explore the shady riparian forests and enjoy the springs near the river, then return

Natural springs along the Blue Dot Trail

the way you came. For those not up for the steep descent into the canyon, walk along the White Rock Canyon Rim Trail at the top, which retains the incredible views for the length of the flat, easy trail.

### MOUNTAIN BIKING

The Los Alamos area is riddled with mountain biking trails, including an underrated but intense bike park at Pajarito Mountain Ski Area. The "tuff" (a rock of volcanic origin) trails have sticky traction, making it great for mountain biking.

In the Los Alamos County trail system, recommended bike trails for beginners include Bayo Point Trail, an easy and fast ride out and back, and Canyon Rim Trail on an easy, paved path with views of the canyon and Santa Fe.

### CLIMBING

*Gallows Edge, White Rock Canyon*

**Getting There:** From NM 4, turn south on Rover Boulevard. Turn left on the first street on your left, Meadow Lane. Stay on Meadow Lane for 1.3 miles and park near 719 Meadow Lane. Please respect the homeowners and don't block mailboxes or driveways. A concrete public access trail heads down between 719 and 721 Meadow Lane. At the end of the concrete, veer slightly left and continue straight toward the cliffs. Follow the trail down to the third shelf.

Climbing at White Rock is not only fun, it's also beautiful. The area boasts gorgeous views of the Rio Grande and the Sangre de Cristo Mountains. There are over 375 documented climbs at three main climbing hubs in White Rock, near Los Alamos. The Overlook is well-loved by experienced climbers, and Gallows Edge offers several beginner climbing options. At Gallows Edge, there are over 20 routes ranked 5.9 and lower. Princess Buttercup, rated 5.6 at

the main wall at Gallows Edge, is great for beginners. Other classics nearby include the Fire Swamp and 99 Red Balloons, both 5.8s.

## 23. Bandelier National Monument

(505) 672-3861

www.nps.gov/band

**Nearest Town:** Los Alamos

**Best Season to Visit:** Year-round, though spring and fall are best. Midsummer is hot and winter snow can cause trail closures.

**Visitor Information:** In busy summer months— mid-May to mid-October—travelers who want to park at the monument must arrive before 9 a.m. Otherwise, visitors will have to take the shuttle from the White Rock Visitor Center located at 115 NM 4.

**Getting There:** Take US 285 from Santa Fe and merge right onto NM 502 to Los Alamos. Continue on NM 502 toward Los Alamos. Bear right and exit onto NM 4 toward White Rock. Continue for 12 miles, passing White Rock. Bandelier's entrance will be on your left.

The park's most famous features are the ladders that climb up into cavates or cliff dwellings carved into the soft rock. My kids were delighted to climb, explore, and learn about the history for the better part of a morning. We sat in the caves carved into the side of a cliff overlooking a vast expanse of juniper and sagebrush and imagined women stone-grinding corn for flatbread, men plucking feathers from the breasts of freshly killed turkey, and children splashing in the nearby creek.

We stopped first at the visitor center and picked up their Junior Ranger packets (appropriate for K–7th graders) and a trail guide pamphlet that informed us about what we were seeing. We returned at the end of our adventure to earn their badges, a surprisingly effective motivator across the National Park system. The visitor center sells water and very few snacks, so be sure to pack your lunch, which you can eat at the park's shady picnic area. Dogs are not allowed on the park trails.

Bandelier National Monument protects over 33,000 acres of rugged but beautiful canyon and mesa country, as well as artifacts from Ancient Puebloan cultures going back over 11,000 years. The monument is located in the southern section of the Pajarito Plateau. Petroglyphs and standing masonry walls showcase the history of nearly 4,000 years of occupation of the Pueblo culture that still survives in the surrounding Native communities.

The visitor complex in Frijoles Canyon is accessible by vehicle; the rest of Bandelier is a hiker's park. Erosion has dissected the plateau into a complex of highly scenic mesas and canyons. A network of trails traverses the rugged backcountry south of Frijoles Canyon. This is high desert country from piñon-juniper and ponderosa pine forests on the plateau to mixed conifer-aspen forests in the mountains.

## HIKE | PUEBLO LOOP TRAIL

**Distance:** 1.4 mile loop
**Difficulty:** Easy
**Getting There:** Trail starts at the Bandelier Visitor Center.
♿ portions of the trail are accessible

Several trails lead up Frijoles Canyon from the visitor center, but this one—with ladders, caves, and the big kiva to explore—is the most interesting for families with children. The trail leads you past the ruins of Tyuonyi, the village and ceremonial site. Next are the cliff dwellings accessed along the Ruins Trail along the cliff base. Portions of the trail are paved and wheelchair and stroller accessible. The cliff dwellings trail returns to the main part of the canyon before long. Cross the small stream, El Rito de los Frijoles, to extend your hike to the

Alcove House. Towering ponderosa pines provide shade along the easy walking trail. Watch for Abert's squirrels, with their tassel ears and bushy tails, and common chipmunks and ground squirrels. In the evening, deer often appear in the meadows seemingly undisturbed by human presence in the canyon.

## CAMPING

Two established campgrounds are located in the monument. Juniper Family Campground for small groups is located near the entrance of the park off NM 4. Restrooms with water are available. Tent, trailer, and large RV accessible.

Ponderosa Campground for groups over 10 is located on NM 4, 6 miles west of the park entrance near the turnoff to NM 501. Reservations are required for this campground at www.recreation.gov, (877) 444-6777.

## HIKE | TSANKAWI RUINS

**Distance:** 1.5 mile loop
**Difficulty:** Moderate
**Getting There:** Near Los Alamos, from NM 502 turn onto NM 4. Less than a quarter of a mile past this turn, Tsankawi will be located on the left-hand side of the road. There are no signs for Tsankawi on NM 4. If you get to the stoplight, you've gone too far. There is an entry fee; no pets are allowed on trails at Bandelier.

The smooth pathways, cavates, and ladders on this hike are a favorite attraction for kids, allowing them to freely explore and engage with the ruins. Walk through this lesser-known site in Bandelier National Monument, which starts in a valley and tops out on a high mesa with long views of the Sangre de Cristo and Jemez Mountain ranges. Walk along the same trails used by Ancient Pueblo people when traveling from their homes at the mesa tops to their farms in the valley below. Thousands of footsteps have carved narrow trenches and rounded stairs into the soft, light-colored tuff. Peer into numerous cavate (caves created by people) cliff dwellings as you wind up the side of the mesa. Pass petroglyphs of people, animals, birds, and other designs. Climb the wooden ladders to arrive at the flat top of the mesa and the central location of the Ancestral Pueblo village of Tsankawi, who lived here in the 15th and 16th centuries. Take in the stunning views from which the Ancient Pueblo people would have overlooked other surrounding villages and enjoyed colorful sunrises and sunsets. Today, short-horned lizards, songbirds, coyotes, and other wildlife are the only remaining permanent residents.

Following in the footsteps of ancestors on the worn steps of Tsankawi Ruins

**TSANKAWI RUINS**
1.5 mile loop

## 24. Jemez Historic Site

(575) 829-3530

www.nmhistoricsites.org/jemez

**Nearest Town:** Jemez Springs

**Best Season to Visit:** Year-round

**Visitor Information:** Open Wednesday–Sunday, but call ahead for special closures.

**Getting There:** From Albuquerque, take US 550 to NM 4. Turn right onto NM 4 and continue for 18.3 miles to the historic site.

♿ accessible

The 700-year-old village of Giusewa was built in the narrow and beautiful San Diego Canyon by the ancestors of contemporary Jemez Pueblo. In 1621, the San José de Jémez Mission arrived, about the time the pilgrims landed at Plymouth Rock. A great kiva has been rebuilt. Climb in to experience their ceremonial center of life, all the more interesting juxtaposed next to the Spanish colonizers' Catholic church and mission compound. The pueblo was abandoned in 1680, when the Jemez participated in the Pueblo Rebellion, which evicted the Spanish from the region until 1692. The visitor center contains exhibitions that tell the story of the site through the words of the Jemez people. An interpretive trail winds through the impressive ruins. Every year around the winter holidays, *farolitos* placed

Gunnison's prairie dog kids wait for their parents' return at Valles Caldera National Preserve

along the ground and ledges of the ruins create a peaceful and magical atmosphere.

## 25. Valles Caldera National Preserve

*Valles Caldera Visitor Center*
(575) 829-4100, ext. 3
www.nps.gov/vall
**Nearest Town:** Los Alamos
**Best Season to Visit:** Year-round
**Visitor Information:** Open daily in the summer 8 a.m.–6 p.m., May 15–October 31; winter season November 1–May 14, 9 a.m.–5 p.m. Limited access for pets. Stop at the contact station for backcountry permits.
**Getting There:** From Los Alamos, take Diamond Drive, then a right on W. Jemez Road to the intersection with NM 4. Take a right, following the signs for Valles Caldera up into the Jemez Mountains. Continue 18 miles on NM 4; the signed entrance gate will be on the right.
♿ accessible

From charismatic prairie dogs and other wildlife, to leisurely fishing and playing in the many creeks, to an active day of biking, hiking, or snowshoeing, the Valles Caldera has a lot to offer families.

The preserve is known for huge

mountain meadows, running with fishable streams and plentiful wildlife. The combination of changes in elevation, abundant rainfall, deep, rich soils, old-growth ponderosa forests, and mixed conifer and aspen forests supports a great diversity of animals, plants, fungi, and wildlife. The large, grassy meadows rife with wildflowers in summer are surrounded by forest-covered volcanic domes, giving the landscape its distinctive look and the feeling of big sky and open spaces.

*Caldera* refers to the geologic history of this locale, when 1.25 million years ago a volcanic eruption created the 13-mile-wide depression that is the preserve. The caldera is dormant, but not extinct, and still displays signs of volcanic life with hot springs and boiling sulfuric acid fumaroles.

All that volcanic activity produced one of the area's greatest resources for past hunter and gatherer peoples: obsidian. Used for tools and weapons, obsidian was traded throughout North America. For more than 10,000 years and continuing today, the Pueblo and tribal people of New Mexico cherish the caldera and visit here for hunting, fishing, and gathering of plants for food, medicine, and ceremony.

During the time of Spanish and Mexican settlement in the late 1800s, the caldera became a hub for sheep and cattle grazing and over many years the land changed ownership, shifting through territories, land grants, and private ranches that transformed the landscape across the Southwest. Evidence of the various past landowners is found in the park's historical cabins and ranch buildings. Valles Caldera was established as a preserve in 2000 and entered a 15-year experiment in multiuse and local land management until it became part of the National Park system in December 2014.

The Contact Station, approximately 2 miles after the entrance, has a small gift shop, bathrooms in the parking lot, and knowledgeable park staff to help plan your visit. Kids can also get their Junior Ranger activity packet and earn a badge while in the park.

About a dozen well-marked trails are scattered throughout the park with a variety of difficulty levels from easy to strenuous, offering something for all levels of hikers. A permit is required to drive into the backcountry to access many of the hiking trails. Thirty-five permits are issued each day during the open season on a first come, first served basis. Besides busy holiday weekends, they almost never run out of permits.

### WILDLIFE

Several thousand elk roam the preserve, as well as healthy but rarely seen mountain lions, badgers, black bears, and coyotes, and endangered Gunnison's prairie dogs form large "towns." From the overlook off NM 4, scan the huge expanse of wet meadow framed by old volcanic domes on the horizon. Along the green ribbon of the East Fork of the Jemez River flowing through the meadows, several hundred elk can often be seen grazing in the late afternoon sun. A drive into the backcountry during the fall season almost guarantees an encounter with rutting elk, given the park's famous, numerous herd. Picnicking at the end of one of the backcountry roads at the edge of forest and meadow will afford the opportunity to at least hear elk bugling. The males' bugles bounce off the rows of trees lining the meadows and sound not unlike underwater whale song. It is one of nature's magical symphonies. Bring binoculars to increase your chances of seeing the full-antlered males face off.

Gunnison's prairie dogs form towns throughout the preserve, but two spots offer the most convenient viewing. A quarter mile west of the main entrance along

NM 4, stop at a pullout where Gunnison's prairie dogs can be spotted crossing the road. On a dry hillside, several dozen animals flit between bare mounds, the entrances to an elaborate underground town. Watch clusters of "kids" crowd together on mounds yelping for their parents, eating, and collecting plants in the surrounding field. When the parents return, or a young one ventures out into the field, they greet each other on their hind legs with nose rubs and face kisses. Another great place to catch their antics is in the fields surrounding the contact station. They seem to be acclimated to the presence of humans in this location, so getting a close look is possible without disturbing them.

### BIRDWATCHING

The National Audubon Society has named Valles Caldera as one of their Important Bird Areas. Birds of the New Mexico high mountains (southern Rocky Mountains) found here include three-toed woodpeckers, red-naped sapsuckers, band-tailed pigeons, Steller's jays, gray jays, white-breasted nuthatches, red-breasted nuthatches, mountain chickadees, ruby-crowned kinglets, western tanagers, house wrens, hairy woodpeckers, mountain bluebirds, hermit thrushes, Townsend's solitaires, MacGillivray's warblers, green-tailed towhees, white-throated swifts, and red crossbills. Red-tailed hawks and turkey vultures can be seen overhead. Occasionally a zone-tailed hawk from nearby Bandelier National Monument can be seen. The caldera contains an isolated breeding population of eastern meadowlarks.

### MOUNTAIN BIKING

Scenic mountain biking is allowed on the generally flat gravel roads that meander through the expansive meadows into the backcountry. For more of a challenge, biking is also allowed on retired and much steeper logging roads that crisscross through the mountain forests.

## FISHING

Waters in the Jemez Mountains are heavily stocked with rainbow trout and some brown trout. The cold-water streams in Valles Caldera are known for large-sized trout and are good for beginner and expert fly fishers. All waters within the preserve are Special Trout Waters, so bag limits and fishing restrictions apply. Anglers must have a NM fishing license. The confluence of the East Fork and Jaramillo has a near-perfect fishing hole.

## CROSS-COUNTRY SKIING/SNOWSHOEING

If you can hike, you can snowshoe on the same trails. The large, snow-covered meadows and valleys surrounded by scenic mountains and hills create one of the most scenic locations for cross-country skiing in New Mexico. Terrain and deeper snows on north slopes in the preserve make for better for cross-country skiing, but skiers are welcome throughout the preserve. The Valle Grande Bookstore in the contact station rents a limited number of snowshoes and poles.

### HIKE | LA JARA LOOP TRAIL

**Distance:** 1.5 round trip
**Difficulty:** Easy
**Getting There:** This trail leaves from the Valle Grande Contact Station.

As a mostly flat hike, this one is easy for the whole family in summer or for a winter snowshoe or cross-country ski to find tracks in the snow. One of the pleasures in midsummer is the abundance of wildflowers, mostly varieties of purple and blue penstemon, along the trail and, with them,

a prairie dog town. The antics of the rare Gunnison's prairie dog kids and their parents are fun to watch from the trail or the contact station where the trail begins. This trail gives a good view of the area with open meadows on one side and wooded mountains on the other. Be sure to pack your field guides for animal scat and tracks to practice identifying elk, coyote, and small mammal signs.

## CAMPING

Valles Caldera is day-use only. Camping is available in the nearby Jemez Mountains.

## 26. Natural Hot Springs

No trip to a volcanic area would be complete without a soak in a natural hot spring. Fortunately, the Jemez has several to choose from. The dramatic geologic history centered around the Valles Caldera's ancient super volcano has left its mark in the form of soothing, natural thermal springs. These are day-use-only primitive springs.

### McCauley Hot Springs
**Distance:** 2 miles one-way
**Getting There:** Trailhead starts in the parking lot to Jemez Falls in the Jemez Falls Campground or at the Battleship Rock Picnic Area.

If you are looking for a quiet soak with just you and your family, this is not it. Soaking here is a well-loved community event. But, as an introduction to hot springs in a serene natural setting, it can't be beat. From the Jemez Falls parking lot, the hike is steady uphill all the way to the hot springs but as long as you are not in a hurry, even most toddlers can manage it. The trail offers great views of the red rock formations and forested hills. Camping is available at Jemez Falls Campground.

### San Antonio Hot Springs

**Distance:** 5 miles one-way if the road is closed

**Getting There:** Off NM 126 on FR 376, 2 miles from the La Cueva junction with NM 4.

The 5-mile road to the San Antonio Hot Springs is a decently maintained gravel road, but it is not always open to vehicle traffic. The hike through lush ponderosa pine forest to these primitive hot springs is well worth it for those who are able, as the hot springs are actually hot and in a stunning natural setting. Built into the side of San Antonio Canyon, a series of rock-edged pools cascade down a hillside with the hottest at the top and a cool river at the bottom. Although you may not have the springs to yourself, the distance keeps the crowds away. No camping is allowed near the hot springs. Across NM 4 from the trailhead parking area, dispersed camping is allowed along the 20+ miles of FR 376.

### CAMPING

### Paliza Campground

**Getting There:** In the lower Paliza Canyon, access to the campground is off FR 10. The last 2 miles are dirt and can be difficult for low-clearance vehicles. High-clearance vehicle recommended.

Nestled in ponderosa pine forest, this 30-site campground is tent only with vault toilets and no water. This campground is a first come, first served facility, no reservations accepted.

### San Antonio Campground

**Getting There:** From the junction of NM 4 and NM 126 at La Cueva, take NM 126 for approximately 2 miles to the campground turnoff.

Located along the San Antonio River in ponderosa pine forests and meadows. This extremely popular campground has 20 sites total, six RV- and trailer-accessible sites, and a large group campground with walk-in sites. Vault toilets and water are available.

Reservation only from mid-May through early September at www.recreation.gov, (877) 444-6777.

### Jemez Falls Campground

**Getting There:** Located on NM 4 approximately 6 miles east from the NM 126/NM 4 junction and 8 miles west from the entrance to Valles Caldera National Preserve. A large Forest Service sign marks the entrance. From the turnoff, continue on approximately 1 mile of paved road to campground.

Located in ponderosa pine forest near the East Fork Jemez River. Campground has 52 sites; some are trailer and RV accessible. Vault toilets and water are available.

The campground is reservation only at www.recreation.gov, (877) 444-6777.

### Redondo Campground

**Getting There:** Approximately 3 miles west of Jemez Falls Campground and 2 miles east of the NM 4/NM 126 junction at La Cueva. Located within the Jemez Mountain Recreation Area.

This is the largest campground in the Jemez, with 62 campsites accessible for tents, trailers, and RVs. There are no utility hookups or water. No reservations accepted at this campground; first come, first served basis.

## 27. San Pedro Parks Wilderness

*Santa Fe National Forest,*
*Cuba Ranger District*
    (575) 289-3264
    www.fs.usda.gov/santafe
**Nearest Town:** Cuba
**Best Season to Visit:** Summer
**Visitor Information:** The road from Cuba is open year-round.

San Gregorio Reservoir is regularly stocked with trout and is a favorite family fishing spot

**Getting There:** The San Pedro Parks lie just to the east of Cuba, New Mexico, in the Santa Fe National Forest.

The rolling, open nature of this area makes it a friendly destination for families. Walking (or running) through the meadows looking for bugs and flowers, trying their hand at fishing, and playing along the edge of streams provided hours of entertainment for my kids. San Pedro Parks is technically in the San Pedro Mountains in the Nacimiento range just west of the Jemez range. In this case, *mountain* is a misnomer. You will find no peaks to stare at or ascend, no jagged rock faces. The range is an uplifted plateau of granite that still manages to create some thigh-burning sections of trail. Even without prominent peaks, the average elevation here is over 10,000'.

The defining features of the 41,132-acre wilderness parks are the large, grassy wildflower meadows framed by dense stands of spruce and mixed conifer trees. Camping is allowed anywhere in the wilderness area. Endless beautiful spots near streams, meadows, and trees will entice you to spend a few days. The Las Palomas Trail will take you into the heart of the parks and connect to the Continental Divide Trail that climbs through this area.

Easily accessible by a short hike, San Gregorio Reservoir is the main body of water in the parks. Various streams cut through the meadows and mountains, supporting the native Rio Grande cutthroat population. Fishing and hiking are popular summer pastimes in the parks, as are cross-country skiing and snowshoeing in winter.

### WILDLIFE

Elk, deer, black bears, turkeys, and other wildlife call this expansive ground their home. Note that San Pedro Parks is also open to cattle grazing for ranchers with permits.

### FISHING

San Gregorio Reservoir, which predates the area's designation as a wilderness area, is 1 mile from the parking area and is a very popular fishing lake for families. The clear streams that wander through the forest and meadows of the park and are usually abundant with trout.

### HIKE | SAN GREGORIO RESERVOIR

**Distance:** 2 miles round trip
**Difficulty:** Easy
**Getting There:** From Cuba, take NM 126 about 6 miles, all but the last half mile paved. Turn onto FR 70 (well-marked and large signs pointing to San Pedro Parks), reaching the trailhead in 3 miles.

Restrooms at the San Gregorio Trailhead are well kept and interpretive signs introduce the area. San Gregorio Reservoir is a lovely man-made high mountain lake surrounded by soggy meadows. It is a popular destination for fishing and is stocked with Rio Grande cutthroat trout and rainbow trout, although some years the lake can dry up. This is a very popular destination on summer weekends, but the lake is also accessible through the winter.

### HIKE | SAN PEDRO PARKS

**Distance:** 8 miles one-way
**Difficulty:** Strenuous
**Getting There:** From Cuba, take NM 126 about 6 miles, all but the last half mile paved. Turn onto NM 70 (well-marked and large signs pointing to San Pedro Parks), reaching the trailhead in 3 miles.

While there are eight other trailheads to enter this wilderness area, the San Gregorio Trailhead is the gentlest way to the high altitude open meadows at the center of the parks. After the reservoir (see above hike), continue on the Las Vacas Trail 51 to the junction with the Continental Divide Trail. Turn left at the trail junction to arrive in the largest section of open meadows. Several trails and creeks cross through this area, providing many great camping spots and day hike options. Pick up a map of the

**SAN PEDRO PARKS** 8 miles one-way

wilderness area at the Ranger Station in Cuba and plan a loop or a shuttle trip.

### CAMPING

Backpacking available throughout the wilderness. Dispersed car camping, including RV-accessible locations, is available on FR 70 on the way to the San Gregorio trailhead.

*Rio de Las Vacas Campground*
**Getting There:** From Cuba, travel 12 miles east on NM 126.

This developed campground offers a peaceful jumping-off point for day hikes into San Pedro Parks Wilderness. The campground has paved RV pads, fire rings, picnic tables, and vault toilets. In the fall, elk can be heard bugling from the campground. The Rio de las Vacas stream runs alongside the east boundary of the campground and offers fishing adjacent to camping sites. Potable water and vault toilets are available in the campground.

*Clear Creek Campground*
Also located on the Rio de Las Vacas stream, 1 mile up the road from Rio de Las Vacas Campground. Open May–October, both campgrounds are first come, first served and can be busy on weekends and holidays.

## 28. Fenton Lake State Park

(575) 829-3630

www.emnrd.state.nm.us/SPD/fentonlakestate
park.html

**Nearest Town:** Jemez Springs

**Best Season to Visit:** Spring–fall; the road may be closed due to snow in winter.

**Visitor Information:** Open and accessible year-round, depending on road conditions. No visitor center in the park.

**Getting There:** From the south, take NM 4 until about 10 miles north of Jemez Springs. Take a right onto NM 126. After about 10 miles, you'll see the sign and entrance to the park.

With paved and gravel roads for kids to ride bikes and a playground for toddlers, Fenton Lake State Park is a great mellow basecamp for your Jemez Mountain adventures. The Jemez Mountains provide the backdrop for this year-round escape nestled in beautiful ponderosa pine forests. It's close to Valles Caldera National Preserve, Bandelier National Monument, and hiking and fishing spots. At 7,650' in elevation, be prepared for warm days and cool nights during the summer. This is not a swimming lake, but fishing and canoeing or kayaking are popular on the 137-acre, motor-free lake. Its calm waters are great for kids to learn paddling and fishing. Two short hiking trails start from the campground and

offer a jaunt through the woods and along the lakeshore. Although most anglers prefer the warmth and comfort of summer, there is also winter ice fishing, which is in itself an adventure kids won't soon forget. The park is also a destination for cross-country skiing and snowshoeing.

### CAMPING

This state park was built for tent camping. The tent camping sites have lovely views into the meadows and valleys. Even though there are electrical hookups for small RVs in a few sites, RVers will find this campground and the small dirt road that winds through the trees difficult to navigate. This is a popular spot on summer weekends; weekdays and the off-season are quiet.

### FISHING

The lake is stocked with rainbow trout from fall through spring and is home to German brown trout. Many find the lake and the Rio Cebolla, which flows through the park, ideal for fly fishing. The lake, only a few miles from Seven Springs Fish Hatchery, is stocked with brown, rainbow, and Rio Grande cutthroat trout with a kids' fishing area.

### LOCAL ATTRACTIONS, BUSINESSES

*Jemez Springs*
Commercial hot springs and lodges that are geared toward relaxation for adults; many do not allow kids under 10 years old. www.jemezsprings.org

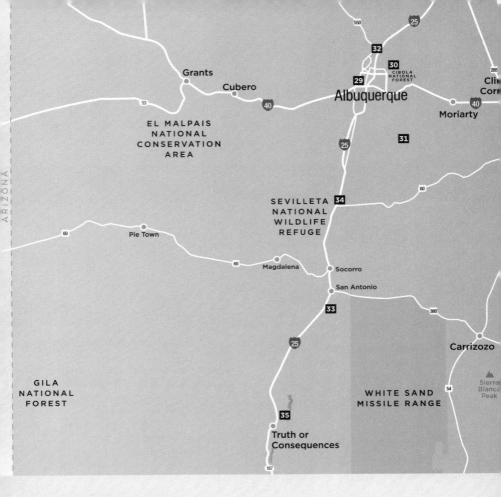

# Albuquerque and Surrounds

Amid the urban sprawl of Albuquerque that occupies much of the Central Rio Grande, open spaces offer recreational opportunities for hiking, birdwatching, kayaking, bike riding, and nature explorations.

Extending from the spillway below Cochiti Dam near Santa Fe to Elephant Butte Reservoir outside of Truth or Consequences, the green ribbon of the Middle Rio Grande is an oasis in the otherwise arid desert Southwest. The bosque is a cottonwood woodland that lines the Middle Rio Grande. This unique riverside ecosystem also includes wetlands, ponds, moist meadows, and willow stands that are home to large numbers of plants and animals.

The Sandia Mountains rise from the populated foothills of Albuquerque to provide a respite from the heat in summer and snowbird opportunities in winter. The rugged Manzano Mountains south of the city provide an opportunity for solitude, extended outdoor adventures, and exciting naturalist experiences. Hiking, camping, backpacking, and mountain biking can be enjoyed in both these mountain ranges.

## 29. Rio Grande Nature Center State Park

(505) 344-7240

www.rgnc.org

**Nearest Town:** Albuquerque

**Best Season to Visit:** Year-round

**Visitor Information:** The visitor center is open daily. Admission fees apply.

**Getting There:** The Rio Grande Nature Center State Park lies within Albuquerque off Candelaria Road NW.

♿ accessible

When the crowds and heat of Albuquerque become overwhelming, escape to the Rio Grande Nature Center State Park. This

entrée into the bosque ecosystem is a shady, forested oasis where the Rio Grande and woodland combine to become one riparian area. Two miles of nature trails wind through tall cottonwoods and past willow thickets to open sand flats alongside the big river. The combination makes the bosque a haven for an unusual variety of flora and fauna that rely on both the river and the forest. Children will delight in looking for animal signs recorded in the sandy soil. The river is shallow in parts but take note that deep pools tend to develop along the shore, so watch kids at the edge. Regular programming at the park includes guided bird and nature walks, lectures, workshops, kids' classes, and three annual festivals.

Inside the visitor center, the kid-focused discovery room is filled with hands-on activities, including an animal-footprint sand table, a magnifying table, and a "rubbing" table for nature drawings. After checking out a pair of loaner binoculars, I sat with my boys for a while in the comfortable chairs of the glassed-in observation room that overlooks a 3-acre pond. My kids enjoyed up-close views of ducks, geese, sunning turtles, and dragonflies while listening to bird sounds pumped in from a microphone set up next to bird feeders.

### BIRDWATCHING

The bosque is located on the Rio Grande flyway, a migration route and birdwatching hotspot throughout the year. This green ribbon in the desert provides food, shelter, and water for large numbers of ducks, geese, sandhill cranes, and a host of other migratory birds. Herons and egrets are common here. Visitors can observe about 250 species of birds, including roadrunners and wood ducks. Migrating songbirds are best viewed in spring and fall. Winter brings sandhill cranes at the river and porcupines in the trees. In summer, lizards skitter across the trails and hummingbirds sip nectar from flowering plants.

HIKE AND BIKE | **PASEO DEL BOSQUE TRAIL**

**Distance:** 16 miles one-way
**Difficulty:** Easy
**Getting There:** Candelaria Road dead-ends at the nature center.
♿ accessible

With easy access from the Rio Grande Nature Center, this 16-mile paved path provides bikers and walkers with a scenic jaunt through the bosque. Other unpaved trails on both sides of the river are used frequently by hikers, horse and bike riders, and birdwatchers. Choose a patch of trail and play a while.

## 30. Sandia Mountains

*Cibola National Forest,*
*Sandia Ranger District*
  (505) 281-3304
  www.fs.usda.gov/cibola

*Sandia Peak Tramway*
  (505) 856-7325
  www.sandiapeak.com

Located in Albuquerque's backyard, these mountains are well-loved and well-used. The wilderness boundary is no more than 1 mile from housing developments where Albuquerqueans can slip into designated open spaces in the foothills such as the Elena Gallegos Picnic Area for a power walk at lunch or a sunset mountain bike ride. Weekends see long waits for the spectacular tram ride up to the Crest Trail and lines of hardy hikers huffing up the steep La Luz Trail. And still, the wilderness with 29 marked trails (over 150 miles) offers so

The view of the Sandia Mountains from Elena Gallegos Open Space

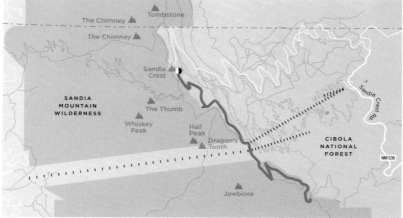

**SANDIA CREST TRAIL** Distance varies depending on your route

many options that you can find a few miles of solitude even in this urban playground.

HIKE | **SANDIA CREST TRAIL**

**Distance:** Varies depending on your route

**Difficulty:** Easy to difficult

**Getting There:** Two main entry points take you to the peak of the Crest Trail, from which you can choose your own adventure through the myriad of trails that branch off from the summit. To drive to the Crest Trail, take I-40 east from Albuquerque. Use Exit 175 to NM 14 North for 6 miles. Then turn left and follow NM 536 for 14 miles to the summit. Find the trailhead marked with a kiosk and restrooms. Or take the scenic Sandia Peak Tramway to the crest line, from which you can easily hop onto the La Luz Trail or Sandia Crest Trail.

The Sandia Crest Trail traverses the entire length of the Sandia Mountains and can be hiked in either direction. While the full 22.1-mile shuttle hike can be done in a day by skilled hikers, there are many alternate routes from easy and difficult to suit your skill level.

Take the Sandia Crest Trail from the Crest House to the Sandia Peak Tram that hugs the edge of the cliff with stunning views of the caprock and outcroppings below the crest. Or try the well-marked Crest Nature Trail with interpretive signage. Despite the crowds, this trail is a delight. Ask children to notice the difference in the plants along the bare cliff faces (low-growing and small to protect from the winds) and the forests (tall and sometimes spindly, searching for the light in the shade). A half-mile from the trailhead is Kiwanis Cabin, where gnarled trees make for great climbing. Kids will enjoy watching the Sandia Peak Tram scale the mountain on thick cables.

**BACKPACKING THE SANDIA CREST TRAIL**

Traverse the entire Sandia Mountain Crest on a grand two-day backpack trip with a car shuttle. Select one of many routes that vary in length and difficulty based on your ambitions. Start at the northern end of the trail at the Tunnel Springs Trailhead and hop onto the North Crest Trail. At the Crest

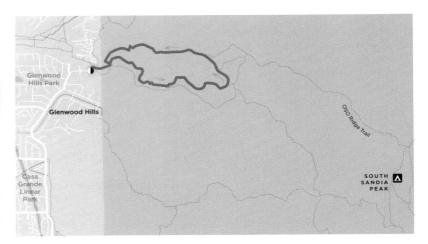

**EMBUDITO CANYON** 4 miles

House, the trail switches names to the South Crest Trail. Finish on the southern end at the Canyon Estates Trailhead. Good dispersed camping sites are located all along the trail, but the crest with shady pine trees offers some of the best camping areas.

## HIKE | EMBUDITO CANYON

**Distance:** 4 miles

**Difficulty:** Easy

**Getting There:** Take Montgomery Boulevard east from Tramway to Glenwood Hills Drive and turn left. Follow Glenwood Hills north and you will see a sign pointing to Embudito Trail. Turn east onto Trailhead Road, which leads you to the large parking area.

Follow this trail through a sandy wash to a lush canyon with a creek. Large boulders along the hills offer fun scrambling for agile kids and adults. The canyon is worth a visit for its pleasant shade, trickling stream, and small waterfall. Taking the 4-mile loop cuts off the steepest part of this trail.

## MOUNTAIN BIKING

*Sandia Peak Ski Area Bike Trails*

**Getting There:** From Albuquerque, take I-40 East to Exit 175, then drive north on NM 14 to the Crest Scenic Byway 536. The road ends at the crest and a large parking lot.

Sandia Peak offers over 30 miles of downhill and cross-country mountain bike trails with three beginner trails: Golden Eagle for downhill, Service Road and Capulin Spring Road are flat trails. The chairlift usually opens to bikes on Memorial Day weekend.

*Sandia Foothills—Elena Gallegos Picnic Area*

**Getting There:** Drive north on Tramway to Simms Park Road.

♿ accessible

A maze of trails networks through the foothills just below the Sandia Wilderness area. Some trails are closed to cyclists, so observe the signs at the well-marked intersections. The lower trails are nice cruisers with limited climbing and great for beginners and children. All the bike trails allow foot traffic, so keep your eyes open.

# 31. Manzano Mountains

*Cibola National Forest,*
*Mountainair Ranger District*
(505) 847-2990
www.fs.usda.gov/cibola

These lightly visited mountains harbor a variety of wildlife, including black bears, mule deer, mountain lions, desert bighorn sheep, and Abert's squirrels. Large patches of bigtooth maples and aspens put on a colorful fall show in the Fourth of July Campground area. The Manzanos are bordered on the north by the Kirtland Air Force Base and the Isleta Pueblo Indian Reservation. The Manzano Mountains Wilderness is composed of nearly 37,000 acres and 64 miles of trails, including the 22-mile-long Crest Trail with the highest summit, Manzano Peak, reaching 10,098'. If you are looking for a weekend of solitude, your family can find it here.

*Manzano Mountains HawkWatch*
www.hawkwatch.org/manzanos
**Visitor Information:** Reservations to visit the observation towers are not needed, but large groups can write to fieldtrips@hawkwatch.org to schedule a visit in advance.
**Getting There:** From Albuquerque, take I-40 East for 13 miles to Exit 175 for NM 337/NM 333 toward Tijeras. Continue onto NM 337 South for 29 miles. Turn right onto NM 55 South and continue for 12 miles. Turn onto County Road B066 and continue for 9 miles up to Capilla Peak (follow the signs to Capilla Peak Campground). The trailhead to reach the observation area can be seen on the west side of the road when you get to Capilla Peak. You can park on the side of the road near the trailhead sign and take the 0.7-mile hike to the observation site. This is a

moderate trail with few rocky sections and little, rolling elevation gain.

Each fall thousands of hawks, eagles, falcons, and other birds of prey migrate south along the crest of the Manzano Mountains, working their way between Canada in the summer and Mexico or Central America in the winter. Since 1985, HawkWatch International has been operating a site in the Manzano Mountains to learn more about raptors and their migration through the southern Rocky Mountain Flyway. Each year, from mid-August to early November, HawkWatch International conducts daily counts of the migrating raptors from lookouts along the Manzano crest. Naturalists teach visitors about migration ecology, raptor identification, and their research efforts. Annual counts typically range between 5,000 and 7,000 migratory raptors of up to 18 species. The experience and somewhat difficult trail will appeal to older children and adults. Spring is also a good time to view migrating hawks here, but the official HawkWatch program only operates in the fall.

HIKE | **FOURTH OF JULY CANYON**

**Distance:** 6.4 mile loop
**Difficulty:** Moderate
**Getting There:** From I-40, take Exit 175 to Tijeras. Follow NM 337 south 29 miles to the T-junction with NM 55. Turn right, going west 3.2 miles on NM 55 to Tajique. Turn right on FR 55 (also marked as A013) and go 7 miles up a gravel road, following the signs to the Fourth of July Campground. Turn right through the gate and park in the hiker parking area if not camping. The gate is locked November–March but you can still access the trailhead about 400' past the gate.

The presence of maples in New Mexico may come as a surprise to many. Meandering from a picnic area along well-established trails to the crest of the Manzano Mountains, this trail offers an awesome fall show of the southwestern species of maple trees. From the picnic area, start out on the Crimson Maple Trail, then catch the Fourth of July Spur Trail and loop back along Cerro Blanco Trail 79, ending with a short jaunt along FR 55 back to the campground. Vistas from the ridgeline stretch for miles in each direction. Leaf-peeping crowds turn out in autumn to see the concentrations of Rocky Mountain maple and golden aspens, but the trails are lightly used throughout the rest of the year.

## 32. Float the Middle Rio Grande

Unlike the intense stretches of whitewater of the Upper Rio Grande, the Middle Rio Grande is a serene, family friendly, Class I/II float with relatively minimal hazards. Local outfitters offer both self-guided and guided adventures that range from a few hours to a full day. Guided outings provide an interpretive aspect so you can learn about the landscape and creatures you see along the way. Floating trips usually begin in Bernalillo or Corrales.

**OUTFITTERS**

*Quiet Waters Paddling Adventures*
A solid choice for a flat-water adventure.
(505) 771-1234
www.quietwaterspaddling.com

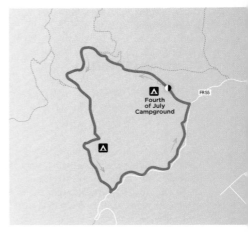

FOURTH OF JULY CANYON 6.4 mile loop

# South of Albuquerque

## 33. Bosque del Apache National Wildlife Refuge

(575) 835-1828
www.fws.gov/refuge/Bosque_del_Apache
www.friendsofbosquedelapache.org

**Nearest Town:** San Antonio

**Best Season to Visit:** November–February for cranes, and year-round for other wildlife.

**Visitor Information:** Visitor center open daily but hours change with seasons; check website for details. The 11-mile refuge driving and biking loop is open daily from one hour before sunrise until one hour after sunset.

**Getting There:** From Socorro, travel south on I-25 for 8 miles. Take Exit 139 following the road through San Antonio. Turn right at NM 1 and follow this road another 9 miles to the refuge.

 accessible

In the dark before dawn, a group of us stood at the water's edge as color began to dance across the sky and water. Through the shadows of twilight, we could see the silhouettes of thousands of white geese (snow and Ross's) and clusters of sandhill cranes stretching their wings to shake off the cold night. Their movements created a harmony of sound spanning several octaves. As the light began to arrive, their excitement and anticipation (and ours) intensified until finally, at the exact moment the sun breached the horizon and spread golden light across their backs, they lifted off the water as one, sending a great *whoosh* through the air with thousands of wings beating in union. Not a single snow goose was left on the water; all moved into the sky and headed north in unison. The ancient sounds of crane calls filled the air.

The morning fly-out is one of the great wildlife spectacles of New Mexico and possibly North America. Sandhill cranes, snow geese, a smattering of ducks and raptors, and an occasional whooping crane occupy the Bosque del Apache National Wildlife Refuge from late October through February each year.

The Rocky Mountain population of greater sandhill cranes is the most abundant and largest variety of sandhill crane that overwinters in the refuge. They stand 4' tall, with a wingspan of over 6'. These birds mate for life and live up to 25 years. Courtship displays by young birds are joyous if short events with bouncing, wing flapping, calling, and dancing often happening in groups. As the sun breaches the horizon in the morning, they take off to feed in the surrounding cornfields during the day and return to the wetland ponds of the refuge at night, where the water protects them from predators.

Though the cranes and geese may be the most charismatic residents, the 57,331-acre refuge is also the year-round home of javelina, coyotes, mule deer, bobcats, mountain lions, and foxes, which can sometimes be seen while driving or biking the 9-mile loop that circles the refuge. In spring, migrating sandpipers and other shorebirds visit the refuge and brightly colored wildflowers decorate the trails. Summer brings

Snow geese getting ready for dawn flight at Bosque del Apache National Wildlife Refuge in February

three species of hummingbirds easily seen at the feeders through the large windows of the visitor center. Many species of songbirds make this a great nature expedition any time of the year.

The Festival of Cranes is a major event on the refuge held each year the week before Thanksgiving. Visitors can participate in crane-behavior talks, photography workshops, guided tours of the wetlands, and even bird banding for kids. In recent years, the festival has been branching out into the cultural and scientific attractions in the surrounding area, such as the Very Large Array, one of the leading astronomical observatories on the planet, and Salinas Pueblo Missions National Monument.

### CAMPING

The refuge is day-use only, but there is basic camping nearby.

*Chupadero Mountain View RV Park*
(575) 518-8264

Located minutes from the refuge gate, this basic, no-frills RV park and campground is about the only accommodations in the area. The knowledgeable owners, Jose and Renata, are friendly hosts and will make you feel very welcome. Campers will appreciate heated bathrooms and RVers the full hookups. The train whistle might wake you up in the middle of the night, but so might the coyote howls; that's all part of the experience. The RV park doesn't have a website and reservations are recommended during crane season.

## 34. Bernardo Wildlife Area

**Nearest Town:** Bernardo
**Best Season to Visit:** October–February
**Visitor Information:** Open daily. The area has bathrooms but no other facilities.
**Getting There:** 50 miles south of Albuquerque

Sandhill cranes feasting in cornfields at the Bernardo Wildlife Area

on I-25, take the Bernardo exit.
♿ accessible

The Bernardo unit of the Ladd S. Gordon Waterfowl Complex provides winter habitat for waterfowl and sandhill cranes. This is a great stop on the way to Bosque del Apache and destinations south. From October to February, thousands of cranes can be seen feeding during the day in the cornfields. Driving another 10 minutes south to the La Joya unit will put you face-to-face with waterfowl, songbirds, and the rare Pecos sunflower that blooms here in large stands in September. Have caution visiting La Joya, as this is also a popular hunting location.

## 35. Elephant Butte Lake State Park

(575) 744-5923
www.emnrd.state.nm.us/SPD/elephantbutte lakestatepark.html

**Nearest Town:** Truth or Consequences
**Best Season to Visit:** Year-round
**Visitor Information:** Open year-round for day use and camping. Entrance fees apply.

**Getting There:** From Truth or Consequences, take NM 51 east. Then take NM 179 for entrance to the north portion of the lake or NM 177 for the south portion.

&#9855; accessible

Elephant Butte is New Mexico's largest state park and largest body of water. It impounds the Rio Grande River. Like Navajo Lake State Park, it has three large marinas renting everything from kayaks to speedboats to houseboats. Stretches of sandy beaches afford an afternoon spent playing in the water and casting from shore.

### FISHING

Record-breaking black, white, and striped bass, as well as crappie, bluegill, blue catfish, largemouth bass, smallmouth bass, and walleye.

### PADDLING

The Rio Grande just below Elephant Butte to just below Williamsburg on NM 187 or to Caballo Lake State Park is a very popular stretch of river for running in kayaks and canoes in the summer when the weather is hot and the water is cool. The passage—to Williamsburg about three hours and five and a half hours to Caballo Lake State Park—is mostly easy flat water with a couple of short or manageable portages when water is high (generally Class II, II+ in difficulty but the one or two sections can be bottom scrapers depending on water level). Check with state park managers for information on seasonal summer dam releases, flows, and projections for best take-out site.

Zia Kayak Outfitters: Located in the City of Elephant Butte, renting single and double kayaks, SUPs, fishing gear, and related accessories. Staff offers free basic instruction for would-be paddlers. (575) 744-4185

Playing on the mudflat islands of the Rio Grande

Sunset on Caballo Lake State Park

### MOUNTAIN BIKING

Mountain Biking along state park roads and nearby Dam Site Road is an intermediate experience with great views of the lake and surrounding rock formations.

### CAMPING

The park has four developed campgrounds, plus dispersed camping is allowed on the beaches.

Paseo del Rio Campground is a small but lovely campground on the Rio Grande below the dam. An accessible beach allows paddlers to put in their boats. Excellent birdwatching here in spring and fall. Pull-through sites have shaded picnic areas.

Nearby Caballo Lake State Park and Percha Dam State Park, both reservoirs along the Rio Grande, are also good fishing waters and summer and fall birdwatching locations.

Percha Dam State Park, where riparian woodlands remain along the Rio Grande, is reported to be one of the best places to watch birds in the state, especially during spring and fall migration. The east side of the park, in the thickets of willows and cottonwoods, has excellent warbler watching. Watch the river for ducks, shorebirds, and kingfishers; the bosque for hawks, owls, woodpeckers, flycatchers, and vireos; and

the scrubland for sparrows. Camping is available in the bosque area along the river.

Caballo Lake State Park has excellent winter viewing of birds. Watch for American pelicans, grebes, raptors, geese, ducks, owls, quail, phoebes, wrens, thrushes, sparrows, and finches. Camping is available in the campground along the river below the dam, and dispersed camping is allowed on the lakeshore above the dam.

### LOCAL ATTRACTIONS, BUSINESSES

*Sandia Peak Tramway*: The longest aerial tram in the Americas, taking you to the peak of the Sandia Mountains. The lines are often long, but the view from the tram is unforgettable. (505) 856-1532, www.sandiapeak.com

*Petroglyph National Monument*: One of the largest petroglyph sites in North America. Usner Boulevard NW at Western Trail, (505) 899-0205, ext. 335, www.nps.gov/petr

*ABQ BioPark*: An aquarium, zoo, and botanical gardens with Tingley Beach Fishing Ponds. (505) 768-2000, www.cabq.gov/culturalservices/biopark

*Albuquerque International Balloon Fiesta*: An enchanted world of balloon rodeos, twilight balloon glows, and mass ascensions. www.balloonfiesta.com

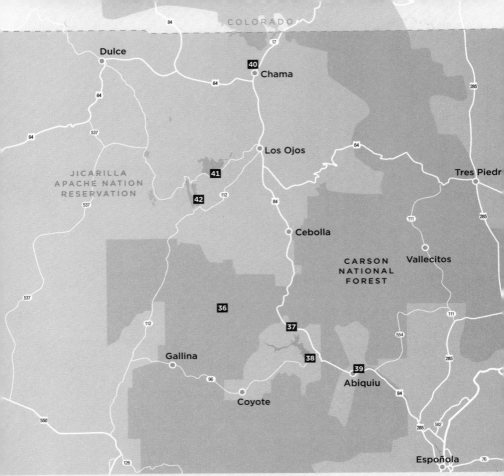

# Abiquiu Area

Kids will appreciate the ample pools and riffles to splash in along the Chama River Canyon and scenic trails to explore on foot or bike. The campgrounds here provide a great basecamp from which to explore a variety of sites within an hour's drive. The Rio Chama passes through some of the most beautiful mountain and desert country in New Mexico. Gently rolling sagebrush-covered plains surround a river that has carved colorful canyons of siltstone and sandstone at times 1,500' deep. Tall cliffs give way to heavily wooded side canyons where ponderosa pine and Douglas-fir cover north-facing slopes and add to the interest and adventure along this wild river.

The Rio Chama originates just north of the Colorado border in the San Juan Mountains and flows for 130 miles through New Mexico to its confluence with the Rio Grande. A 24.6-mile portion starting at El Vado Dam is designated as Wild and Scenic River, preserving its flow and natural character. For more than three centuries, an estimated 1,500 Puebloans built villages, farmed, and hunted along this river, leaving behind evidence of their lives in rich archaeological sites. One preserved side canyon showcases evidence of the river's earliest residents: dinosaur tracks.

Several trails take hikers from the sandstone cliffs of the uplands down to the river. FR 151 parallels the river for 12 miles. Developed campground and primitive camping sites provide easy access to the river.

## WILDLIFE

Rainbow and brown trout often flourish in the river. Mule deer, black bears, elk, coyotes, and mountain lions leave signs of their presence and movements onshore. Varying canyon elevations create a wide range of vegetation and habitat for about 80 different bird species. Keep your binoculars up to spot raptors, hawks, and owls perched along the canyon walls and surrounding trees.

## HIKE | CONTINENTAL DIVIDE TRAIL-OJITOS SEGMENT

**Distance:** 2 miles to 13.1 miles round trip, depending on turn-around point

**Difficulty:** Moderate

**Getting There:** Turn onto FR 151 from US 84 heading west, then northwest along the Rio Chama for 9.1 miles to Skull Bridge. A small parking area is located downstream of the bridge.

Short legs will appreciate this mostly flat, scenic portion of the Continental Divide Trail that crosses the Rio Chama and enters the sagebrush flats surrounded by pastel cliff faces. The trail is well marked with CDT posts and easy to follow. Make a game with children to see who can spot the next post first. The first 10 miles of the trail are relatively flat and easy hiking for children. Some portions of the trail have tall

**CONTINENTAL DIVIDE TRAIL-OJITOS SEGMENT** 2 miles to 13.1 miles round trip

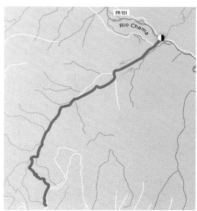

ponderosa pines for shade, which make good resting points, but most is exposed to the sun, so bring hats and water. Hike this trail early or late in the day. My boys especially enjoyed watching the flocks of scrub jays that entertain with their loud social behaviors along the trail. We spotted several other sagebrush-loving birds as well. From April to early June, wildflowers can be abundant after winter rain and snow.

### FISHING

The best trout fishing on the Chama River is within several miles of El Vado Dam. Fish species include trophy-sized brown trout, rainbow trout, and kokanee salmon. Kids will like the abundance of fish and adults will like their large size.

## 36. Rafting the Rio Chama

The first 6 miles of the Rio Chama pass through a narrow gorge suitable for expert kayakers only. Private land and fences cross the river, making the stretch from Chama to Tierra Amarilla impassable for boaters. The 15 miles between Tierra Amarilla and El Vado Reservoir is a deep canyon with ponderosa pines on the shores and several rapids, including the largest, dubbed Big Mama Chama.

A mile below the El Vado Dam, the privately owned Cooper Ranch serves as the put-in for a highly scenic 30-mile river trip on the Rio Chama to the Big Eddy take-out on FR 151. This stretch of the Chama is mostly a gentle float, punctuated by easy rapids that speed up near the trip's end. This section of the Chama is often done in three days/two nights. Experienced guides will take the time to stop and let kids

The Ojitos Segment of the Continental Divide Trail crosses the Rio Chama Valley

explore a historic homestead that was a hideaway for horse thieves, a hot spring, a ghost town, and, to the delight of budding paleontologists in the family, fossilized dinosaur footprints.

After the normal runoff season concludes in mid-June, water is released on summer weekends for boaters. Access to this popular stretch, with Class II and III rapids, is rationed with a lottery for the noncommercial boating public. Permits and can be obtained from the Bureau of Land Management's Taos Field Office. Commercial trips are also limited. During the week, families can enjoy an easy canoe or kayak on the quiet waters of the Rio Chama Canyon along FR 151. There are many put-ins and take-outs for those that want to float for an hour or two.

## OUTFITTERS

*New Wave Rafting Company*
Embudo, NM
(800) 984-1444
www.newwaverafting.com

*Los Rios River Runners*
Taos, NM
(575) 776-8854
www.losriosriverrunners.com

## CAMPING

*Rio Chama Campground*
**Getting There:** From US 84, travel 12 miles west on FR 151 to the campground; this road can be very slippery when wet from snow or rain.

The Rio Chama Campground is located on the Rio Chama with nine individual and two double sites tucked into husky juniper

trees that provide good shade. Paved loop roads in the campground are great for little bikers. All sites have picnic tables and fire rings. Two vault toilets and trash disposal are also available in the campground, but no potable water or RV hookups. Open from mid-May to late October.

Dispersed camping is found throughout the Wild and Scenic valley and sites are popular with rafters and kayakers on the weekends.

*Santa Fe National Forest,*
*Coyote Ranger District*
    (575) 638-5526

*Bureau of Land Management,*
*Taos Field Office*
    (575) 758-8851
    www.blm.gov/office/taos-field-office

## 37. Ghost Ranch

    (505) 685-1000
    www.ghostranch.org

**Nearest Town:** Abiquiu
**Best Season to Visit:** Spring and fall
**Visitor Information:** Open year-round. Check in at the visitor center upon arrival.
**Getting There:** From Abiquiu, take US 84 north for 13 miles. Turn right at the entrance gate.

From mid-May to October, families can enjoy all that Ghost Ranch has to offer, including a campground, dining hall meals, hiking trails, horseback riding, archery, and proximity to adventure on Abiquiu Lake and Rio Chama. Renowned painter Georgia O'Keeffe found inspiration in this beautiful countryside of red cliffs, green river valleys, and vast skies, which she made famous through a lifetime of work. Her former home and studio are now the 21,000-acre Ghost Ranch Retreat Center owned by the Presbyterian Church. This land of shifting light, towering rock, and vivid colors is

a favorite among photographers and travelers alike. Eight trails crisscross the Ghost Ranch property and entry to all is all included in the day-use fee. Kids will also enjoy the geology and paleontology museum just across the road from the conference center.

HIKE | **KITCHEN MESA TRAIL**

**Distance:** 3.7 miles out and back
**Difficulty:** Moderate
**Getting There:** The trailhead is located on the Ghost Ranch. Turn off NM 84 to the Ghost Ranch on Road 1708. Stop at the Retreat Center to pay the day-use fee if you are not camping on the property. Follow Road 1708 past the dining hall; watch for signs that point the way to Kitchen Mesa. Turn onto Road 1709 and find a parking area where the road is closed.

A climb to the top of a mesa through an appropriately challenging slot in the rocks will delight kids and guardians alike. Follow coffee cans painted green with a white stripe nailed onto small posts to striking views of the landscape. Where the trail is steep, take your time to admire the many layers of geologic time laid down in rock. Some layers were created from sediment deposited in ancient oceans; others are fossilized sand dunes. Ask children if they can tell which is which. The rich red rock comes from traces of iron. Ask kids what minerals might make the other colors.

The trail has some steep parts and drop offs, and the scramble up to the ridge of the mesa is steep but doable. The views from the top are well worth scrambling through the final slot. The trail is extremely slick when wet. Hike early in the morning during summer months to avoid the afternoon heat.

### HORSEBACK RIDING

Trail rides are offered for people ages 8+ of all levels of experience. Hour and a half rides during the day and special sunset rides are available. The ride includes interpretation of the locations in which Georgia O'Keeffe painted and lived. Reservations are required. Book online or at the retreat visitor center.

### ARCHERY

A few days a week in the afternoons, kids and adults can try their hand at hitting the bullseye at the Ghost Ranch's outdoor archery area. Sign up in the Retreat Center. Instruction included.

### CAMPING

The campground is open year-round. Tent and RV sites with full hookups are available. The campground has water and bathrooms with showers. Only a few sites have shade. Campers can opt to eat meals in the retreat center's dining hall.

## 38. Abiquiu Lake

*US Army Corps of Engineers*
(505) 685-4371
www.spa.usace.army.mil/Missions
/Civil-Works/Recreation/Abiquiu-Lake

**Nearest Town:** Abiquiu
**Best Season to Visit:** Year-round; late summer–early fall for water play.
**Visitor Information:** Visitor center has interpretive displays and information; call ahead for hours.
**Getting There:** Located 13 miles north from the town of Abiquiu. Turn left at the entrance sign.
&#9855; accessible

Sage- and juniper-dotted shores surround one of New Mexico's larger lakes, made

Cooling off with water play at Abiquiu Lake

from an earthen dam on the Rio Chama. Swimming beaches offer a great way to cool off on hot summer days. Fishing is a favorite activity from the shores or from boats. Several well-marked trails leave from the shores with gorgeous views of the Flint Mountains. Skimming the often-calm waters of the lake in a kayak or canoe is an enjoyable way to pass the day. There's plenty of boating, waterskiing, and jet skiing going on too; the lake's size leaves ample room for anglers, powered watercraft, and paddle craft to share. Kids will delight in the heart-pumping adventure of jumping off steep cliffs.

### PADDLING

The lake is popular with power boaters, so if you're new to canoeing or flat-water kayaking, you'll want to stick close to the shores. As with most places in New Mexico,

Echo Amphitheater's echo chamber

Abiquiu Lake does get windy in the afternoon, so plan accordingly. When the winds do pick up, you can still paddle around the leeward side of the many small islands and coves on the northeast side of the lake.

### CAMPING

*Riana Campground*
Located on a 150' bluff overlooking Abiquiu Lake with scenic views to the red bluffs, mesas, and mountains surrounding the lake. There are 41 tent sites and 37 RV and trailer sites. Potable water and bathrooms with a shower house in the campground. Open April 15–October 15.

### FISHING

Largemouth and smallmouth bass are plentiful in the reservoir, as well as rainbow trout, walleye, kokanee salmon, channel catfish, white crappie, bluegill, and brown trout.

### POINT OF INTEREST: ECHO AMPHITHEATER

Seventeen miles north of Abiquiu, a concavity carved by erosion in the sandstone, the Echo Amphitheater is known for its unique echoing auditory properties. When we visited for a short stop on our drive to points north, my kids (and their parents) had fun throwing our voices off the cliff wall and listening to them bounce and fade. There's also a campground, toilets, and interpretive signage along the short-paved path to the amphitheater.

### HIKE | PLAZA BLANCA

**Distance:** Variable
**Difficulty:** Easy
**Getting There:** On the grounds of the Dar al Islam education center and mosque. Turn right onto NM 554 for about 0.6 miles, then turn left onto CR 155, a small but paved track through the desert. Go 3.3 miles, driving past the small houses of local residents on this back road to the Dar al Islam gate. Take the dirt track for 0.6 miles. At the fork, take a right toward Plaza Blanca. Park here and hike the remaining quarter mile into the valley.

The unique and beautiful rock formations of Plaza Blanca were made famous by Georgia O'Keeffe's painting of the "White Place," or *Plaza Blanca* in Spanish. Now located on the grounds of the Dar al Islam Mosque and Islamic Education Center that welcomes visitors. There are no official hiking trails here, so families can explore and wander to their hearts' content.

## 39. Purple Adobe Lavender Farm

(505) 685-0082
www.purpleadobelavenderfarm.com
**Nearest Town:** Abiquiu
**Best Season to Visit:** Summer
**Visitor Information:** Open April–October.
**Getting There:** Located off of NM 84 in Abiquiu, between mile markers 210 and 211. Look for the purple flags.

The owner, Elizabeth Inman, welcomes kids to the farm to experience the long, scented rows of purple flowers. For many kids, this stop is less about the lavender fields than the gift shop for lavender-infused gelato, scones, and chocolate-raspberry truffles, but both are enjoyable. The farm sits just outside Abiquiu, among the dramatic red cliffs of the Rio Chama valley. Take a walk through the aromatic fields and down to the river. Lavender is a natural calmative, perfect for parents working to keep up with kids on a weekend adventure.

## Chama Area

### 40. Edward Sargent Wildlife Management Area

*New Mexico Department of Game and Fish*
(505) 756-2585
www.wildlife.state.nm.us

**Nearest Town:** Chama

**Best Season to Visit:** Year-round

**Visitor Information:** Access is restricted during elk calving May 15–June 30 and to nonhunters (except hunters' guests) during elk hunts.

**Getting There:** At the north end of Chama, turn left onto First Street at the Chama Medical Clinic sign. Go one block, then turn right on Pine Avenue, which becomes gravel after 1 mile. After 200 yards, watch for two iron gates. If the first iron gate is locked, the area is closed to all access; the second gate down the road remains locked year-round. There is horse and bike access to the left of the second gate.

Kids will enjoy searching for wildlife, or at least plentiful animal signs, and tracks in this vast preserve. Colorful kestrels hovering above the meadows and dive bombing their prey are especially enjoyable to watch. The edges of this lush basin rise up to meet thickly forested hills and the rugged Chama

Wildflowers and mountains provide a stellar backdrop on a hike through Edward Sargent Wildlife Management Area in Chama

Peak. A small trout stream, the Rio Chamita, flows through the site. Follow the level dirt road on foot, horseback, or mountain bike about 10 miles to the Colorado border, or turn right onto a graded dirt road—about 3.5 miles for the entrance—that leads to Nabor Lake, a small reservoir. Keep to the left as the road forks.

## WILDLIFE

Excellent dawn/dusk viewing of elk, with best viewing dates July–mid-September. Frequent glimpses of mule deer, coyotes, porcupines, and black bears; resident mountain lions and snowshoe hares are rarely seen. Look for beaver sign and western chorus frogs at Nabor Lake and along the Rio Chamita. Wildlife viewing is not recommended during elk hunts (October–December).

## BIRDWATCHING

Common summer birds include American kestrels, mountain bluebirds, broad-tailed and black-chinned hummingbirds, northern flickers, Steller's jays, Clark's nutcrackers, mountain chickadees, brown creepers, warbling vireos, common nighthawks, red-winged blackbirds, and northern shrikes. Occasional wild turkeys or blue grouse.

## CROSS-COUNTRY SKIING/SNOWSHOEING

The craggy mountains surrounding Chama rise to a high point at Cumbres Pass, a great jumping-off point for several trails that offer some of the best powder conditions for cross-country skiing and snowshoeing in the state. In January each year, the town hosts the Chile Ski Classic and Winter Fiesta, a family-friendly event featuring cross-country skiing and snowshoe races, yurt and ski tours, live music, ski clinics, and prizes.

HIKE | ELK INTERPRETIVE TRAIL

**Distance:** 1 mile round trip
**Difficulty:** Easy
**Getting There:** Trailhead is in the first parking lot after entering the Wildlife Area.

The brief Elk Interpretive Trail entices even short-legged hikers with gorgeous views of alpine meadows and the mountains around Chama. The gravel pathway meanders through meadows, a riparian area good for birdwatching, and up onto a hill with striking views. Early morning or late afternoon is the best chance to view elk from the trail. Cross-country skiing is also excellent on this trail in winter.

## 41. Heron Lake State Park

(575) 588-7470
www.emnrd.state.nm.us/SPD/heronlake
statepark.html
**Nearest Town:** Tierra Amarilla
**Best Season to Visit:** Year-round
**Visitor Information:** Open for day use and camping. Entrance fees apply.
**Getting There:** From Tierra Amarilla, take US 84 W for 2.6 miles. Turn left onto NM 95 and follow for 9.5 miles to the park.
♿ accessible

Rimmed by ponderosa pine forest with panoramic views of the Pine Bluffs and Brazos Cliffs in the distance, Heron Lake offers a serene setting for a weekend getaway. The no-wake waters prohibit fast motorboats, affording kayaking, canoeing, sailing, or SUPs a peaceful paddle.

## FISHING

This cold-water lake offers good trout and kokanee salmon fishing. Ice fishing is also possible in winter when safe ice forms. Explore the 35 miles of shoreline with no-wake boats. The lake is accessible for fishing from most of the shoreline. Four

## Cliff Swallows

Paddling around on the glassy waters of Heron Lake in late spring, my family and I came across one of nature's wonders. As we launched the boat, I noticed birds with metallic blue backs and red rumps gathering on the muddy shores. Erratically fluttering their wings, they repeatedly dipped their beaks in the mud. We paddled across the lake to the far bank and leisurely made our way back along the shore. Natural rock cliffs gave way to man-made walls as we approached the dam that birthed Heron Lake.

Next to the dam, we noticed a flurry of activity in the air. Metallic blue cliff swallows swooped low over the water, feasting on winged bugs—likely a hatching of mayflies, given the time of year. As we approached, one of the boys accidentally hit the side of the canoe with the paddle, making a loud *ping*. Thousands of birds suddenly took to the air and circled overhead. Their squeaks

and purr-like alarm calls echoed across the lake. There weren't enough of them to block out the sun like the passenger pigeons of yesteryear, but their numbers were impressive.

Cliff swallows form mud into round pellets and transport it in their beaks, which is what those by the boat launch were doing. Clinging to a vertical wall, they form clusters of 900–1,200 individual mud pellets into gourd-shaped nests. Several males sat defending their finished nests. Their puffed-up red faces peeking out an opening, ready to pounce on would-be intruders. Hundreds of new nests were being built as we watched. These birds are common, forming colonies on bridges, overpasses, and culverts across the country. Their communal antics are remarkable to behold. We stayed a while to watch their aerial acrobatics and territorial battles as they vied for mates and occasionally knocked each other into the water for a swim.

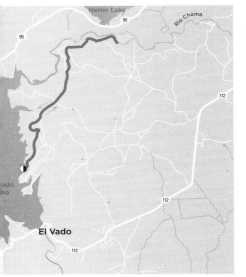

**RIO CHAMA TRAIL** 5.5 miles one-way

boat launch ramps and four docks are available to assist boat owners. Portage canoes and kayaks from several convenient locations around the lake.

### HIKE | RIO CHAMA TRAIL

**Distance:** 5.5 miles one-way

**Difficulty:** Moderate

**Getting There:** Trailhead at Heron Dam. Gate at north edge of campground is locked in fall and winter, which adds about a half mile onto the hike on gravel road.

The dramatic caprock stairway at Heron Dam and crossing the Rio Chama Gorge on a suspension bridge served to keep my kids engaged while hiking this trail. The trail takes hikers by scenic rock formations, cliff walls, and high-altitude arid forest land and

El Vado Reservoir's rocky shoreline

connects to neighboring El Vado Lake State Park. The trail is easy to follow but not always maintained. Best hiked in spring, fall, or winter when no snow or ice is present.

### CAMPING

The state park's campground lines the shores of the lake with 250 developed campsites, 54 electric campsites, two picnic group shelters, and bathrooms.

## 42. El Vado Lake State Park

(575) 588-7247
www.emnrd.state.nm.us/SPD/elvadolake
statepark.html

 accessible

At the other end of the Rio Chama Trail sits another of New Mexico's remote, large reservoirs that impound the Rio Chama. This lake sits at almost 7,000' in elevation and is over 5 miles long. It does not restrict speedboats, so the lake is popular with water skiers and jet skiers. Two boat ramps afford easy access for all boats. The rocky shores provide ample supply for kids to spend an afternoon skipping rocks and fishing.

### FISHING

Quiet coves around the lake are great places to catch trout and kokanee salmon.

### CAMPING

Three campgrounds in the state park have 100 sites with vault toilets, playgrounds, and bathrooms. Primitive camping on the shores of the lake away from any crowds is allowed at Sands Cove and Hargroves Point Primitive Camping Areas off CR 322.

### LOCAL ATTRACTIONS

*Cumbres and Toltec Scenic Railroad*: Occasional trips just for kids and families explore the mountains around Chama and into Colorado aboard a classic steam train. Trips range from a few hours to all day with buffet lunch offered at the Osier dining hall about halfway through the trip. Other special themed train rides include wildflower, music, and dinner trains. (888) 286-2737, www.cumbrestoltec.com

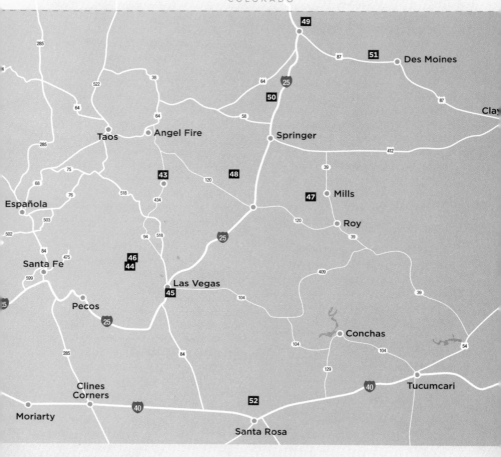

E astward over the mountains from Santa Fe, the Sangre de Cristo Mountains of New Mexico subside into the Great Plains. The once Wild West town of Las Vegas, now the seat of United World College, provides entry points into the rugged canyons and steep climbs of the eastern side of the Pecos Wilderness or the waving shortgrass prairie stretching east to Texas. The northeast section of the Pecos includes about 25,000 acres in Carson National Forest, the least visited portion of the wilderness.

In the sparsely inhabited plains, long stretches of two-lane highway meander through rolling meadows under a vaulted blue sky. Prehistoric animals roamed the eastern plains, leaving evidence of their lives in the Dinosaur Trackways at Clayton Lake State Park.

Comanches and Kiowas thrived on the plains, but it was the Jicarilla Apaches that controlled the area when Spanish colonizers arrived 500 years ago. While Santa Fe and the Rio Grande Valley were settled by Europeans in 1609, the northeastern area remained open and was primarily used for its trade routes for the next 60 years. The Santa Fe Trail, the remnants of which can still be seen in the Kiowa National Grasslands, is the most famous of these routes.

By the late 1880s, the Plains Indians were forced onto reservations. Ranches with sheep, cattle, and agricultural fields began transforming the landscape. Life on the arid plains was never easy. A prolonged period of drought in the 1920s and 1930s, known as the dust bowl, literally blew the land away and took a toll on farming and ranching. Scattered ranches and a few small villages still dot the northeast today in a patchwork of public and private lands. The area's Spanish influence and culture are as prevalent today as they were 400 years ago. You'll still find rock corrals, division fences, and acequias (ditch irrigation) on small *ranchitos* of the original settlers.

Watching the shortgrass prairie wave in the wind through the window of your car inspires daydreaming. But don't be fooled into thinking there is no adventure to be had in this vast expanse. Hidden gems like lakes, volcanoes, river canyons, rock climbing hotspots, accessible wildlife, and excellent bird-watching supply plenty of family fun for a weekend or longer. Your discoveries will have you wanting to return throughout the seasons.

### WILDLIFE

Mule deer and pronghorn are often spotted standing among the short grasses. The stretch of road from Ocate to Wagon Mound offers some of the best viewing of pronghorn in the state. Prairie dog towns can span several acres, which badgers and burrowing owls also use. In late summer, black bears sometimes venture out from the wooded areas in search of food before they enter their winter hibernation. Turkeys are numerous, as are coyotes and foxes.

A great horned owl rests along the river before heading out for a night hunt

### BIRDWATCHING

Several refuges, small wetlands and lakes, and the Canadian River offer excellent birdwatching, especially during spring and fall migrations. For more details, visit New Mexico True's interactive birding map for the northeast region of the state: www .newmexico.org/things-to-do/outdoor -adventures/birding/.

## Las Vegas Area

### 43. Coyote Creek State Park

(575) 387-2328
www.emnrd.state.nm.us/SPD/coyotecreek
lakestatepark.html Nearest
**Town:** Mora
**Best Season to Visit:** Summer
**Visitor Information:** Open year-round.
**Getting There:** From Mora, take NM 434
for 17 miles.
&#9855; accessible

This is a peaceful park where you can spend a quiet weekend playing and relaxing in nature. Coyote Creek is a small state park nestled in the eastern foothills of the Sangre de Cristo Mountains along a meandering stream at about 7,000'. Enclosed by a forest of spruce and pine, the small valley displays abundant wildflowers and beautiful fall foliage. Kids will enjoy playing in the creek with plenty of fishing action. In fact, Coyote Creek, a tributary of the Mora River, is the most densely stocked trout stream in New Mexico. A 2-mile trail circles through the park, crossing the creek twice and passing through a flowery meadow. Take a side trip to the high-tech Mora National Fish Hatchery up the street. Tour the visitor center and operations. The hatchery is dedicated to recovering the endangered Gila trout, which live in cold mountain streams in southern New Mexico.

### WILDLIFE

Mammals known to inhabit the immediate area include black bears, cougars, elk, mule deer, red and gray foxes, bobcats, coyotes, skunks, and porcupines. Beavers have created small pools along the creek with their dams.

### BIRDWATCHING

Numerous bird species have been identified in the park, including great horned owls and the endangered southwestern willow flycatchers that nest and breed along Coyote Creek.

## FISHING

The beaver ponds have benefited the game fish, which include rainbow trout, brown trout, Rio Grande cutthroat trout, and white suckers.

## 44. Montezuma Hot Springs

**Nearest Town:** Las Vegas
**Best Season to Visit:** Year-round
**Visitor Information:** The private hot springs allow free public access 5 a.m.–midnight.
**Getting There:** From Las Vegas, take NM 65/ Hot Springs Boulevard for about 6 miles. The hot springs parking area will be on the right.

Bathing suits are required, making this a family-friendly natural hot spring. When my kids got bored of soaking in the hot water, they could switch to playing by the creek. The mineral pools of Montezuma Hot Springs capture warm, bubbling springs along the Gallinas River. Rustic open-air cement pools remain from the days when the Montezuma Hotel invited guests to these rejuvenating waters in the 1890s. The slightly ostentatious hotel, in eyeshot of the pools, now serves as the administration building of the United World College–USA. Several small soaking pools range from warm to very hot, in addition to larger rock pools christened the "lobster pot" at a steaming 120°F.

## 45. Las Vegas National Wildlife Refuge

(505) 425-3581
www.fws.gov/refuge/Las_Vegas
**Nearest Town:** Las Vegas
**Best Season to Visit:** Spring and fall
**Visitor Information:** Visitor center is open with limited hours; check website for details. The refuge trails are open all year sunrise to sunset. No entrance fee is required.
**Getting There:** From Las Vegas, take I-25 south to Exit 345. Turn east on NM 104 for 1.5 miles.

Turn south on NM 281 for about 4 miles and follow the signs to the refuge headquarters.
 accessible

Las Vegas (Spanish for "the meadows") sits on a plateau in the Sangre de Cristo Mountains foothills. River canyon walls drop below the refuge on three sides. With the Rocky Mountains rising in the west, the Great Plains stretching to the east, and the Chihuahuan Desert to the south, three ecosystems meet at the Las Vegas National Wildlife Refuge, creating an edge effect where diversity of plants and animals is greater than in any one of those ecosystems. In addition, the refuge is located along the Central Flyway, an important resting, feeding, and wintering area for migrating geese, ducks, and cranes. All of these combine to make an excellent wildlife viewing and birdwatching area in the right season.

Driving the 8-mile horseshoe loop along CR 22C and NM 281 allows visitors to enjoy scenic views and excellent wildlife viewing opportunities in a diversity of habitats, including ponds, lakes, marshes, grasslands, cottonwood stands, and brush thickets. Stop at the Fred Quintana Overlook at Crane Lake, one of the best areas from which to view wildlife. Kids will appreciate the educational displays at the visitor center.

Walk the 1.75-mile Gallinas Nature Trail that meanders through fields of wildflowers, past historic ruins, and descends approximately 250' into a box canyon.

### WILDLIFE

Keep a look out for pronghorn, Rocky Mountain elk, badgers, ground squirrels, and mule deer.

### BIRDWATCHING

The Las Vegas NWR bird list records 271 species, many that ebb and flow with the seasons. Out of the list, 80 species nest here, 50 are neotropical migrants that winter here, and 14 species of raptors glide through during their spring and fall migrations. Migrating shorebirds, like long-billed dowitchers and sandpipers, probe the mudflats in early fall and spring. Kids will enjoy the unique feeding styles of colorful avocets and long-billed curlews that nest on the refuge. Some 20 bald eagles spend winters here, attracted by open waters and hundreds of ducks and geese. Mallards, canvasbacks, and wigeons peak in October and November. You'll find highest numbers of ruddy ducks, northern shovelers, northern pintails, and gadwalls in March and April. Visit in fall and winter to see sandhill cranes and Canada geese.

## 46. El Porvenir Canyon

One of several rugged canyons that lead into the southeastern portion of the Santa Fe National Forest and Pecos Wilderness. In this less-visited but still well-used area, the forests are lush, the wildflowers are abundant, the rivers run year-round, and trails climb into the high alpine with spectacular views.

HIKE | **HERMIT'S PEAK**

**Distance:** 8.1 miles round trip

**Difficulty:** Strenuous

**Getting There:** Trailhead is in El Porvenir Campground.

Hermit's Peak is a broad, flat-topped summit with towering cliffs on its eastern escarpment. It rises notably on the far southern border of the Pecos Wilderness. The peak is named for a hermit who supposedly lived in a cave near the summit. Although this is a steady climb to the peak, determined youth can make it to the summit for impressive views of the mountains to the north and Great Plains stretching to the east. It took my family six hours (and a bag of marshmallows as motivation for our

### Sewing Shorebirds

Las Vegas National Wildlife Refuge is especially known for its variety of migrating shorebirds. The gray-brown long-billed dowitchers match the color of their muddy feeding sites. It's not their coloring that makes them stand out from other shorebirds but rather their quirky feeding style—they move like a sewing machine! The shorebird quickly probes into the refuge's mudflats with its long bill, sometimes to the point of sticking their head in the mud, and then bobs back up. Their long migration extends as far north as Alaska and as far south as the Yucatán Peninsula. And, although both sexes share incubation of the eggs, only the male takes care of the young once they hatch.

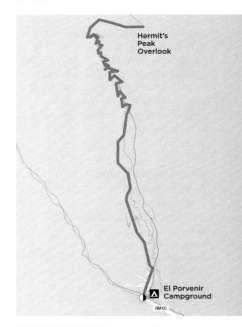

**HERMIT'S PEAK** 8.1 miles round trip

Hermit's Peak towers over the plains of eastern New Mexico

smallest one) to summit. Our hike included a twisted ankle and hiding out from a hailstorm underneath a tree, but they remember the accomplishment and the view from the top the most.

### CAMPING

From Las Vegas, a winding, scenic drive ends at El Porvenir Campground, tucked into the beautiful pine forests on the eastern side of the Sangre de Cristo Mountains with Beaver Creek running through it. Conveniently located at the trailhead for Hermit's Peak. My kids enjoyed bike riding along campground roads and swimming and playing along Beaver Creek, which is hikeable for several miles out of the campground. To get there from Las Vegas, take NM 65/Hot Springs Road for 16 miles, dead-ending in the campground.

*Santa Fe National Forest—*
*Las Vegas District*
    (505) 438-5300
    www.fs.usda.gov/recarea/santafe

## 47. Mills Canyon/Kiowa National Grasslands

**Nearest Town:** Roy

**Best Season to Visit:** Spring–fall

**Visitor Information:** Campgrounds with vault toilets are the only facilities. Pack out your trash.

**Getting There:** From Las Vegas, go north on I-25 to Wagon Mound (71 miles), east on NM 120 to Roy (33 miles), then north on NM 39 for 10 miles. Look for the road sign to Mills Canyon or the Mills Canyon Road street sign. Proceed west on this gravel road for 10 miles to the rim of Mills Canyon. The road from the rim to the bottom of the canyon is narrow with several sharp switchbacks. It is not suitable for motor homes or vehicles with long trailers.

Hidden in the vast grasslands of northeastern New Mexico, the Canadian River has carved a dramatic rift for 30 miles through the surrounding shortgrass prairie. Twelve miles of the rift are within the Kiowa National Grasslands, and Mills Canyon lies smack in the middle of it. Named for Melvin W. Mills, a territorial-era politician and businessman, Mills Canyon is the site of the homestead he established in the 1880s. In its heyday, the ranch boasted fruit and nut orchards, vegetable gardens, and cattle. It was even a stop on a treacherous 100-mile Santa Fe Trail shortcut. Mills abandoned the canyon in 1916 after a flood plunged him into financial ruin. When we visited, my boys enjoyed exploring the ghostly remnants of his homestead in the canyon at dusk. Old irrigation ditches and a handful of buildings remain, including Mills's two-story stone house and an adobe bunkhouse where signs interpret the history.

### HIKING

No official trails exist in the canyon, but the hiking is pleasant on the floodplain. Generally, follow the course of the Canadian River as it meanders between the sloping 800' red sandstone canyon walls. During the monsoon season (late June through August) and in springtime, hikers should be wary of the kind of flash flood that ruined Mills.

### WILDLIFE

Several side canyons branch off from the main river canyon, where you may find wildlife, including deer, pronghorn, black bears, mountain lions, or Barbary sheep (a large African import with curved horns, introduced in the 1950s).

A Bullock's oriole visits Mills Canyon in spring

### BIRDWATCHING

Mills Canyon has excellent birdwatching during spring and fall migrations. Watch for year-round resident golden eagles, song sparrows, and rufous-crowned sparrows. In summer, the canyon attracts common poorwills, white-throated swifts, and yellow-breasted chats. Migrants include summer and western tanagers, Wilson's warblers, lazuli buntings, and Bullock's orioles.

### CAMPING

*Mills Rim Campground*
Mills Rim Campground sits on top of the 1,000'-deep canyon carved by the Canadian River.

*Mills Canyon Campground*
Mills Canyon Campground lies at the bottom of the canyon and has pit toilets, picnic tables, and fire rings. There is no running water or trash disposal, and campers are asked to pack out everything they pack in.

### CLIMBING

The cliffs along the Canadian River have become a legendary spot for bouldering. Most climbers begin at Mills Canyon Area Trailhead in the Mills Rim Campground. Best time of year for climbing here is November–April; summer is hot.

*Cibola National Forest–Kiowa and Rita Blanca National Grasslands*
(505) 374-9652
www.fs.usda.gov/cibola

## 48. Charette Lakes Wildlife Area

(505) 827-7882
www.emnrd.state.nm.us/SPD/BOATINGWeb
/CharetteLakes.html

**Nearest Town:** Springer

**Best Time of Year to Visit:** March–October

**Visitor Information:** The two lakes are managed by the New Mexico Department of Game and Fish. Open March 1–October 31. The campground has bathrooms but otherwise no facilities.

**Getting There:** From I-25, take Exit 404 (Colmor) and head west on Highway 569 for 13 miles. The gravel road crosses private ranch land and then turns to pavement as it wends its way to the top of the mesa.

Two lakes formed from a natural depression in volcanic rock sit atop a remote grassy mesa southwest of the town of Springer. Even though the lakes are not especially noteworthy, they offer a quiet family retreat with good wildlife viewing and consistent fishing. When we visited, my kids were most excited about the herd of pronghorn that raced alongside our car on the dirt roads surrounding the lake (they won) and spotting a pair of bald eagles fishing along the shores.

The lakes in this 2,000-acre refuge are fed with water from Ocate Creek. The nearby town of Colmor is now a ghost town, with ruins on private lands visible from the frontage road between Charette Lakes turnoff and Wagon Mound. Hikers will enjoy exploring the creek flowing through a deep canyon off the southeast corner of the lake. Perched on a high mesa, the lakes are a great spot to watch summer thunderstorms sweep over the outlying plains.

### FISHING

The lower lake has always boasted a good population of trout and perch. Fishing from the shore is easy due to the lack of vegetation around the lake. According to the book *Fishing in New Mexico* by Ti Piper, Charette Lakes are best fished in the fall with a woolly bugger or gray-hackle peacock fly suspended below a bubble and cast out onto the lake with a spinning rod.

### BIRDWATCHING

All year look for eared grebes on the lake, as well as horned larks and western meadowlarks in the prairies. In winter, find charismatic buffleheads.

### WILDLIFE

Browsing pronghorn are plentiful around the lakes.

### CAMPING

Primitive camping is available on the shore of the larger lake with vault toilets. No water is available.

# Raton Area

## 49. Sugarite Canyon State Park

(575) 444-5607 (park office)
(877) 664-7787 (reservations)
www.emnrd.state.nm.us/SPD
/sugaritecanyonstatepark.html

**Nearest Town:** Raton

**Best Season to Visit:** Late spring–fall for camping; winter for day-use cross-country skiing.

**Visitor Information:** Visitor center is open daily. Fees apply.

**Getting There:** From I-25, take Raton Exit 452. At the stop sign, turn right (east) on NM 72 for 3.8 miles. Where NM 72 turns sharply east, continue straight on NM 526.

&#9855; accessible

After summer rains at Sugarite Canyon State Park

When my family camped at this remote state park in the middle of summer, we found lots of adventure to fill our days. The roomy campground has great views of passing thunderstorms and subsequent rainbows, plenty of room to roam, open meadows, and shady oak forests in which to build forts. My boys especially liked fishing from canoes in Lake Maloya while they paddled across the lake to an empty beach. They managed to catch several trout, even though they tipped their canoe and fell in the water on the way back. Easy hikes, dirt roads to bike on, crags for rock climbing, a small store and educational displays at the visitor center, and wildlife appearances made this one of our favorite state parks. It's also a great basecamp for day trips to other points of interest in northeast New Mexico, like Capulin Volcano National Monument and nearby wildlife refuges.

Sugarite's (pronounced *sugar-reet*) 4,000 acres offer two lakes, 20 miles of hiking trails, two campgrounds, and the remains of a historic coal camp. Wooded mountains and meadows painted with wildflowers and butterflies make this park a prime location for wildlife viewing and birdwatching. Two streams run through the valley, flanked by basalt cliffs. Bartlett and Little Horse Mesas rise in the west and Horse Mesa in the east. The park was heavily forested with ponderosa pine and Gambel oak forests before a wildfire burned most of it in 2012. The forests are slowly coming back. Along Chicorica Creek at lower elevations, a riparian forest of willow and cottonwood offer cool shade over the hiking trail. On the flat top of Little Horse Mesa, a grassy meadow and ponderosa pine park opens to expansive views of cinder cones and extinct volcanoes on the southern horizon.

The park visitor center is open daily and has a small store and interpretive displays.

Outside the center, year-round feeders attract resident hummingbirds and other birds. In the summer, the park typically hosts events on birds and butterflies. Several trails leave from the visitor center.

Coal mining in the canyon began in 1894. The town of Sugarite was established as a coal-mining town in 1912 and had a population of nearly 1,000 at its peak. The mines began to shut down in 1941 and now make up part of the human history and educational displays in the park's visitor center. The Coal Camp Interpretive Trail winds through the ruins of the Sugarite coal camp.

### WILDLIFE

Wildlife is abundant and visible in this park. During a weekend trip, a black bear crossed the road in front of our car, a mountain lion approached the lake for a drink as we fished, elk and mule deer fed along the roadways, resident gray foxes visited our campsite, and hummingbirds attempted to sip nectar from my sunglasses. An annual butterfly festival invites participants to count and identify butterflies in the meadows near Lake Dorothey, a reservoir that sits on adjacent land across the Colorado border. This family-friendly event is a fun way to spend a day.

### BIRDWATCHING

The park's many meadows, edged by forest and varied terrain, make for great birdwatching. In fact, some of the most colorful birds we saw in the park were in the trees around our campsite and were easily spotted by my boys, who were still getting used to binoculars. The 120-acre Lake Maloya boasts many waterfowl species. In spring and fall, migrating ospreys may be seen fishing. Watch for red-naped sapsuckers, dark-eyed juncos, woodpeckers (Lewis's, hairy), Woodhouse's scrub-jays, Steller's jays, black-capped chickadees, American goldfinches, pine siskins, broad-tailed and black-chinned hummingbirds, belted kingfishers, eastern phoebes, gray catbirds, cedar waxwings, rufous and calliope hummingbirds, bald eagles, and ospreys.

### CROSS-COUNTRY SKIING

Cross-country skiing is a popular activity through the winter along the roads and trails. Some roads and facilities are closed during the season.

### FISHING

The two artificial lakes in the park, Lake Maloya (130 acres) and Lake Alice (3 acres), are stocked with rainbow and brown trout. Lake Alice is open year-round for those interested in ice fishing.

### PADDLING

Canoeing, flat-water kayaking, and sailing are allowed on Lake Maloya. Ramps are located on the northwest side of the lake. Gasoline motors are prohibited, but small electric motors are allowed. Swimming is prohibited since the lake provides drinking water to the town of Raton below.

### CLIMBING

The caprock cliffs of Sugarite boast several rock climbing opportunities. Climbing is permitted in the state park, although attaching permanent anchors is not. For experienced climbing families, routes are set on the face of Little Horse Mesa, a south-facing 70'-high basalt cliff with over 40 traditional routes. Routes can be led or top-roped. Routes range in difficulty from 5.8 to 5.12, with the majority of routes at 5.9 and 5.10.

### CAMPING

Lake Alice Campground has 11 sites with electric hookups. Soda Pocket Camp-

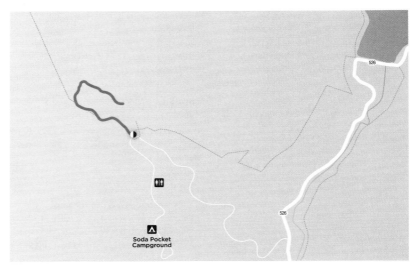

**LITTLE HORSE MESA** Under 2 miles out and back

ground has tent camping, vault toilets, and water. Group shelters are located in Gambel Oak Group Area.

HIKE | **LITTLE HORSE MESA**

**Distance:** Under 2 miles out and back
**Difficulty:** Moderate
**Getting There:** From the visitor center, continue 2.4 miles farther north to a left turn to Soda Pocket Campground. This dirt road is generally open from April to November. Drive 1.3 miles and park in a small pullout on the right, which is the trailhead.

With colorful wildflowers, easily visible wildlife signs, stunning views, and a mostly flat trail with a short, challenging climb, this trail will be fun even for reluctant little hikers. From the parking area follow signs left to Lake Maloya, Segerstrom Valley, and Little Horse Mesa. The trail climbs steadily away from the road. Watch for purple and white asters, dragonhead (of the mint

family), cutleaf coneflower, and other abundant wildflowers that line the trail in summer. After .4 miles oscillating between open meadows and shady oak groves, arrive at a trail junction where a sign indicates Lake Maloya is 4 miles to the left. Turn right to climb a quarter mile to the top of Little Horse Mesa. While steep, the minimal length of this climb makes it doable. On top of the mesa, find a large meadow dotted with ponderosa pines. Go on a scavenger hunt with children to find the abundant but often hidden wildflowers among the grasses. Follow the trail to the right to an overlook on the southern edge of the mesa. Look down Sugarite Canyon, where peaks of volcanic cones rise in the distance. Return the way you came or continue along the trail to Lake Maloya; the rest of the trail is easy going.

## 50. Maxwell National Wildlife Refuge

(575) 375-2331, ext. 200

www.fws.gov/refuge/Maxwell

**Nearest Town:** Raton

**Best Season to Visit:** Year-round

**Visitor Information:** Visitor center is open weekdays. When the visitor center is closed, a welcome kiosk next to the driveway provides maps, bird checklists, and other information.

**Getting There:** From I-25, take Maxwell Exit 426. At the stop sign, turn right (north) on NM 445 for 0.8 miles. At NM 505, turn left (west) for 2.5 miles. Turn north on Lake 13 Road at the refuge entrance sign. Go 1.25 miles to the visitor center.

 accessible

Short hikes through the refuge, miles of drivable roads for wildlife spotting, and an interesting visitor center make this refuge a memorable day trip or a couple-hour stop on the way to other points of interest in the area. Pick the right season (spring or fall) and time of day (morning or evening) to maximize wildlife viewing opportunities.

The refuge sits in an open basin surrounded by views of the Sangre de Cristo Mountains and protects migratory birds and native wildlife. A mix of shortgrass prairie, lakes, wetlands, woodlots, and agricultural fields fill the preserve's 3,699 acres. The refuge has a visitor center with educational displays and information. A 10-mile auto tour winds through the refuge with several pullouts from which visitors can take short hikes. Bring your own water and snacks and binoculars or a scope to get the best view of wildlife. The refuge operates with a small staff, so call ahead to make sure the visitor center is open. Refuge roads are open to the public seven days a week.

### WILDLIFE

Residents include mule deer, white-tailed deer, beavers, muskrats, badgers, bobcats, coyotes, striped skunks, raccoons, porcupines, long-tailed weasels, black-tailed prairie dogs, black-tailed jackrabbits, desert cottontails, six species of bats, and a wide variety of rodents that are typical of the area grasslands. The lakes harbor several species of frogs, salamanders, and dragonflies.

### BIRDWATCHING

The refuge is located in the Central Flyway, a route traveled every spring and fall by migratory birds. It provides feeding and resting areas for wintering waterfowl. Migratory grassland birds rely on short-grass prairie for habitat, which is declining across the West. The refuge is an essential sanctuary for birds that depend on this habitat, including the highest density of grasshopper sparrows in the state. Spring and fall bring migrating sandpipers. Summer attracts flocks of American white pelicans. Provided the lakes are not frozen during winter, good numbers of waterfowl can be spotted. Also watch for wild turkeys, Wilson's snipes, burrowing owls, eastern kingbirds, cackling geese, tundra swans, common goldeneyes, American tree sparrows, western sandpipers, and long-billed dowitchers.

### FISHING

Fishing is allowed at Lake 13 beginning yearly on March 1. A New Mexico State Fishing License is required.

### CAMPING

Primitive camping is allowed around Lake 13. Amenities are vault toilet only; bring your own water. Open March 1–October 31.

## 51. Capulin Volcano National Monument

(575) 278-2201

www.nps.gov/cavo

**Nearest Town:** Capulin (cap-u-LEEN)

**Best Season to Visit:** Year-round. Volcano Road may be closed by snow for a few days each winter.

**Visitor Information:** The visitor center is open daily, except for major holidays. The park has no food service, lodging, or camping. Fees apply.

**Getting There:** From Raton, travel 30 miles east on NM 64/87. At Capulin, turn north on NM 325 and travel 3 miles. Enter the park from NM 325.

♿ accessible

When we took a day trip here from our basecamp at Sugarite Canyon State Park, we began our visit at the small but informative visitor center. The boys picked up their Junior Ranger packets and dug into the videos and educational displays to learn about the geology and ecology of the area in order to earn a badge by completing the workbook. If you arrive at the right time, the rangers also lead a variety of interesting and fun interpretive programs throughout the park.

We all enjoyed the drive to the top of the extinct volcano and the hike around the rim on a paved path. Circling around the 360-degree 2-mile road to the top was an adventure in itself. Each direction offered a different view: the Rocky Mountains to the north, the Great Plains stretching in all directions, and other cinder and shield volcanoes that rise up on the horizon surrounding the monument.

Capulin is near the center of the Raton-Clayton volcanic field. *Capulin* is the

### Convergent Lady Beetle

In late summer, a generation of ladybugs arrives at Capulin Volcano from the surrounding aphid-rich fields or the wheat fields of Texas. They seek out companionship at their annual ladybug gathering. They coat rocks, tree limbs, and other vegetation with their colorful bodies. Convergent Lady Beetle is named for the converging white lines on its thorax. They usually have 13 black dots on a reddish-orange shell. Thousands of ladybugs congregate, seeking the same spot where their parents and grandparents gathered. Scientists believe they find it by following pheromones—a chemical trail—left by last year's ladybugs. Once they arrive, they crawl on each other as females seek a mate. Then they bed down in logs and crevices to hibernate through the winter on the highest points of the volcano. They emerge again in early spring to take care of any unfinished business—namely, mating. Surviving beetles then catch a warm current to the south off the volcano in February. During a lifespan of a few months, the females lay up to 500 eggs on leaves and twigs. The eggs hatch and the larvae gorge themselves on the aphids until they pupate. Since the larvae usually clean the area of their favorite food (aphids), the next generation of adults migrates back to Capulin Volcano. There they feed on small insects, pollen, spores, and vegetation and await the early spring, when they can ride the wind back to the aphid-rich areas and lay their eggs.

With their bright colors and docile nature (unless you're an aphid), ladybugs are a favorite with kids. These nature ambassadors are unfortunately on the decline across the nation. Kids can help scientists keep track of them by participating in a citizen science project called the Lost Ladybug Project (www.lost ladybug.org).

Spanish word for chokecherry, a shrub that grows throughout the park. This diverse landscape of volcanic cones, domes, and lava flows stretches for 80 miles across northeast New Mexico, covering 8,000 square miles between the towns of Raton and Clayton, hence its name. Capulin Volcano erupted about 60,000 years ago, covering the surrounding plains in four distinct lava flows and shooting lava fragments and ash into the air. Over a couple years, the volcano grew to 1,300', twice as tall as the average cinder cone (the smallest type of volcano). Capulin is one of the youngest cinder cones in the volcano field and its steep slopes are well preserved. The volcano straddles two habitats: the grassland of the plains and the forested mountains. Annual sunflowers and other wildflowers thrive in the volcanic soil.

The national monument has 5 miles of hiking trails that cover the range of ecosystems from the lava flows at the base to the rim trail that circles the steep top. Trails provide unique wildlife viewing opportunities at the right time of year.

## BIRDWATCHING

In early fall, mountain bluebirds gather in large numbers on the volcano, becoming the most numerous bird in the park for a time. The powder-blue male is among the most beautiful birds in the West. Their bright color stands out against the muted tones of the Capulin landscape. Watch for them among the piñon and juniper trees and in open fields. Bluebirds forage by hovering in the air and dropping down to catch their prey—grasshoppers and other insects. They also perch on low branches and dart out to catch insects in midair.

Other species to watch for include Woodhouse's scrub-jays, juniper titmice, bushtits, mountain bluebirds, pine siskins, canyon towhees, Cassin's kingbirds, barn swallows, rock wrens, and chipping sparrows.

## HIKE | CRATER RIM AND CRATER VENT TRAILS

**Distance:** 1.2 miles for both
**Difficulty:** Moderate
**Getting There:** From the visitor center, drive the 2-mile spiral road to a parking area at the top of the volcano.

Capulin is one of few volcanoes in North America that allow an up-close experience. Kids will enjoy the view, the many benches for resting, and interesting interpretive signs along this trail. The 1-mile loop rim trail takes about an hour to complete, accounting for stops and a slow pace up the steep sections. From the rim, panoramic views of lava-capped mesas illustrate the rich volcanic history of the Capulin region. On clear days, you can see all the way to Oklahoma, Texas, Colorado, and even Kansas before the horizon finally falls beneath the Earth's curvature. After hiking the rim trail, descend 400' into the mouth of the volcano, where hikers can stand in what was once an epicenter and imagine the dangerous and violent lava eruptions and explosions.

# Santa Rosa

## 52. Santa Rosa Lake State Park

(575) 472-3110
www.emnrd.state.nm.us/SPD
/santarosalakestatepark.html

**Nearest Town:** Santa Rosa
**Best Season to Visit:** Fall–spring. Summer is very hot during the day.
**Visitor Information:** A small information center is located by Shoreline Trailhead.
**Getting There:** Take Exit 273 from I-40. Turn left onto NM 91 and follow signs to the lake for about 12 miles.
♿ accessible

Santa Rosa Lake at sunset

This 3,800-square-foot reservoir is located on the eastern plains. The lake and surrounding attractions make for a nice stopover when spending a weekend in the area. Boating, jet skiing, fishing, camping, hiking, and abundant birdwatching are all available in the park. Kids will enjoy seeing turkey vultures soaring over the lake. They also roost in flocks in the trees along the Pecos River in spring and fall, making quite a spectacle with their large numbers. In years with good spring rains, wildflowers of the Great Plains are abundant in the meadows and limestone rocks around the lake.

### HIKE | SHORELINE TRAIL

**Distance:** 3 mile loop
**Difficulty:** Easy
**Getting There:** The trail begins across the road from the visitor center at the kiosk for South Shoreline Trail.

This trail follows the shores of Santa Rosa Lake along the layers of limestone cliffs. Wildflowers are abundant from March to May, including immense prickly pear cactus, which bloom in May and June. My kids delighted in seeing striped skunks, jackrabbits, and foxes in the early morning and late afternoons along the trail. Several side trails lead to outlooks of the lake where dispersed camping and picnicking are allowed. Skeletons of juniper trees still remain along the lake's beaches from the time when the lake was created by damming the Pecos River and flooding the canyons.

### PADDLING

Canoeing, flat-water kayaking, and speedboats all share the lake. The Pecos River Canyon on the western side of the lake below the dam is well suited for kayaking.

### BIRDWATCHING

Year-round, watch for western grebes, double-crested cormorants, red-tailed hawks, turkey vultures, curve-billed thrashers, and yellow-rumped warblers. Northern harriers may also turn up in the winter. The three northern arms of the lake and the Pecos River Canyon have excellent birdwatching.

## FISHING

Anglers often catch bass, walleye, and catfish. Motorized boats are allowed on the lake. The boat ramp is located next to Juniper Campground.

## CAMPING

Three campgrounds offer 78 sites for tents, RVs, and trailers. Equestrians and primitive camping are welcome at Tano Campground. Juniper Campground sits adjacent to the boat ramp. Rocky Point has electric hookups for RVs. The campgrounds have bathrooms, drinking water, showers, kids' playgrounds, and a dump station. Reservations can be made online.

## LOCAL ATTRACTIONS, BUSINESSES

*Blue Hole Lake and Dive Center*: This 80'-wide and 130'-deep sinkhole lake's crystal-clear water attracts scuba divers from around the world for a unique diving experience. The lake is fed by a natural spring that releases 3,000 gallons of water a minute. Kids will delight in cliff jumping and swimming in the refreshing 62°F water.

*Scenic Highway 91*: Take a drive down scenic Highway 91 to Puerto de Luna. The two-lane highway crosses several bridges and meanders through red rock cliffs that line the Pecos River Valley. Raptors and other interesting birds can be seen flying along the riverway. The highway ends in the historic Spanish town of Puerto de Luna. History buffs will revel in the knowledge that Billy the Kid reportedly ate his last Christmas Eve dinner here in 1880, while being transported to trial in Las Vegas, Nevada, in the custody of Pat Garrett. An adobe church still stands near interpretive signs describing the history of the town.

*Blue Hole Cienega Nature Preserve*: Most of the year, this 116-acre nature preserve is not much to look at, but in September, acres of the wetland turn into a sea of gold when the federally threatened Pecos sunflower blooms en masse. The preserve is managed by the NM Forestry Division and protects three endangered plant species. An endemic species of round-nose minnow can be found swimming in the Blue Hole spring run that connects Blue Hole Lake to the preserve. Interpretive trails and signs are planned for the preserve.

*Clayton Lake State Park Dinosaur Trackways*: The park is a man-made oasis set among arid rolling prairies and sandstone bluffs. If you have a dinosaur fanatic in your bunch, you'll want to stop here to check out the dinosaur trackways, the most extensive one of its kind in North America. The fossilized footprints are best viewed in early morning and late afternoon.

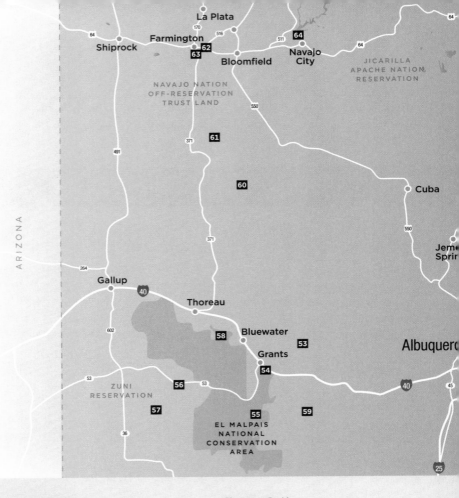

For nature-loving families who are looking for a rustic and remote landscape to explore, there is adventure aplenty to be found in northwestern New Mexico. This is a land of fire and ice, moonscape badlands, and fast rivers flowing through high desert scrublands. National parks, monuments, and wilderness preserve the cultural history and geologic and biological treasures in this area. Volcanic activity has left its mark on the region, forming intriguing lava flows, ice caves, and towering dormant volcanoes. Unique wildlife and plants make their homes in this arid landscape dotted with large reservoirs and rivers.

## Grants Area

### 53. Mount Taylor

**Nearest Town:** Grants

**Best Season To Visit:** Year-round

**Visitor Information:** The road to La Mosca is only open June–October and is impassable in wet weather.

**Getting There:** From Grants, take Lobo Canyon Road (FR 547), which turns into FR 239 where the pavement ends at mile 13. Turn right onto FR 453. A high-clearance vehicle is necessary to make it the last 2 miles to the saddle.

Mount Taylor is the main landscape feature in the Four Corners area, and kids will enjoy getting to know its fire lookouts, forests, beaver ponds, trails, and long views from the summit. Its towering profile is clearly visible from Albuquerque, 50 miles to the west. The volcano rises up from the high desert, standing alone on the edge of the Zuni Mountains and lava flows of El Malpais. The summit is not above the tree line, but only the northwest slope is forested. The rest of the mountain is covered in alpine meadows that burst with wildflowers in late summer.

The forested side of the mountain provides some of the best mushrooming in the state in August and September. Children will delight in the variety of colors and shapes of mushrooms found here. The deadly but colorful amanitas are common on the mountain; look for their red caps with white flecks. Take a moment to talk with your children about the importance of never eating any wild mushroom unless they've been identified as edible by an expert. Amanitas are indeed dangerous. One child reportedly died from eating just a third of an amanita mushroom cap.

The view from the 11,301' peak is nearly 360 degrees of spectacular. The mountain is regarded as one of the four sacred mountains by the Navajo and is popular with hikers in the summer and backcountry skiers in winter. Mount Taylor is also the site of the annual Mount Taylor Quadrathlon, a grueling race involving running, biking, skiing, and snowshoeing.

La Mosca lookout sits across the saddle from Mount Taylor. Built in the 1960s, it is now on the National Register of Historic Places. FR 453, a rocky and rugged road, provides access to the parking area at its base. The lookout is still staffed, and friendly rangers will allow you to climb to the top and take in the views. The saddle between the lookout and volcanic peak makes a great spot for dispersed camping for a night or two. Previous campers have left fire rings in the best spots. Several hiking trails branch out from the saddle into watery canyons or to the peak.

Wildflowers color the meadows on the way to summit Mount Taylor

## WILDLIFE

The route from Grants to the La Mosca saddle has some of the best opportunity to view wildlife in the area. Watch for black bears, mule deer, elk, and wild turkeys.

## BIRDWATCHING

Raptors are common, especially in the alpine area. Watch for band-tailed pigeons, pine siskins, Steller's jays, Clark's nutcrackers, and various nuthatch species.

### HIKE | SUMMIT MOUNT TAYLOR

**Distance:** 2 miles one-way

**Difficulty:** Moderate

**Getting There:** Take FR 239 to FR 453, following signs for La Mosca Peak. At 4.6 miles from the turnoff, in the saddle between La Mosca and Mount Taylor, the road forks. The left fork leads to the fire lookout on La Mosca, and the right leads to Mount Taylor and

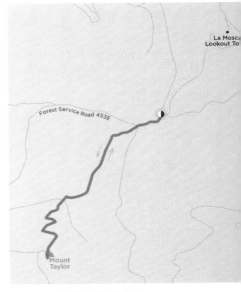

**SUMMIT MOUNT TAYLOR** 2 miles one-way

Water Canyon. Take the right fork and park. The road to Water Canyon continues down the hill; the road up Mount Taylor is to the right. In between is the short trail up Mount Taylor, sometimes marked with a Gooseberry Trail sign, often unmarked with a cairn. Another option: a 6-mile hike up to the summit is available by starting at the Gooseberry Trailhead on FR 193.

**Getting There:** From the Mount Taylor District Ranger Station on Lobo Canyon Road, take a left onto NM 547, which becomes FR 239. After 11 miles, at the end of the pavement, turn right onto FR 193. After 4.7 miles from turnoff, reach the trailhead parking lot on the right in a grove of aspens. The trailhead is across the street from the parking lot.

Kids will enjoy this relatively easy 2-mile climb through wildflower meadows and shady, mushroom-packed forests to the peak of a massive stratovolcano where views of lava-covered landscape stretch for miles. Along the way to the top, you might be able to spot a Clark's nutcracker, a resident of high alpine forests.

From the Gooseberry Trail sign (or unmarked cairn) off FR 453E, walk through the meadow and enter a patch of conifer trees. The trail then sidehills up the backside of Mount Taylor through a wildflower meadow, dives into the cool shade of spruce-fir woods, and pops you out onto the summit. Children are able to easily distinguish spruce and fir trees from their needles. Show them how to roll the needles between their fingers. The needles that roll are spruce and the flat ones that don't are fir.

Views from this 11,301' ancient stratovolcano are spectacular; the peak is wide open in three directions, with dense forest on the northwestern slope. The La Mosca Fire Lookout and cell phone antenna farm are visible a mile to the northeast, a wind farm to the north, the Zuni Mountains to the west, and the lava flows and sandstone bluffs of El Malpais National Monument to the south.

## 54. El Malpais National Monument

(505) 876-2783

www.nps.gov/elma/index.htm

**Nearest Town:** Grants

**Best Season to Visit:** Year-round, though August and September have the best weather.

**Visitor Information:** Visitor center open daily, except for major holidays. Admission fees apply.

**Getting There:** Visitor center is located just south of I-40 at Exit 85. Two paved state highways, NM 53 on the west side and NM 117 on the east side, provide access to the larger monument and conservation area off I-40.

♿ some areas are accessible

Choose your own adventures in this unique landscape. From spelunking in lava caves, climbing bluffs, watching masses of bats fly at twilight, and finding camouflaged wildlife, there's a lot for children to delight in and families to enjoy in this public land. From the summit of Mount Taylor, it's easy to see how this landscape earned the moniker El Malpais (Spanish for "the Bad Land"). Thirty cinder cones rim the broad valley of the monument on the west, yellow sandstone rimrock on the east, to the south stretch vast dry plains, and in between are miles of black lava. The Malpais lava flows range in age from about 2,000 years old to more than a million.

American Indians nearby El Malpais tell similar but unique stories of the "Black Rock River" and the devastation wrought by volcanoes in the region. Rivers of hot lava flowed down valleys and canyons. Showers of ash, cinders, and volcanic bombs landed on the earth. Earthquakes signaled new eruptions and dangers. For the people who lived here while the volcanoes were active, the eruptions meant loss of life and entire villages.

But people persisted, nonetheless. Archaeologists have found sites dating from 12,000 years ago until the present. The big game hunting Paleo-Indians set up camps in the area, and Ancestral Puebloans followed, gathering plants and eventually settling into farming here. Around 500 years ago, Navajo and Apache Indians moved in and still live here today. The Zuni-Acoma Trail, which crosses rugged and sometimes sharp lava flows on the northeastern edge of the monument, served as an important trade route between the two pueblos.

These tribes were some of the first to be contacted by the Spanish conquistador Francisco Vázquez de Coronado, who led expeditions north from Mexico City in the 1500s. Settlers and homesteaders came in with railroads and logging companies. By the 1950s, most of the conifer forests that cover the Zuni Mountains to the west had been clear-cut. Logging still takes place today.

The monument was created in 1987 to protect the natural and cultural resources of the area. Many acres within the El Malpais National Monument and Conservation Area have been identified as having wilderness characteristics and await official designation and further protection.

Spend a day or two driving and stopping throughout the monument to take in the harsh yet starkly beautiful landscape. The many lava tube cave systems, ice caves, cinder cones, spatter cones, and other intriguing volcanic features can be explored on scenic drives, at overlooks, and by hiking short trails.

Each season has its benefits and challenges due to the weather in this dramatic country. With some preparation and research ahead of time, any time of year can be enjoyed. That said, the high desert ecosystem explodes with life after the summer monsoon rains of late June and July. In August and September, grasses and wildflowers light up in a rainbow of colors. This surge in plant activity draws out an abundance of mammals, insects, toads, frogs, and other hidden life. Milder temperatures in the later part of summer and into late fall make this a great time of year to visit.

From the visitor center, start your exploration with the half-mile interpretive hiking trail that begins just off the parking area to get a sense for the area and how volcanoes and lava have shaped the landscape. Pets are permitted on this trail.

CAVING

Underneath the lava flows of El Malpais lies a hidden world of lava tube caves with their ice, rock, and mineral formations. Most of them don't have set trails and require scrambling over boulders and rocks. A kid's dream! With a free caving permit from the visitor center and proper equipment, you

## Bats in the El Calderon Area

At least 14 species of bats are found in the monument. During the summer months, thousands of bats fly from the entrance of Bat Cave in the El Calderon Area at dusk to forage for insects. A colony of about 40,000 Mexican (a.k.a. Brazilian) free-tailed bats use this cave as a summer home and migrate south for the winter. Other bats, like little brown bats and Townsend's big- eared bats, live here year-round and hibernate in this cave. Bat Cave is closed to entry year-round, but you can watch the evening flight from the entrance. Ranger-led programs at the Bat Cave are scheduled weekly from June throughout September. Wildflowers can blanket the ground in the El Calderon Area after the monsoon rains.

can explore several caves in the park. Junction Cave is the easiest cave to access. The Big Tubes Area, which requires a high-clearance vehicle to reach, accesses several caves that can be explored underground. The invertebrates and microorganisms in each cave have evolved separately from those in other systems. Bats, owls, blind crickets, and unusual plant species found nowhere else are just some of the interesting creatures that live in and use the caves. Decontamination of cave gear (clothes, boots, flashlights, helmets, and gloves) is required for entry into the caves to preserve the health of the species that live there. Adult chaperones are required for kids to enter the caves. See the monument's website for more details on caving (www.nps.gov/elma).

## WILDLIFE

In the lava flows, watch for wood rats, mice, and various reptiles that exhibit melanistic coloring—an adaptation that causes darker colors in their coats and skins, allowing them to blend in with the surroundings. The sandstone rimrock country is home to black bears, mule deer, coyotes, prairie dogs, and bobcats. More than two dozen bison were transplanted into the monument in 1992. Pronghorn thrive in the grasslands of the southern portion of the monument.

## BIRDWATCHING

A total of 210 species have been identified in the monument, many abundant upland desert species. Watch for burrowing owls in prairie dog towns, red-tailed hawks, American kestrels, turkey vultures, violet-green swallows, and canyon wrens close to cliffs where peregrine falcons have also been sighted. Common birds include western bluebirds, ravens, pinyon jays, northern mockingbirds, and black-chinned hummingbirds.

POINT OF INTEREST | SANDSTONE BLUFFS OVERLOOK

Located along the NM 117 drive through the monument, the colorful Sandstone Bluffs rise from the lava fields of El Malpais below and afford a 360-degree view of the surrounding area. See sweeping vistas over black lava, forested mesas, and Mount Taylor rising dramatically in the north. Fossils emerge from the rocks in places, and depressions in the sandstone (called tinajas) can fill up with rainwater, creating a nice reflection of the sky. Water striders, whirligigs, and tadpoles of spadefoot toads thrive in this shallow water. The rocks on the bluffs make a great setting for a game of hide and seek. The area has a nice picnic area and vault toilets. Enjoy a picnic dinner while watching the sunset. The cliffs are steep, so watch kids carefully around the edges. At the base of the bluffs there is more to explore. Animals leave their tracks in the power-soft sand underfoot. There are no official trails, but wandering around will reveal natural arches, places to scramble, side canyons, Native American rock art, and several archaeology sites.

## 55. El Malpais National Conservation Area

(505) 876-2783

www.blm.gov/visit/el-malpais-nca

**Nearest Town:** Grants

**Best Season to Visit:** Year-round; spring and fall have the best weather.

**Visitor Information:** Ranger station open to visitors; check website for hours and days.

**Getting There:** Located 9 miles south of I-40 Exit 89 (Quemado) on NM 117.

The El Malpais National Conservation Area extends the protected beauty of the national monument with additional sites and hiking trails off NM 117. Managed by the BLM, the area covers 200,000 acres, two wilderness areas, and several wilderness study areas. Stop at the ranger station for information on the area and walk the 1-mile loop interpretive trail. Whether backcountry camping or just taking a scenic drive, the area offers a whole lot of solitude, space, and interesting geology.

### HIKE | LA VENTANA ARCH TRAIL

**Distance:** 0.25 miles
**Difficulty:** Easy
**Getting There:** Trailhead off of NM 117.

This trail is an easy entry into the vast wilderness, taking you to one of the largest natural arches in New Mexico set into colorful sandstone cliffs. The trail starts on a paved path and changes to gravel when you cross the boundary into the Cebolla Wilderness Area. Here you are surrounded by dramatic sandstone cliff formations, piñon and juniper trees, a variety of shrubs and grasses, and colorful wildflowers in the late summer.

### CAMPING

Joe Skeen Campground in the high desert is set back from the highway and has 10 primitive sites for campers that fill on a first come, first served basis. Some pull-through sites accommodate large RVs. Two vault toilets but no water on site.

### ICE CAVE

(888) 432-2283
www.icecaves.com
**Nearest Town:** Grants
**Best Time of Year to Visit:** April–October, though open year-round
**Visitor Information:** Privately run operation offers self-guided tours. Open daily. Check their website for education info.
**Getting There:** From Grants, take Exit 81 on I-40 and turn south on NM 53. Follow the road 25 miles to an entrance gate clearly marked with posts and signs. Take a left and follow the driveway for a half mile to the parking lot.

The Ice Cave and Bandera Volcano are a privately owned attraction adjacent to the monument. The David Candelaria family has managed the area since the 1990s and has developed educational information about it on their website. They offer self-guided tours into the Ice Cave and into the Bandera Volcano. The volcano, an erupted cinder cone, was active about 10,000 years ago, creating a lava tube system over 17 miles long. Most of the lava tube collapsed, but some sections remain intact, like the Ice Cave.

We started our tour of these attractions with the volcano. A half-mile trail winds around the side of the volcano on a gradual incline. Standing at the edge of the caldera, I talked with my kids about the explosive force of hot lava able to shoot hot boulders from its center; many still sit where they fell. It is one of the best examples of a cinder cone in North America.

A 10-minute walk and 69 steps take you into a one-room cave with just the right conditions to form a natural icebox; temperatures never rise above 31°F. While there's no access to the ice floor, my kids were still impressed and relieved by the stark temperature drop from the hot desert as we descended the stairs into the cool Ice Cave. Every year, rainwater and snowmelt drips through the roof of the cave to freeze and form new layers of ice. The ice has been forming in the cave for over 3,400 years. Tell your kids that people have been visiting the cave for the last 1,200 years. Imagine what ancient peoples used their chipped ice blocks for: A cool summer drink? Preserving meat from the latest hunt?

Tent and RV camping are available on the grounds, as is a trading post that sells snacks and goods from the neighboring tribes.

## 56. El Morro National Monument

*El Morro Visitor Center*
(505) 783-4226, ext. 801
www.nps.gov/elmo

**Nearest Town:** Grants
**Best Time of Year to Visit:** Spring and Fall
**Visitor Information:** Open year-round, except on major holidays. Hikes must be completed by 5 p.m.
**Getting There:** From Albuquerque, take I-40 west to Grants. At Exit 81, go south on NM 53 for 42 miles to El Morro National Monument.
♿ accessible

Water in the desert attracts life. At El Morro National Monument, a natural pool at the base of a great bluff collects snowmelt and rain runoff, making it a valuable water source and resting place for centuries of Puebloan people, explorers, travelers, and wildlife. Children will be intrigued by the ancient names, symbols, and petroglyphs carved into the rock face around the pool.

They will also enjoy exploring the ruins of a large pueblo built in the 1200s located on top of El Morro. This town was vacated by the time the Spaniards arrived in the late 1500s. Spanish explorers found the pool and added their carvings and messages to the rock; some, like Juan de Oñate and religious leaders, were controversial, infamous figures. These brief notes in stone give a thumbnail sketch of New Mexico's Spanish history and their attempts to conquer the area. As settlers arrived, El Morro became a break along the trail for those passing through and a destination for sightseers.

To preserve the history carved here, El Morro was established as a national monument in 1906. The Zuni and Acoma Puebloan peoples continue to live on the border of this small monument today. The visitor center has interpretive displays and a small bookstore.

The Headland Trail will take you on a

Bleached sandstone on the Headlands Trail at El Morro National Monument; courtesy of NPS/Lanny Wagner

2-mile loop past the pool and wall of inscriptions to the top of the bluff for long views. Kids will love the climb up the natural sandstone stairs. At the top, find the Atsinna ruins, where up to 600 people lived in this pueblo with 355 rooms from 1275 to 1350 AD.

Camping is available in the monument, with nine tent sites, vault toilets, and water during the warm months.

## 57. Wild Spirit Wolf Sanctuary

(505) 775-3304

www.wildspiritwolfsanctuary.org

**Nearest Town:** Ramah

**Best Season to Visit:** Spring–fall

**Visitor Information:** Reservations needed for tours and camping. Check website, as tour hours vary through the year. If you plan to stay overnight, you'll need a high-clearance vehicle to reach the campground.

**Getting There:** From Grants, take NM 53 west for 45 miles. Turn left on Indian Service Route 125 and right on Indian Service Route 120. Turn left on Jubilee Trail.

A guaranteed encounter with wildlife is a rare thing in New Mexico, so animal lovers of all ages won't want to miss the Wild Spirit Wolf Sanctuary. Unreleasable, rescued, and captive-born wolves and wolf-dog mixes roam the sanctuary's large natural habitat enclosures. We first met Flurry, a white arctic wolf that is one of the sanctuary's ambassadors, at an event at the public library. The wolf, sitting at the front of the room with the sanctuary's director, Leyton, commanded the attention of a room full of kids. Flurry kept a wolfy eye on everyone but remained calm and engaged the entire presentation. When Leyton informed us that we could visit the wolves at their home and even stay overnight, we knew we had to go.

After traveling down a remote gravel road, we arrived and were welcomed by the soulful sound of the wolves howling. Visitors are not able to wander the sanctuary alone and must stay with the group. We took the standard tour and were guided by a staff member on a quarter-mile walk. She told us about each wolf—from behavior to what they like to eat—and about the sanctuary's conservation efforts. Most of the canines end up here from the exotic pet trade. Our tour guide explained the difference between wild wolves and domestic dogs, emphasizing that wild wolves are not pets and should not be kept as such. None of the canines are forced to interact with the public here, so while there are about 60 canines on site—including some foxes, dingoes, and singing dogs—not all are seen by the public. Kids over 7 with their adults can take a leashed wolf for a walk on a special tour. The staff selected one that was ready for some interaction that day and afforded us the opportunity to get closer than we imagined and observe their particularly reserved behavior compared to our pet dog.

The sanctuary offers four standard tours a day. Other specialized tours are available with advanced reservations, but other than the wolf walk and feeding tour, most are limited to 18 and older. The ultimate experience is to stay overnight camping or in one of the sanctuary's on-site cabins. The remote, forested primitive campground made for great stargazing and, much to the kids' delight, we heard wolves howl from our tent.

## 58. Bluewater Lake State Park

(505) 876-2391

www.emnrd.state.nm.us/SPD/bluewater lakestatepark.html

**Nearest Town:** Grants

**Best Season to Visit:** Year-round

**Visitor Information:** Open year-round. Gates are locked in evening; check website for details. Entrance fees apply.

&#9855; accessible

This reservoir, set in a small canyon surrounded by piñon-juniper-covered hills on the north flank of the Zuni Mountains, makes a great basecamp for exploration in the region. If you've been sightseeing in the high desert monuments and volcanoes in the area, this big, serene body of water is a refreshing respite from the arid landscape. Kids will enjoy the playground, campground roads to bike on, and skipping rocks or fishing from the lakeshore. The campground's 150 sites accommodate tents and have full hookups for RVs. A second site across the lake, Las Tusas Campground, allows primitive camping on the beach. The bathrooms have showers and there's a small visitor center. Short hikes around the lake take you to scenic views. Swimming, fishing, and boating are all allowed. The lake is stocked with rainbow and brown trout, but most anglers come for the tiger muskies.

## MOUNTAIN BIKING

Maintained trails through scenic high desert, sagebrush scrublands, and other-worldly badlands have made northwest New Mexico an increasingly popular destination for mountain bikers. Active families will find trails for all levels of riders here. Nearby, Gallup has three major mountain biking areas. The High Desert Trail System has 22 miles of singletrack trail with great vistas and caprocks. This fast-riding mountain bike-designed trail system is very well marked and offers a remote backcountry feel.

The Zuni Mountain Trail System is 25+ miles through ponderosa pine forest and grassy meadows, plus another 18 miles in the Twin Springs Area along primitive singletrack. Beginners should check out the Strawberry Canyon Trail in the Zuni Mountains.

Hogback Trail follows an open ridge through the high desert. Most of these trails are intermediate level, but a few easy trails are accessible to beginners and families.

Anglers try their luck at Bluewater Lake

## 59. Acoma Pueblo

(800) 747-0181

www.acomaskycity.org

**Nearest Town:** Grants

**Best Season to Visit:** Year-round

**Visitor Information:** Tours operate daily. Closed on major holidays and for tribal ceremonies. Check website for up-to-date information.

**Getting There:** From I-40 heading west, take Exit 102. At the roundabouts, take Pueblo Road for approximately 3.5 miles to Pinsbaari Drive. Turn left on Pinsbaari Drive and drive about 8 miles. Turn left on Haak'u Road and continue for 5 miles. Arrive at the Sky City Cultural Center and Haak'u Museum.

Acoma is the oldest continuously inhabited settlement in North America, and one of the most beautiful. A visit to the pueblo is only possible on a guided tour, and although children are allowed, they must stay with the group without wandering or climbing on things. The tour is best suited for older youth who would benefit from hearing the stories and history during the 1.5-hour tour.

The mesa top settlement is perched on a sheer-walled, 367' sandstone bluff in a valley studded with similar monoliths. A trip to the village and museum offers a window in time where Native people carry on traditions of their ancestors and share their culture and history with visitors. Most people don't live in the Sky City today but return for cultural occasions and events. Adults will appreciate Acoma pottery, recognized for their thin walls and geometric designs. Many potters still work in studios in the village.

After the tour, visitors can walk down from the mesa, an adventurous hike after being with the group. Check with your guide and ask them to point out the trail.

# Farmington Area

## 60. Chaco Culture National Historical Park

(505) 786-7014

www.nps.gov/chcu/index.htm

**Nearest Town:** Gallup

**Best Season to Visit:** Year-round; summers can be very hot and winter nights cold.

**Visitor Information:** The park is open sunrise to sunset. The visitor center is open daily; times vary with season. The road into the park is slick and can flood during rain events. Entrance and camping fees apply.

**Getting There:** From Cuba, travel 42 miles on US 550. Turn left at the Red Mesa Express gas station onto dirt road 7940. The route to Chaco is well signed and the road can be a bumpy washboard if weather has taken its toll.

&#9855; accessible

Late afternoon in June, we pulled up to Chaco in our rented RV, tired after 40 minutes of rattling and shaking on the washboard road that leads to the park. At the visitor center, a friendly ranger filled us in on all the tours and events available to us during our stay and pointed the way to the campground. Nestled into large canyon walls with intriguing rock formations, the campground includes a small ruin, which we immediately explored. The grandparents settled in to enjoy the view from their camp chairs with a cool drink and the boys made friends with the kids camping the next site over. The peace and beauty of the ancient place quickly rejuvenated our spirits.

At sunset, we rode our bikes to get a closer view of Fajada Butte, 442' of capstone that dominates the canyon entrance and serves as a landmark throughout the park. A small herd of elk crossed the road in front of us, continuing to graze undisturbed by our presence. As we watched them, the

Visiting the ruins at Chaco Culture National Historical Park

evening sky took on a rose-pink hue. We rode on to an interpretive sign that informed us about the Sun Dagger on top of the butte. Light passing through three boulders onto a spiral petroglyph marks the sun's position during the solstices and equinoxes. Chacoan and modern-day Pueblo peoples use the sun, the stars, and the seasons to plan their agriculture and ceremonies. This impressive creation was just a first taste of the mysteries that unfold in Chaco Culture National Historic Park. Back at camp, we settled in for the night beneath dark skies filled with stars for a good night's rest before continuing our adventure the next day.

Chaco Culture National Historic Park preserves what was once, and for some still is, the center of Ancestral Puebloan culture and the universe. For more than 300 years, this high-desert valley nurtured a thriving culture of impressive scale and complexity. Chacoans used unique and specialized building skills to construct massive buildings of multiple stories that contained hundreds of large rooms. Structures were often oriented to solar, lunar, and cardinal

directions. The community began in the mid-800s, and by 1050 its sphere of influence was extensive, connected by a network of roads and trade routes to villages through the San Juan Basin and beyond. Aztec, Mesa Verde, and many other sites in the Four Corners area all bear the mark of Chacoan culture. Chaco remains an important spiritual and cultural center to many modern Southwest Indians who are descendants of ancestral Chacoans. The ruins can be visited on guided tours or on your own, which is likely preferable for families with smaller children. Be sure to stop at the visitor center to join the Junior Ranger program.

In addition to the fascinating cultural stories told here, Chaco is an island of protected biodiversity in a landscape otherwise besieged by development, grazing, and extraction that have had a significant impact on the ecosystem.

### WILDLIFE

Watch for elk, deer, bobcats, rabbits, badgers, porcupines, bats, snakes, lizards, and amphibians.

### MOUNTAIN BIKING

Biking is encouraged in the canyon and is a great way to explore the park and ruins with children. The 9-mile paved Canyon Loop Road is nearly level and open from sunrise to sunset. Begin your bicycle tour at the park's visitor center. Ride west and follow the signs that direct you around the circuit tour. Along the tour, there are bicycle racks at the various archaeological sites, like the impressive ruins of Pueblo Bonito and Casa Rinconada. Park your bike and walk through these historic structures. The circuit ends at the bike rack back at the visitor center.

## Mexican Spadefoot Toad

A fascinating resident of Chaco is the Mexican spadefoot toad. For most of the year, this animal stays buried beneath the sands of Chaco's arid landscape; the toads can survive underground for over a year if necessary. When the heavy rains of July and August form small, temporary pools of water, the toads rehydrate in the nearest puddle and eat voraciously. During the rainy season, the males begin a raucous chorus, calling for females while floating on the water. The females lay up to 1,000 eggs, and within 48 hours, the tadpoles emerge and begin feeding. They metamorphose from tadpole to juvenile in two to three weeks, a feat that makes them one of the fastest-growing amphibians in the world. As the season cools, both adults and juveniles will dig a winter burrow and stay there until the next summer's rainy season. Then the phenomenon begins all over again.

HIKE | **PUEBLO ALTO TRAIL**

**Distance:** 5.4 miles or less round trip
**Difficulty:** Moderate to strenuous for children
**Getting There:** Find the trailhead at the Pueblo del Arroyo parking lot and the end of the park's loop road, where a parking area and toilet are located between the ruins of Pueblo Bonito, Pueblo del Arroyo, and Kin Kletso.

Before your hike, stop at the park's visitor center and museum. The more kids understand of the history and mysteries of Chaco culture, the more they will take interest in the sites along the hike. In New Mexican Spanish the word *chaco* means "desert," which is what you'll find in the arid, treeless country of Chaco today. This hike takes you through and above the remains of the remarkable civilization that flourished here

some 1,000 years ago. At least 11 "great houses" fill the canyon, some four and five stories high.

At the trailhead, follow the signs pointing toward the ruins of Kin Kletso and the trails to Peñasco Blanco and Pueblo Alto. After a quarter mile, follow the signs for Pueblo Alto Trail, which branches to the right and arrives at the base of a cliff. The trail heads up the cliff and is far less difficult than it first appears. My children enjoyed knowing that we were following a route the feet of Ancestral Puebloans carved into a cleft in the rocks.

Emerge onto a broad sandstone ledge overlooking the valley. Walking along the mostly level cliff, you'll pass stone circles, handmade basins, rock chambers, lizards, and other mysteries to be explored. Take in the impressive views of Chaco below.

Arrive at a bench overlooking Pueblo Bonito. This makes a good turnaround point for tired legs needing a shorter hike. Or chose one of the branches of the trail that splits at this point. Both continue past examples of Chacoan roads and stairs cut into the rocks. They meet at Pueblo Alto or "High Town," named for its location atop the mesa. Take the branch to the northeast for the most direct route back to Pueblo Alto. The other continues along the mesa rim to view Chetro Ketl and to explore the roads that converge from other Chacoan towns in the Southwest.

**DARK SKY NIGHTS**

Chaco's commitment to nighttime darkness, reducing light pollution, and educational events has qualified it as a certified International Dark Sky Park. You'll notice that no permanent outdoor lighting exists in the park to preserve the nighttime ecosystem and for the nocturnal wildlife that depend on darkness for survival. The dark, clear skies also mean Chaco is one of the best places in the world for stargazing, a perk of camping in the park. The Albuquerque Astronomical Society provides interpretive programming at Chaco's domed observatory. Night sky programs are presented on Friday and Saturday evenings at sunset from April through October. Staff presentations on archaeoastronomy (ancient celestial knowledge and practices), cultural history, and other topics are followed by telescope viewing of celestial objects. Special events happen on spring and fall equinox and summer and winter solstice. Star parties often take place in May and October.

## 61. Bisti/De-Na-Zin Wilderness Area

*Bureau of Land Management*
*Farmington Office*
  (505) 564-7600
  www.blm.gov/visit/bisti-de-na-zin-wilderness

**Nearest Town:** Farmington
**Best Season to Visit:** Spring and fall
**Visitor Information:** No amenities or water available in the area; bring with you everything you need. When it rains, the ground turns into deep mud and rushing creeks.

**Getting There:** To reach the Bisti Access Parking Area, drive NM 371 just under 36 miles south of Farmington and turn east on Road 7297 (a gravel road). Drive Road 7297 for approximately 2 miles to a T-intersection and turn left. Drive just under 1 mile to the Bisti Access Parking Area, which is just south of a broad wash on the east side of the road. There is another, smaller parking area a quarter-mile farther north.

Hoodoos, labyrinths, petrified trees, dinosaur eggs, arches, and spires converge to create an otherworldly desert landscape that is the Bisti Badlands. After setting up camp in the primitive parking lot, we

Hoodoos of Bisti Badlands at sunset

passed through the fence and set out to explore this strange land. No official trails exist in this 45,000-acre wilderness. Navigate by following the general direction of the wash in and out.

We hiked for a while under a cloudless, blue sky, admiring a rainbow of earth-toned rock and mud revealing strange forms as we approached. We crested a tall clay hill and looked down upon a maze of valleys, narrow canyons, small caves, and sculpted rocks. My boys' eyes grew wide and we all agreed—this was an epic location for a game of hide and seek. For several hours we scrambled, hid, slid, and clambered around. We emerged dirty, tired, and happy and hiked out of the fantasy moonscape hungry for dinner.

Adventure-loving families will enjoy a day or two in the Bisti (pronounced "bees-tie"). Once a coastal swamp of an inland sea that was home to many large trees, reptiles, dinosaurs, and primitive mammals, much of the area is now devoid of vegetation and animal residents. It's the rocks and shapes that provide hours of entertainment and interest. Hike up the wash about 2 miles to reach the dinosaur eggs, rocks that look like cracked-open eggs covered in sinuous patterns. Near to the eggs, also find giant logs of petrified wood resting on eroded mud platforms. Follow canyons to find endless galleries of caprocks and hoodoos. If you want to aim for seeing specific features in the wilderness area, I highly recommend a thorough internet search beforehand and GPS in hand.

#### MORE BADLANDS

While Bisti is the best-known of northwest New Mexico's badlands, there are several others that are worthy of a visit.

*Angel Peak Scenic Area* overlooks 10,000 acres of rugged, scenic landscape. Short hikes from picnic areas and the small campground provide views of the area's stunning features, like Angel Peak and the Castle. Sunrise and sunset are especially scenic here. Dirt roads on the outskirts of Bloomfield provide access to the Kutz Canyon badlands below. *Getting There:* Drive in on Road 7175 off of US 550, about 20 miles south of Bloomfield.

*Ah-Shi-Sle-Pah Wilderness Study Area* offers more spectacular geologic formations to explore on unmarked hikes. Of special note are the Alien Throne, King of Wings, and Valley of Dreams formations. *Getting There:* On US 550, 7.5 miles northwest of Nageezi along NM 57.

#### THE URBAN OUTDOORS IN FARMINGTON

Along the Animas River, Farmington has developed a National Recreation Trail system for hiking, biking, and paddling that connect several parks, playgrounds, and a nature center. Animas and Berg Park are main access points to the 8 miles of trail great for birdwatching and playing in the river.

## 62. Riverside Nature Center

(505) 599-1422

www.fmtn.org/252/Riverside-Nature-Center

**Nearest Town:** Farmington

**Best Season to Visit:** Year-round

**Visitor Information:** Hours vary. Check their website for regular tours and events.

**Getting There:** Located in town at 145 Browning Parkway, Farmington, NM 87402.

♿ accessible

This nature center in Farmington overlooks wetland connected to the Animas River. The center has a host of educational displays and activities for kids, including duck feeding and skunk observing from their large windows. The staff is friendly and knowledgeable about wildlife in the area.

A bald eagle perches along the San Juan River after a rainstorm

## 63. Animas River Whitewater Park

(505) 326-7602

www.farmingtonnm.org/listings/animas
-river-white-water-park

During spring runoff, rafters and kayakers enjoy Class I and II rapids from Animas to Boyd Park, but paddling is enjoyable here year-round. On the weekends, families can spend a day meandering down the Animas River on tubes. The locally owned Animas Outdoor provides tube and bike rentals and car shuttles Fridays to Sundays; (505) 947-5683.

## 64. Navajo Lake State Park

*Navajo Lake State Park*
(505) 632-2278
www.emnrd.state.nm.us/SPD/navajolake
statepark.html

*Navajo Lake Marina*
(800) 582-56587
www.navajomarina.com

**Nearest Town:** Bloomfield
**Best Season to Visit:** April–October
**Visitor Information:** Visitor center with educational exhibits open daily.
**Getting There:** From Bloomfield, travel 25 miles northeast on US 64 and NM 511.
♿ accessible

New Mexico's second largest reservoir lake has plenty of developed tourism services for those who want a guided adventure. Navajo Lake accommodates everything from large houseboats for spending several days exploring the canyons to kayaks for a few hours of paddling along the shoreline. The marina has a restaurant, store, and rental area for kayaks and paddleboats and offers guided fishing tours. The state park has multiple campgrounds and two boat docks. The San Juan River below the dam offers world-class, year-round fly fishing for rainbow, brown, and cutthroat trout.

## WILDLIFE

Beavers and muskrats inhabit the waters. Also watch for mule deer.

## BIRDWATCHING

Good winter viewing of bald eagles, golden eagles, mallards, common mergansers, common goldenheads, gadwalls, American wigeons, buffleheads, and cinnamon and blue-winged teals.

## MOUNTAIN BIKING

Farmington's Glade Run Recreation Area is a massive trail system and OHV area that can be accessed from town. Most of the trails are intermediate and above. A network of trails also extends from town, offering families and beginners easy access. Beginners can check out the Anasazi Bike Trail, a fast-paced singletrack with no major climbs or descents, just gentle grades. Near Aztec, check out the Alien Run, which flows through the high desert mesas.

## LOCAL ATTRACTIONS, BUSINESSES

*Zuni Pueblo*: Zuni Pueblo offers a variety of tours and experiences to learn about their culture and way of life. These tours are best suited for older kids who can remain respectful and attentive for the length of the tour. www.zunitourism.com

*Sherman Dugan Museum of Geology*: Located at the San Juan College in Farmington, this museum is a rewarding stop off for rock hounds and fossil-lovers. The collection features over 100 minerals, rock specimens, and fossils—each one a small universe of intriguing color and shape. The exhibit includes the skull and jawbones of a 35-million-year-old brontothere and a full pterosaur skeleton. An interactive augmented reality sandbox geology display will entertain the kids. Entrance to the museum is free. The facility is open Monday–Friday.

# SOUTHEAST MOUNTAINS TO DESERT

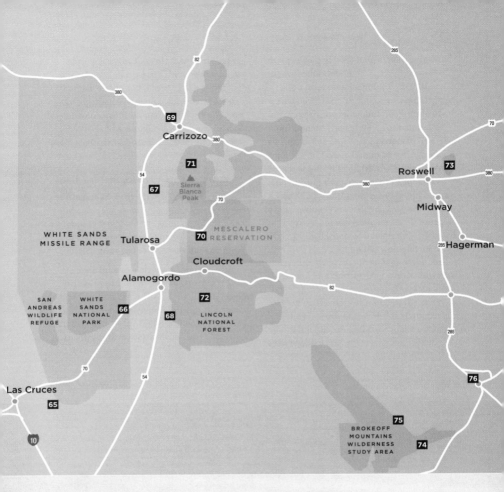

O n a trip to the southeastern corner of New Mexico, families can play in white sand dunes, walk across miles of black lava, cool off in underground caves, climb jagged mountains, and drive through large expanses of desert—providing kids free rein to fully engage with their environment.

Here, isolated mountain ranges with 360-degree views are surrounded by huge expanses of desert. The Lincoln National Forest includes two wilderness areas. Ski Apache is the southernmost ski area in the state and offers winter and summer fun. The mountain towns of Ruidoso and Cloudcroft will surprise you with their quaintness and delicious Texas-style BBQ. The larger city of Las Cruces is an excellent jumping off point for adventure.

## Las Cruces

### 65. Organ Mountains-Desert Peaks National Monument

(575) 522-1219

www.blm.gov/visit/dripping-springs
-natural-area

www.organmountains.org/

**Nearest Town:** Las Cruces

**Best Season to Visit:** Spring and fall

**Visitor Information:** Open daily, except winter holidays. Day-use fees apply.

**Getting There:** The Dripping Springs Visitor Center is located 10 miles east of Las Cruces, on the west side of the Organ Mountains. From Exit 1 on I-25, take University Avenue/ Dripping Springs Road east to the end.

The most jagged of New Mexico's mountains, the Organs, rise above the desert floor, creating a picturesque backdrop to colorful spring wildflowers, stormy summer weather, and the city of Las Cruces. The steep, needlelike spires resemble the pipes of an organ. Peaks jut to an elevation of 9,000'. Year-round springs in the Organ Mountains make this critically important habitat for wildlife. Spring is an especially lovely time to visit the Organ Mountains when the lowlands flush with orange

Mexican poppies and white evening-primroses, followed by bright red claret cup cactus. Summer is extremely hot, with several days over 100°F. Late summer monsoons cool things off and bring another flush of color of white and yellow wildflowers. Snow does fall in the Organs in winter, though it rarely stays on the ground for long.

The Desert Peaks—which also include the Robledo Mountains, Sierra de las Uvas, and Doña Ana Mountains—are arid mountains that rise sharply from the desert floor. These "sky islands," as they are known, are isolated from other mountain ranges by the surrounding desert. This isolation has resulted in several types of endemic cacti and wildflower.

The Potrillo Mountains—the most remote section of the monument, located southwest of Las Cruces—is composed of a volcanic landscape of cinder cones, lava flows, and craters. The Doña Ana Mountains have extensive pedestrian, equestrian, and mountain bike trails, rock climbing routes, and some limited vehicle routes.

Families hiking in the Organ Mountains

### WILDLIFE

Mule deer, mountain lions, pronghorn, jackrabbits, bobcats, coyotes, bats, rock squirrels, and other rodents can be found throughout the monument.

### BIRDWATCHING

Golden eagles, hawks, and owls are abundant in the summer in rocky cliffs. Great horned owls, Swainson's hawks, and peregrine falcons nest in the Potrillo Mountains. Grassland areas harbor rare birds, like aplomado falcons, Baird's sparrows, and Montezuma quail.

### HIKE | PINE TREE TRAIL

**Distance:** 4.5 mile loop

**Difficulty:** Moderate

**Getting There:** Trailhead located in Aguirre Springs group campsite across from a small parking lot between campsites 31 and 32.

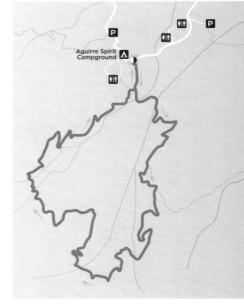

**PINE TREE TRAIL** 4.5 mile loop

Taking in the view from Aguirre Spring Campground

Located on the eastern slope of the Organ Mountains, this loop trail starts in juniper-piñon forest and climbs into high-elevation ponderosa pine forest. Kids will enjoy the varied terrain, with opportunities to climb around in the wet canyons with jagged peaks towering overhead. The trail meanders at the base of the Organ peaks, crossing several seasonal streams. Resting spots with benches and shady ancient alligator junipers offer stunning views of the Tularosa Basin and White Sands beyond.

### HIKE | DRIPPING SPRINGS

**Distance:** 3 miles out and back
**Difficulty:** Easy
**Getting There:** Trail starts in the visitor center parking lot.

Kids will delight in this hike's destination of a lush, wet box canyon filled with trees and historic buildings that tell interesting stories. From the visitor center, head left to the Dripping Springs Trail Head. Follow the old gravel road to the junction with the Crawford Trail, and take the right fork to stay on to the Dripping Springs Trail. Enjoy the beautiful views of the mountains and rock formations. There's not much shade on the first part of the trail, so it's best to do this in the morning. Take a right at the next trail fork and arrive at the old Boyd Sanatorium. Read the interpretive signs explaining the history of this place. Kids may want to know about tuberculosis and why this center for healing was created. The trail continues past the first set of buildings, veering right into a lush, shady canyon. Arrive at the base of a waterfall, or "dripping spring." Follow the path up to the right to see the sanatorium's old historic kitchen and Van Patten Mountain Camp. Follow the stairway up and left to the area above the waterfall to see the springs and dam that fed the camp. After exploring the camp, return to the main trail and the visitor center.

## MOUNTAIN BIKING

### Baylor Canyon Road

**Distance:** 6.8 miles one-way with car shuttle
**Getting There:** Start in the parking lot for Sierra Vista Trail off of Dripping Springs Road.

Burn off some energy on Baylor Canyon Road, a two-lane road that stretches north–south and parallels the western edge of the Organ Mountains. The road is paved, well-maintained, and wide, providing a moderately easy family bike ride. Kids will enjoy stopping at several pull-offs along the way to enjoy the wildflowers, huge barrel cactus, and interesting desert landscape.

### Sierra Vista Trail National Recreation Trail

This 29-mile National Recreation Trail extends from the Organ Mountains south to the Franklin Mountains in El Paso, Texas. Try biking the 7.2-mile stretch of trail from Soledad Canyon to Pena Blanca. This portion of singletrack trail rolls across the desert at the base of the mountains, crossing several arroyos. Watch for rocks and thorny plants that literally grab your attention—and your pants. Most of this trail is on gravelly uplands.

## CLIMBING

### La Cueva, Organ Mountains

**Getting There:** From Las Cruces, go east on University Avenue, which turns into Dripping Springs Road. Follow this road into the recreation area and turn left into La Cueva Picnic Site. Hours vary seasonally.

The Organ Mountains abound with rock climbing locales. Many require several miles hiking to get to. But the La Cueva crag is the one of the closest climbs to Las Cruces, and the views of the jagged Organ Mountains from here are stunning. Note that the rock quality is often quite poor, as are some of the old fixed anchors. Still, my family had fun climbing and scrambling here for a few hours. Climbing is not permitted above the cave, but other routes can be found on the north side of the rock formations. Routes vary from 5.7 to 5.10.

## CAMPING

(575) 525-4300
www.blm.gov/visit/aguirre-spring-campground

Aguirre Spring Campground has 55 campsites and two group sites at the base of the dramatic cliffs and needlelike spires of the Organ Mountains. Upon arrival, my kids immediately disappeared into the canyons to play in trickling creeks, stake their claims on large boulders, and build forts under tree cover. The campground overlooks the Tularosa Basin and White Sands. There are vault toilets in the campground; potable water is available at the entrance gate. Group sites can be reserved, all others are first come, first served.

Primitive camping is also available at the Sierra Vista Trailhead and Baylor Canyon West Trailhead.

## Alamogordo

### 66. White Sands National Park

(575) 479-6124

www.nps.gov/whsa

**Nearest Town:** Alamogordo

**Best Season to Visit:** Spring and fall

**Visitor Information:** The entrance and exit times for the monument vary depending on season. Check ahead for details. Fees apply.

**Getting There:** From Alamogordo, head west on US 70 for about 15 miles. The visitor center is just off the highway.

Sledding and playing in the sands of White Sands National Park

Shimmering, wavelike sand dunes cover 275 square miles of desert in southeast New Mexico. As one of the most unique places on earth, the park service has preserved a major portion of this landscape for the rare plants and animals that live here. To every visiting family's delight, the park service also allows the gypsum sand to be used as a huge, outdoor playground. (The playground is handicapped accessible.)

On a spring afternoon, we pulled into White Sands, bought our circular sleds and wax, and headed out into the white wonder. We spent the afternoon climbing up and sledding down dune after dune, carving a track over time that sped our flight to the bottom as the afternoon wore on.

The kids buried each other in the sand, dug holes several feet deep, and, with their hands and feet, drew massive designs soon to be blown away in the winds. As the sun set, we meandered farther into the dunes. The sand took on the hue of the late afternoon light, changing from white to bright yellow and orange to cooling rose and blue. A profound calm and quiet came over the park as families across the dunes settled into the warm sand, kids sitting on parents' laps. We watched as a full, pink, strawberry moon rose over the Sacramento Mountains to the east, disappearing and reappearing behind colorful layers of clouds on the horizon. We slipped our tuckered-out little ones into the car and drove back to the campground in the Organ Mountains. They drifted off to sleep with ear-to-ear smiles on their faces.

#### WILDLIFE

Watch for subtle signs of wildlife in tiny prints and tracks in the sand made by darkling beetles, snakes, lizards, and rodents. It takes a keen eye to spot the park's wildlife that has adapted to their surroundings by taking on a white coloration. Bleached earless lizards and occasional kit foxes can be spotted in midmornings; white pocket mice and white insects tend to be nocturnal.

#### HIKE | DUNE LIFE NATURE TRAIL

**Distance:** 1 mile

**Difficulty:** Easy

**Getting There:** Trailhead along the main road in the park.

The family-friendly Dune Life Nature Trail has unique characteristics that are not found in the heart of the dunes. Katie the

SOUTHEAST MOUNTAINS TO DESERT
ALAMOGORDO

Kit Fox, the trail mascot, describes the animals and other dune life on 14 trailside signs. Although the animals are rarely seen during the day, this is a great place to practice tracking skills. Tracks in the sand tell the stories of the previous night's activities in the dunes. Look for the tracks of kit foxes, badgers, birds, coyotes, rodents, and reptiles.

### CAMPING

Backcountry camping among the glistening gypsum dunes under the star-studded night sky of White Sands is an unforgettable experience. Summer and fall are the best seasons to camp in the dunes. Spring is generally windy and can result in whiteout storms. Winters can drop to below freezing at night. Setting out for camp in late afternoon and returning in late morning avoids the midday summer heat. Camps are generally within a mile of the trailhead. Permits are required and can be obtained at the visitor center on a first come, first served basis each day.

## 67. Three Rivers Petroglyph Site

*BLM–Las Cruces Field Office*
(575) 525-4300
www.blm.gov/visit/three-rivers-petroglyph-site

**Nearest Town:** Tularosa
**Best Season to Visit:** Year-round, though it can be hot in the summer.
**Visitor Information:** Open year-round; daily times vary with seasons. Fees apply.
**Getting There:** From US 54, 24 miles south of Carrizozo or 18 miles north of Tularosa, turn east onto FR 579 at the sign for Three Rivers Petroglyph Site and Campground and follow the signs for 5 miles to the entrance.
♿ accessible

Kids and adults alike will be awed by the more than 21,000 glyphs of birds, humans, animals, fish, insects, and plants, as well as numerous geometric and abstract designs that are scattered over 50 acres. Ask your kids why the ancient peoples left these signs here. What were they trying to communicate about this place? Are the markings art? Do they tell stories? What do the glyphs look like to them?

The petroglyphs at Three Rivers date back to between about 900 and 1400 AD and were created by Jornada Mogollon people who used stone tools to remove the dark patina on the exterior of the rock. The number and concentration of petroglyphs make this one of the largest and most interesting rock art sites in the Southwest. A rugged half-mile trail begins at the visitor shelter and links many of the most fascinating petroglyphs. Another short trail begins on the east side of the picnic area and leads to a partially excavated prehistoric village.

### HIKE | THREE RIVERS TRAIL

**Distance:** 5–11 miles out and back
**Difficulty:** Moderate to strenuous
**Getting There:** Trailhead located in the Three Rivers Campground.

Water features, rock caves, and mountain tops keep kids' interest along this rugged hike. From the campground, hike along a cascading stream through old growth forest and huge ponderosa pines. Pass under towering cliffs and abundant wildflowers in the summer. As you pass through different life zones along the trail, talk to kids about why plants grow where they do. Are there more plants in the arid forest or along the river? What do plants need to thrive?

Climb the steep western side of the Sacramento Mountains into alpine meadows for stunning views of the Tularosa Basin and mountains beyond. Follow Trail 44 to White Horse Hill for the full hike, or for a moderate 5-mile hike, stay in the lush, green valley and turn around at the Cave Rock.

### CAMPING

Limited tent and RV sites are available at the Three Rivers Petroglyph Site. Three Rivers Campground, a rustic and remote campground, is located about 7 miles beyond the Petroglyph Site on the western slope of the Sacramento Mountains. Twelve sites accommodate tents and trailers. Potable water and vault toilets on site.

## 68. Oliver Lee Memorial State Park

(575) 437-8284

www.emnrd.state.nm.us/SPD/oliverlee statepark.html

**Nearest Town:** Alamogordo

**Best Season to Visit:** October–April

**Visitor Information:** Open year-round. State park fees apply.

**Getting There:** Eight miles south of Alamogordo via US 54 and 4 miles east via Dog Canyon Road.

♿ accessible

Oliver Lee Memorial State Park is at the base of the western escarpment of the Sacramento Mountains of New Mexico. Its main feature, Dog Canyon, is one of several canyons on the west side of the mountains. The park features a historic ranch house and quiet camping in the Chihuahuan Desert. But it's the unique oasis of pools of water under the cottonwood trees of Dog Canyon that kids—and their parents—will

### THREE RIVERS TRAIL

5–11 miles out and back

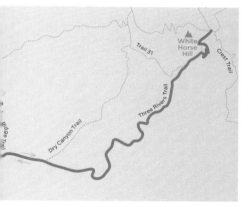

The desert mountains of Oliver Lee Memorial State Park

find most appealing in this arid canyon. The canyon is bisected by a perennial stream, which creates a riparian environment, a rarity in the Chihuahuan Desert. The stream is fed by rain and snowmelt and from seeping springs that naturally occur in the limestone formations of the park. The riparian area supports a small variety of insects and amphibians, but no fish.

Water in the desert has attracted human presence in this canyon for millennia, with the earliest evidence from 9500 BC. The Mescalero Apaches established their presence here by 1400; as a mobile tribe, they left evidence of their hunting and gathering practices in the area. The Apaches defended their territory from incursions of settlers from Spain, Mexico, and elsewhere. Numerous conflicts are recorded between the Apaches and Anglo-Americans from 1848 until 1912. The US military and the Mescaleros had many confrontations within Dog Canyon itself over this time period during the Apache Wars. The park is named after Oliver Lee, a controversial but influential figure who ranched just south of Dog Canyon, served as a New Mexico senator, and brought the railroad to Alamogordo in 1898.

## WILDLIFE

Watch for collared peccaries, ground squirrels, mule deer, black-tailed jackrabbits, and desert cottontails. Also, larger mammals like black bears, cougars, and bobcats occasionally pass through the park but are elusive. Other mammals include badgers, porcupines, raccoons, white-nosed coati, and several species of bats and skunks. Two species of rattlesnakes are found in the park, western diamondback and black-tailed, as well as several species of lizards, skinks, geckos, turtles, and nonvenomous snakes. The Texas horned lizard—which is threatened by loss of habitat, pesticides,

and development in Texas and Oklahoma—is thriving in the park.

## BIRDWATCHING

Turkey vultures, red-tailed hawks, mourning doves, broad-tailed and rufous hummingbirds, greater roadrunners, northern orioles, western tanagers, mockingbirds, Bewick's and canyon wrens, great horned owls, curve-billed thrashers, warblers, and Gamble's quail can be found here.

## HIKE | RIPARIAN NATURE TRAIL

**Distance:** Less than a mile
**Difficulty:** Easy
**Getting There:** Trailhead in parking lot of visitor center.

The short but refreshing Riparian Nature Trail loops above and along a narrow riverbed lined with wild grapevines, yellow columbines, prickly pear cacti, cane chollas, hackberries, and desert willows. Talk with your kids about the unique desert plants. Ask them how the plants growing out of the side of the rock faces manage to set seed and survive there.

In the rocky hills that jut above, ocotillo blooms in flames of red on its spindly tips. Tell your kids that when there's enough moisture in the soil, small oval leaves about 2" in diameter will sprout from its brown stems. When the water dries up, the leaves will fall and the plant will rely on the chlorophyll inside its stems to photosynthesize. This process can happen four or five times a year, depending on the amount of rainfall. When the water is flowing, small pools form in bedrock, making a perfect spot to take a cool dip in the water.

## CAMPING

Oliver Lee Campground has 44 sites, 16 of which have electrical hookups. Full-service bathrooms and water available.

A paved boardwalk meanders through the lava flows of Valley of Fires Recreation Area

## Ruidoso/Cloudcroft

### 69. Valley of Fires Recreation Area

575-648-2241

www.blm.gov/visit/valley-of-fires

**Nearest Town:** Carrizozo

**Best Season to Visit:** October–April

**Visitor Information:** A small visitor center is located in the campground. Fees apply.

**Getting There:** Drive 4 miles northwest along US 380 from the junction with US 54 at Carrizozo.

&#9855; accessible

The Valley of Fires Recreation Area (not to be confused with the larger Valley of Fire State Park in Nevada) provides a wonderful diversion on the road to the high mountains of Ruidoso and Cloudcroft. Just outside Carrizozo, a short side road takes you to a BLM-managed campsite sitting atop a ridge of Dakota sandstone. The ridge is a remnant of what the land once looked like before molten lava seeped out of the earth and covered it in black rock. The campground overlooks a large expanse of lava extending over 10 miles. The volcanic activity was relatively recent, between 2,000 to 5,000 years ago, making the area one of the youngest lava flows in the continental United States. Little Black Peak erupted about 5,000 years ago, spreading lava for 44 miles and filling the Tularosa Basin with molten rock. The resulting lava flow is 4 to 6 miles wide, 160' thick, and covers 125 square miles. Its largess is visible from the peaks in the White Mountain Wilderness on the western horizon. Its southern edge stops just 14 miles from White Sands National Park, and the resulting contrast of the black lava and white sands is used to navigate from space.

Rather than barren rock, the area has a greenish hue separating it from the stark black of other deposits in the Southwest. Volcanic rock's ability to hold water, combined with soil accumulating over millennia in pockets, has allowed plants to colonize the lava flows. Many varieties of grasses, small shrubs, cactus, and wildflowers typical of the Chihuahuan Desert are found here. The pink blooms of cholla and bright spring wildflowers offer a colorful contrast to the dark rocks, as does the occasional white dusting of a winter snow.

Native American people of several different cultures lived in the area prior to the arrival of European settlers. Occasional bits of pottery testify to visits by Native Americans of the Jornada branch of the Mogollon Culture. The region later became the domain of the Mescalero Apaches, who resisted the intrusions of immigrant settlers. The lava flow provided a great variety of plants used for food and fiber and as a source for grinding stones.

The area is well preserved, with interesting geologic features such as lava caves, pressure ridges, collapsed gas bubbles, and two types of lava—rough blocks and ropy flows of pahoehoe. Only one official trail exists in the recreation area, though hiking across the lava field is permitted. Beware that the lava is like walking on broken glass and is unforgiving to skin and clothing if you slip and fall. A cross-lava hike may not be suitable for small children or grandparents, but families that crave an extra adventure can hike to Little Black Peak, which has intact lava tubes radiating out from it.

The visitor center has informative books, a free book exchange library, and Valley of Fires souvenirs. The staff and volunteer campground hosts are friendly and knowledgeable about the area.

### WILDLIFE

Watch for desert cottontail rabbits, bats, roadrunners, quail, cottontails, mule deer, lizards, and introduced Barbary sheep. Some animals have adapted their coloration to the lava to survive and blend into the environment, allowing them to better hide from predators. Two examples you may see here include rabbits with darker hair and lizards with darker skin than the same species found elsewhere.

### BIRDWATCHING

Birdwatching is surprisingly rich in the lava fields. Watch for great horned owls, burrowing owls, turkey vultures, hawks, towhees, gnat catchers, cactus wrens, sparrows, harriers, red-tailed and Swainson's hawks, and golden eagles.

### HIKE | MALPAIS NATURE TRAIL

**Distance:** 1.5 mile loop
**Difficulty:** Easy
**Getting There:** The trailhead is located in the picnic grounds.

The paved boardwalk is dotted with interpretive signs that provide interesting information about the plants, geology, and human history of the area. The trail descends from the picnic area in the campground on long switchbacks and then loops through the lava field. Touching and

Mountain deathcamas on Lookout Peak in the Sacramento Mountains

walking on the lava is allowed and affords an intimate and engaging experience of the unique formations.

## CAMPING

The campground has 19 sites, all with tables, grills, drinking water, and metal shelters. Some sites have electric hookups. Views to the west look over the lava fields and to the east Sierra Blanca, the tallest peak in southern New Mexico at 11,981', rises on the horizon. The place is quite exposed and often very windy. The night we stayed here, we watched in awe as a lightning storm passed to the west. While the storm didn't cross our path, the resulting winds sent our tent across the campground while we were eating dinner.

## 70. Sacramento Mountains

*Lincoln National Forest*
    Smokey Bear Ranger District:
    (575) 257-4095
    Sacramento Ranger District: (575) 682-2551
    www.fs.usda.gov/attmain/lincoln

The Sacramento Mountains are a unique and special New Mexico treasure running north–south for 85 miles through the southeastern part of the state. It is split into two sections: the Sierra Blanca range that lies in the north, and the Guadalupe Mountain range that runs south into Texas. The surrounding desert physically separates these mountains from other mountain ranges, turning them into isolated habitat. These "sky islands" harbor a variety of endemic (found nowhere else in the world) species, including 13 plant species, five bird species, and at least one small mammal. The two major mountain towns of Ruidoso and Cloudcroft are rife with coffee shops, grocery stores, outdoor gear shops, good restaurants, and many activities geared toward tourists.

## Bighorn Sheep Return to the Sacramento Mountains

Two types of bighorn sheep—desert and Rocky Mountain—are native to New Mexico. Both types nearly went extinct in the state due to overhunting, loss of habitat, and disease. Desert bighorn sheep were listed as endangered in 1980, but through the efforts of wildlife biologists to reintroduce bighorns to the state, they were taken off the list in 2011. Today, their numbers are increasing and both species are doing well in New Mexico. In fall of 2018, New Mexico Game and Fish decided to translocate (move from one area to another) desert bighorn sheep from the nearby San Andres Mountains in southern New Mexico to the Sacramento Mountains. These mountains provide good habitat for bighorns, but they've been absent here for about 80 years. Moving bighorns is quite a production. They are captured with a net from a helicopter, fitted with GPS collars that will allow biologists to track them in the future, placed on a truck, transported to their new location, and then released into the wild. Forty sheep were released into the Sacramento Mountains and a second group is planned for the future. If you are lucky, you might now catch sight of them grazing in the high mountains or see the rams battling for mates in the fall on your hikes through the Sacramentos.

Desert bighorns can also be seen in the Peloncillo, Little and Big Hatchet, Caballo, Sierra Ladrones, and San Andres Mountains of southern New Mexico.

Rocky Mountain bighorns are often spotted in the Pecos, Wheeler and Latir Peaks Wilderness, Culebra Mountains, and the Rio Grande Gorge in northern New Mexico, the Manzano Mountains outside Albuquerque, and in the Mogollon Mountains in the Gila National Forest.

## New Mexico Checkerspot Butterfly

Another treasure of the Sacramento Mountains is the delicately patterned orange, brown, and white New Mexico checkerspot butterfly (*Euphydryas anicia cloudcrofti*). It pollinates and feeds on a variety of plants, one of its favorites being sneezeweed. But like many other butterflies, it lays its eggs on only one host plant—the New Mexico penstemon, which itself is only found in the Sacramento and nearby Capitan Mountains. This butterfly lives in the Sacramento Mountains only in high-elevation meadows between 7,800' and 9,000' on a 3-square-mile patch of forest near the town of Cloudcroft. The county government has a conservation plan for this butterfly not currently listed on the Endangered Species list, but further protections may be needed. Climate change may spell disaster for this high-elevation species: if either the butterfly or the penstemon shifts its range due to changing temperatures or weather patterns, host and guest may miss each other, and the butterfly could vanish forever.

A checkerspot butterfly, an endemic species in the Sacramento Mountains, stops for a sip of nectar

### WILDLIFE

Watch for rare Peñasco least chipmunks inhabiting the area around Lookout Mountain. Other abundant wildlife in these mountains includes elk, mule deer, black bears, porcupines, bobcats, badgers, feral hogs, coyotes, gray foxes, skunks, various rodents, and recently reintroduced desert bighorn sheep. The Sacramentos are also a hotspot for butterflies, including rare species.

### WILDFLOWERS

Thirteen species of wildflower are endemic to these mountains, including Sacramento Mountain paintbrushes, New Mexico penstemons, White Mountain alumroots, Sacramento prickly poppies, Sacramento Mountain thistles, and Sierra Blanca lupines. Many are locally abundant but are not found outside these mountains.

### BIRDWATCHING

The White Mountains are critical habitat for five listed threatened or endangered species: red-breasted nuthatches, Townsend's solitaires, Clark's nutcrackers, northern three-toed woodpeckers, and golden crowned kinglets.

### GONDOLA RIDE

*Ski Apache*
575-464-3600
www.skiapache.com

Kids will delight in riding the glass-sided gondola to the top of the ski area, taking in the expansive views on the way up. At the top, we turned left at the bottom of the staircase and walked a quarter mile to the summit of the 11,580' Lookout Mountain. We reveled in the panoramas from the circular viewing area. Ask kids to name the distant mountains with the help of the interpretive signs. Nearby Sierra Blanca, the highest peak in southern New Mexico, rises to the south. The mountain sits on land belonging to the Mescalero Apaches, who consider it sacred. At the time of writing, hikers are not allowed to climb the peak, though occasionally the tribe will open it. Sierra Blanca, a huge extrusive volcano that rises 7,800' above the Tularosa Valley to top out at 11,981', and its surrounding ridges and summits are the only features in southern New Mexico to rise above the tree line, forming alpine tundra.

While you meander around the summit of Lookout Mountain, talk to your kids about the dwarfed wildflowers in the alpine habitat. Ask them to consider what conditions (icy, cold spring winds, hot sun, lack of water) keep these wildflowers small, while the same flowers at lower elevation grow much larger. Remind them that alpine environments are fragile and it's best not to pick or step on the flowers so they can grow another year. Try to get a glimpse of the rare Peñasco least chipmunk that resides on this mountain. Ride the gondola back to the base of the mountain or pick up the lower portion of the Lookout Mountain Trail to the right (north) of the gondola and descend 3.4 miles to the Scenic Trailhead. Arrive back at Ski Apache, usually serving lunch on the grill. Downhill mountain biking is also popular along the ski trails in the summer.

### MOUNTAIN BIKING

Excellent mountain biking can be found at the Grindstone Trail System around Ruidoso. The 18 miles of singletrack were designed by the International Mountain Bicycling Association.

## 71. White Mountain Wilderness

The White Mountain Wilderness is part of the larger Sacramento Mountain range and contains some of the best alpine habitat in this corner of the state. It includes 48,266 acres and covers much of the Sierra Blanca range and part of the Mescalero Apache Reservation. The west side of this ridge is extremely steep and rugged, with avalanche chutes, high-rising rows of cliffs, and prominent rocky outcroppings. The eastern side is gentler, with broader, forested canyons and some small streams. Some of the streams are large enough to flow year-round and carry a few small trout. Stitching it together is more than 50 miles of trail, including the 25-mile-long Crest Trail, a highland gem rich with aspen groves, mountain meadows, and alpine vistas.

Several fire lookouts are located throughout the Lincoln National Forest. The picturesque Monjeau Lookout on the border of the wilderness is listed on the National Register of Historic Places. It was built in 1940 by the CCC and is still in active use today. Surrounded by wildflowers in the summer, visitors can climb the lookout to take in an unending view. The lookout makes a great day-trip destination or a launching point for a weekend backpacking trip into the wilderness.

Day-hike routes abound in the White Mountain Wilderness, as do overnight backpacking trips. Spreading a hike over two or three days will give you a good taste of these unique "sky island" mountains that rise up from the desert floor. Trails traverse glacial scars and pass abandoned mines, summits routinely top 11,500'.

HIKE | **CREST TRAIL–WHITE MOUNTAIN WILDERNESS**

**Distance:** Varies depending on route
**Difficulty:** Easy to moderate
**Getting There: For Argentina Canyon and Big Bonito Trailheads:** Drive about 12 miles north of Ruidoso on NM 48 and turn left (west)

onto NM 37. Drive 1.3 miles on NM 37 and then 9 miles on FR 107 to the end of the road, passing Bonito Lake. The road turns to gravel at the South Fork Campground turnoff, which has been closed since the 2012 wildfire. Find the Argentina Canyon and Big Bonito Trailheads in the parking area.

**For Crest Trailhead near Monjeau Lookout:**

Take NM 48 north of Ruidoso for 5 miles to the junction with NM 532. Follow it for 0.9 miles to the turnoff for FR 117. Continue 4.7 miles to the Crest Trailhead parking lot. Monjeau Peak Lookout is just beyond the trailhead at the end of the road.

Families will enjoy spending a day or several days hiking along the high, lush ridge of White Mountain Wilderness, with spectacular views and unique wildflowers abundant in the late summer. The Crest Trail is 25 miles long and has several trailheads from which to create an out-and-back hike or a longer traverse if you have a car shuttle. A few of the more scenic areas start at the Crest Trail near Monjeau Lookout, which begins on the high ridge, or Argentina and Bonito Canyon, which start at the base in a creek canyon and climb into the high meadows. Much of the Crest Trail is above the tree line, with panoramic views in all directions. From the alpine meadows, you'll look out across the Great Plains that unroll like parchment to the east, the snow-capped Sangre de Cristos to the north, and the serrated teeth of the Organ Mountains glinting in the west. The trail is easy to follow (after the snow melts) and is relatively flat, with moderate climbs and drops as the trail crosses from one drainage to another. There are many excellent dispersed campsites just off the trails.

Above the tree line, the weather can change quickly. Be prepared for sudden storms with lightning and hail in the summer monsoon season. Take plenty of water. The main springs (Turkey Canyon,

Argentina, Spring Cabin, Bonito, and Ice) are unreliable.

## ACTIVITIES

### Ski Apache

www.skiapache.com

(575) 464-3600

Run by the Apache Mescalero tribe, New Mexico's southernmost ski area, Ski Apache, offers dozens of skiing and snowboarding trails in winter and in summer a super long zipline, downhill mountain biking trail, 5 miles of hiking trails, and gondola rides into the high alpine tundra. Fees apply.

### Ruidoso's Winter Park

(575) 336-7079

www.ruidosowinterpark.com

Winter sledding is taken to a whole new level with this snow tubing adventure park. Spend a winter day tubing down hills and jumps and riding the Magic Carpet Lifts back to the top.

## CAMPING

A campground is located at the trailhead for Argentina Canyon/Big Bonito Trails. Tent and RV sites available with vault toilets. Dispersed camping is also allowed along the creek leading up to the campground. Oak Grove Campground, tucked into an oak forest with views of Sierra Blanca Peak, makes a great basecamp for a weekend of day hikes and adventures in the Sacramento Mountains. There are 30 campsites with vault toilets. No potable water on site. Open mid-May through mid-September.

The Milky Way rises over Monjeau Fire Lookout

## 72. Bluff Springs National Recreation Area

**Nearest Town:** Cloudcroft

**Best Season to Visit:** Summer

**Visitor Information:** Open year-round. No facilities.

**Getting There:** From Cloudcroft, take NM 130. Take a right on Sunspot Highway. Turn left onto Upper Penasco Road; look for Bluff Springs on the right.

Located at the site of a spring-fed waterfall, Bluff Springs is surrounded by a network of trails that range from 1.5-mile loops to full 12-mile treks into the forest. With dispersed camping and a vault toilet, it serves as a great jumping off point for any number of activities in the greater Cloudcroft area.

Located in the western portion of the Lincoln National Forest, the recreation area is a popular destination for RVs, families, and campers during the summer. From the beautiful Sunspot Ridge Trails that overlook the White Sands National Monument below to the High Rolls area hikes that follow the 19th-century railroad tracks up the canyon and into the forest, there's no shortage of beauty to be found.

### HIKE | WILLIE WHITE SPUR TRAIL

**Distance:** 2 miles one-way

**Difficulty:** Easy

**Getting There:** Trailhead at Bluff Springs National Recreation Area.

A lovely walk in the woods along a historic railroad route with a waterfall and summer wildflowers. With your kids, examine the remnants of the railroad and mining operations. Imagine what the metal pieces left along the trail were used for. To extend your hike several miles, turn on T113 to hike through a forest and canyon.

Cross-country skiing and mountain biking are popular on hiking trails in the area. Most trails, except in designated wilderness, can be biked. The trails around the Silver-Saddle-Apache Campground, tucked into the forest, are especially nice for skiing or snowshoeing and are maintained in the winter. Try the Little Apache Trail at 2.8 miles long and the Fir Trail at 1.9 miles.

### CAMPING

Silver-Saddle-Apache Campground Complex is located in Lincoln National Forest just north of Cloudcroft. These three campgrounds are located off the same paved road and together offer ample tent camping, hookups for RVs, and hiking trails among pine trees. Tucked into dense conifer forests, they are conveniently located near many outdoor activities in the area. Dispersed camping is allowed in the Bluff Springs National Recreation Area. RVs will find flat areas in the parking lot and tent campers can venture down to the stream or take the stairs up above the waterfall for some solitude. A vault toilet is the only amenity.

# Roswell

## 73. Bitter Lake National Wildlife Refuge

(575) 662-6755

www.fws.gov/refuge/Bitter_Lake/wildlife _and_habitat.html

www.friendsofbitterlake.org

**Nearest Town:** Roswell

**Best Season to Visit:** September

**Visitor Information:** The refuge is open every day from one hour before sunrise to one hour after sunset. The visitor center, with impressive educational displays, is open Monday–Saturday. Admission fees apply.

**Getting There:** From Roswell, take US 380 (Second Street) east about 3 miles to Red Bridge Road. Follow Red Bridge Road north to Pine Lodge Road and travel east to the refuge entrance gate.

 accessible

Over 100 species of dragonflies are found at Bitter Lake National Wildlife Refuge

Naturalist families will enjoy birdwatching, wildlife viewing, and exploring this unique area. One of the best times to visit is the first Saturday in September, when the annual Dragonfly Festival is celebrated and the federally threatened Pecos sunflower is in bloom. The refuge has documented more than 100 species of odonates—dragonflies and damselflies—making it home to one of the most diverse populations of odonates in North America. Spend the festival day participating in educational activities, tours of the refuge, a monarch butterfly release, fishing tournaments, food, and more family fun. The visitor center's interpretive exhibits are impressive, informative, and staffed by knowledgeable rangers and volunteers.

Bitter Lake is located at the meeting of the Southern Great Plains with the Chihuahuan Desert, the wetlands of the Roswell Artesian Basin, and the Pecos River Valley. As with any edge in nature where two or more ecosystems meet, the result is a high diversity of plants and animals. Bitter Lake is a great example of this diversity, with 357 documented species of birds on the refuge and a variety of rare plants, mammals, and aquatic creatures. Scattered across Bitter Lake National Wildlife Refuge are more than 70 natural sinkholes of different shapes and sizes. Created by groundwater erosion, these water habitats form isolated communities of fish, invertebrates, amphibians, and other wildlife. Added to that are the flowing streams, rivers, playa lakes, and brackish waters of the refuge's namesake, Bitter Lake.

**POINT OF INTEREST: BOTTOMLESS LAKES STATE PARK**

Located about 30 minutes from Bitter Lake is a series of eight cenotes, or small but deep sinkhole lakes, formed when the ground eroded and filled with water from natural springs. Swimming is allowed in the largest of the lakes, Lea Lake. The clear blue-green water makes a great side trip to cool off on a hot day. Camping is available in the park.

## Carlsbad

### 74. Carlsbad Caverns National Park

(505)785-2212

www.nps.gov/cave/index.htm

**Nearest Town:** Carlsbad

**Best Season to Visit:** Year-round

**Visitor Information:** Visitor center hours are 8 a.m.–5 p.m., with the last entrance tickets sold at 1:45 p.m. Sign up for a ranger-led tour online ahead of your visit. Fees apply.

**Getting There:** Located 20 miles southeast of Carlsbad. Turn north from US 62/180 at Whites City. Enter the park gate and continue on the entrance road, Carlsbad Caverns Highway, for 7 miles to the visitor center and cavern entrance.

 accessible

We started our adventure to this underground world with the 750' descent through a series of steep switchbacks on the 1.25-mile Natural Entrance Trail. My kids were impressed with the colling temperature as we descended underground. Ask your kids why the temperature changes. The trail eventually meets up with the Big Room Trail, close to the elevators.

Spotlights highlight the natural art of the caves, decorated with draperies, ribbons, curtains, and other formations developed over millions of years by the action of water dripping from the surface, drying, and depositing minerals attached to the ceiling and floors. The result is a magnificent, moist underground world that can be explored on self-guided or ranger-led tours by elevator or by hiking in near the bat viewing area. Kids will enjoy the bouncing echoes in the caves, although you are asked to speak quietly when others are around. Be sure to bring sweatshirts, as even on 100°F summer days on the surface, the caves are cool.

The park has been aptly described as the Grand Canyon with a roof on it. The more than 119 limestone caves are outstanding in the profusion, diversity, and beauty of their formations. They are some of the longest and largest caves in the world. While most of the world's caves are formed from the eroding effect of carbonic acid, which occurs in all surface water, these caves were formed from sulfuric acid. As the Guadalupe Mountains uplifted over time, this aggressive "acid bath" dissolved the underground passageways and caverns at the level of the water table along fissures, faults, and cracks in the limestone. Around 4 to 6 million years ago, this left behind what visitors now know as the Carlsbad Caverns, plus many yet unexplored passageways and caverns under the desert mountains. These marvels left an impression on my kids, who walked through the caves in awe and wonder and snapped pictures the whole way (flash photography is allowed; just be considerate of other visitors). For kids older than 12, try the ranger-led candlelit tour to the deepest part of the caves open to the

Hall of Giants at Carlsbad Caverns National Park; courtesy of NPS/Peter Jones

public. Even sardonic teenagers will be thrilled by the blackout experience. For true spelunkers at heart, other ranger-led tours get rough and dirty crawling around in small spaces, through narrow passages, up and down ladders, and over slippery surfaces. Check the website for more details.

### WILDLIFE

Drive along the Desert Scenic Loop, a one-way, 9.5-mile scenic drive, for wildlife viewing. Watch for desert bighorn sheep, coyotes, and mule deer. After sunset in the summer, watch for nocturnal ringtails and hognose skunks. Raccoons are often seen near the amphitheater.

## BIRDWATCHING

The largest nesting colony of cave swallows in the United States can be seen at the mouth of the caverns from spring through fall. Rattlesnake Springs south of the main park area is one of the best birdwatching spots in New Mexico, especially during spring and fall migration.

## HIKE | GUADALUPE RIDGE TRAIL

**Distance:** 100 miles one-way

**Difficulty:** Strenuous

**Getting There:** Rattlesnake Canyon Trailhead is located on Desert Loop Road, past interpretive marker #4.

The Guadalupe Ridge Trail is a designated National Recreation Trail and, at 100 miles long, provides hikers and backpackers with a true wilderness experience in the Chihuahuan Desert and Guadalupe Mountains. The trail begins atop the highest point in

## Bat Flight

We sat in silence with several dozen tourists in the bat amphitheater waiting for a sign—a bat sign. The ranger told us to look for v-shaped figures that distinguish them from the swallows that spend their days in the cave entrance. Observations made by bat researchers have shown that bats who are used to total darkness and silence are disturbed by sounds and light, which can cause changes in their behavior. So, we sat in the dark and waited. After several minutes of silence, several dozen bats began to appear in the blue twilight. They zoomed over our heads and elicited gasps of delight from my boys. Within minutes, hundreds of bats are swirled around our heads in the sky above. Their leathery wings didn't make a sound, but we could hear them clicking and squeaking.

While bats are almost blind, they use sound, or echolocation, to build an extremely accurate audio map of their surroundings to find their prey and guide their flight. The park hosts 17 different bat species, but it's the Brazilian free-tailed (a.k.a. Mexican free-tailed) bats that make up the large colonies that fly from the mouth of the cavern and wow visitors.

At sunset each evening from late May through October, Brazilian free-tailed bats that live in Carlsbad Cavern emerge to feast on insects in a mass exodus. Bats migrate in spring and fall. In some years, their numbers have reached nearly 1 million. The resident colony is around 300,000 to 400,000 bats. The best bat flights normally occur in August through September when baby bats, born in early summer, join the flight, along with migrating bats from colonies farther north.

Each year on the third Saturday of July, the park hosts Dawn of the Bats, when visitors can gather with rangers at sunrise to watch the creatures dive back into the cave. Bat-related activities at the visitor center throughout the day celebrate this natural phenomenon. The 1-mile paved Chihuahuan Desert Nature Trail is dotted with interpretive signs explaining the plants, animals, and landscape of the Chihuahuan Desert. A short spur trail leads to the second natural entrance of Carlsbad Caverns and historic ruins of guano mining. The trail is closed during bat flight times.

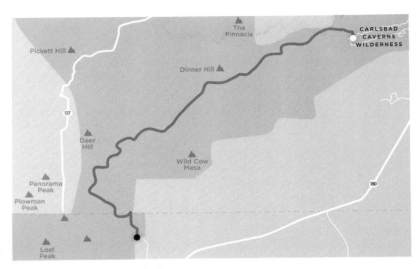

**GUADALUPE RIDGE TRAIL** 100 miles one-way

Texas, Guadalupe Peak—located in Guadalupe Mountains National Park—winds through the high desert of New Mexico, stops at Sitting Bull Falls Recreation Area, and ends at Carlsbad Caverns National Park's eastern boundary in Whites City, NM. The trail winds through Carlsbad Caverns National Park for 21 miles. You can hop on and walk a few miles or start a multiday backpack at the Rattlesnake Canyon Trailhead. Find a map and more at http://guadaluperidgetrail.com/.

#### CAMPING

Only backcountry camping is allowed in the park with a free permit, which can be obtained at the visitor center.

The White's City RV Park near the national park entrance gate offers pull-in spaces for RVs, some tent sites, and a small grocery store. (505) 361-3665, www.white citynm.com/rv-campground.

Pine Springs Campground is in the

Guadalupe Mountains National Park, about 30 miles south on Highway 62 just over the border into Texas. The Guadalupe Mountains are a worthy family adventure location on their own, but you'll have to wait for the Texas version of this book for more about that. The campground has 20 tent sites and a paved parking lot where RVs are allowed. Two group campsites can be reserved online, and the rest are available on a first come, first served basis. Bathrooms and drinking water available. Fees apply.

## 75. Sitting Bull Falls Recreation Area

**Nearest Town:** Carlsbad

**Best Season to Visit:** Fall–spring

**Visitor Information:** Rock shelters and bathrooms are the only amenities.

**Getting There:** From US 285 north of Carlsbad, turn west onto NM 137. Continue on NM 137 for about 20 miles until you find CR 409. Turn right on this road and continue. The

After an hour drive from Carlsbad, the road ends in a green semicircular basin with steep walls and a 150' spring-fed waterfall, an icy-cool oasis in the Chihuahuan yucca and mesquite desert country. This is a popular location with families looking to cool off from the desert heat. Water creates a lush microhabitat with thriving madrone, willow, big-toothed maples, and oaks providing plentiful shade. To the left of the main waterfall, a shaded, secondary falls can be found down the rocky path about 50 yards. A paved path will take you through the picnic area to the waterfalls and an overlook at the top. The falls pour over a high travertine bluff made from the mineral deposits in the water. The reed- and willow-lined ponds at the base of the waterfall offer a chance to take a dip and cool off from the desert heat. Maidenhair ferns and abundant wildflowers cling to the cliffs and crevices around the falls.

In 1940, the Civilian Conservation Corps built rock shelters for shade, each with picnic tables. Several hiking trails branch off from the area and lead up the steep cliffs to the top of the canyon. Visit in the spring and fall, as summer temperatures regularly rise to about 100°F. The area is thought to be named after a local American Indian chief, not to be confused with Sitting Bull, the famous war chief. This Sitting Bull was chief of a small band that lived in the area in the 1880s. The Apache name for the area is Gostahanagunti, which means "hidden gulch."

## WILDLIFE

Small fish, abundant dragonflies, and frogs occupy the ponds and creek around the waterfall. Bats and lizards are also abundant in the area. Year-round, find rock squirrels, black-tailed jackrabbits, ringtails, and mule deer. Mountain lions often leave their mark at Last Chance Spring. Best viewing is early morning or late evening midweek.

## BIRDWATCHING

The canyon and surrounding riparian area offer very good viewing of canyon wrens, western and hepatic tanagers, Cassin's kingbirds, white-throated swifts, black-headed and blue grosbeaks, black phoebes, and other songbirds mid-April through October.

## CLIMBING

**Getting There:** From US 285, head west about 38 miles on NM 137 to Queen. On the far end of Queen, just after mile marker 18, turn right onto FR 525. There are numerous spur roads; just follow the main track. You will encounter two cattle guards and two gates. After about 3 miles, make a hard left onto 525A, and continue 1 mile to the parking lot overlooking the canyon.

Last Chance Canyon in the Sitting Bull Falls Recreation Area is home to some of the best sport climbing in New Mexico. The canyon currently hosts about 120 bolted routes, ranging in difficulty from 5.4 to 5.13+. A favorite climb among families is Frosted Flake. Easy moves up the rock with lots of footholds and handholds rated at 5.7 makes this a great climb for beginners or a warm-up for more experienced climbers.

## HIKE | SITTING BULL FALLS T68

**Distance:** 2.5 miles one-way
**Difficulty:** Moderate
**Getting There:** Take the marked T68 on the opposite side of the parking lot from the paved falls trail.

Kids will enjoy this trail that follows the stream above the waterfall to the spring through varied terrain and beautiful views of the Guadalupe Mountains. The trail climbs 200' up to a small plateau at the top of the falls. After half a mile, you will reach the creek, which flows through several ponds before the falls. The trail continues another 0.8 miles to the spring through riparian vegetation along a rushing creek. This is the most scenic part of the trail. Return the way you came from this point or continue to 2.5 miles, where the trail meets with NM 137, for a longer hike.

## 76. Living Desert Zoo and Gardens State Park

(575) 887-5516

www.livingdesertnm.org

**Nearest Town:** Carlsbad

**Best Season to Visit:** Fall–spring

**Visitor Information:** Visitor center offers educational displays and activities; check website for hours.

**Getting There:** Located on the northwest edge of Carlsbad off US 285.

&#9855; accessible

The zoo cares for more than 200 animals, representing 40 species that have been rescued and rehabilitated after injury in the wild, including mountain lions, black bears, bobcats, bison, and pronghorn. Endangered Mexican wolves here are part of the captive breeding program to introduce the wolves back into the wild in New Mexico, Arizona, and northern Mexico. The views of Carlsbad and the Pecos River Valley from parts of the trail are breathtaking. A 1.3-mile, approximately 1.5-hour self-guided tour takes visitors through the local sand dune, mountain, and desert ecosystems.

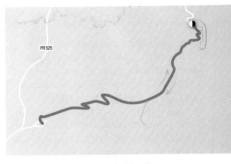

SITTING BULL FALLS T68 2.5 miles one-way

LOCAL ATTRACTIONS, BUSINESSES

*Smokey Bear Historical Park:* (575) 354-2748, www.emnrd.state.nm.us/SFD/ SmokeyBear/SmokeyBearPark.html

*Sunspot Solar Observatory:* (575) 434-7190, https://sunspot.solar/

*New Mexico Museum of Space History:* (575) 437-2840, nmspacemuseum.org

*International UFO Museum and Research Center:* (575) 625-9495, roswellufomuseum.com

*Tularosa Basin Gallery of Photography:* (612) 963-1499, photozozo.org

*Happy Hiker:* (575) 315-0123, www.happyhikerruidoso.com

*High Altitude Outfitters:* (575) 682-1229, www.highaltitudenm.com

SOUTHWEST MOUNTAINS TO DESERT

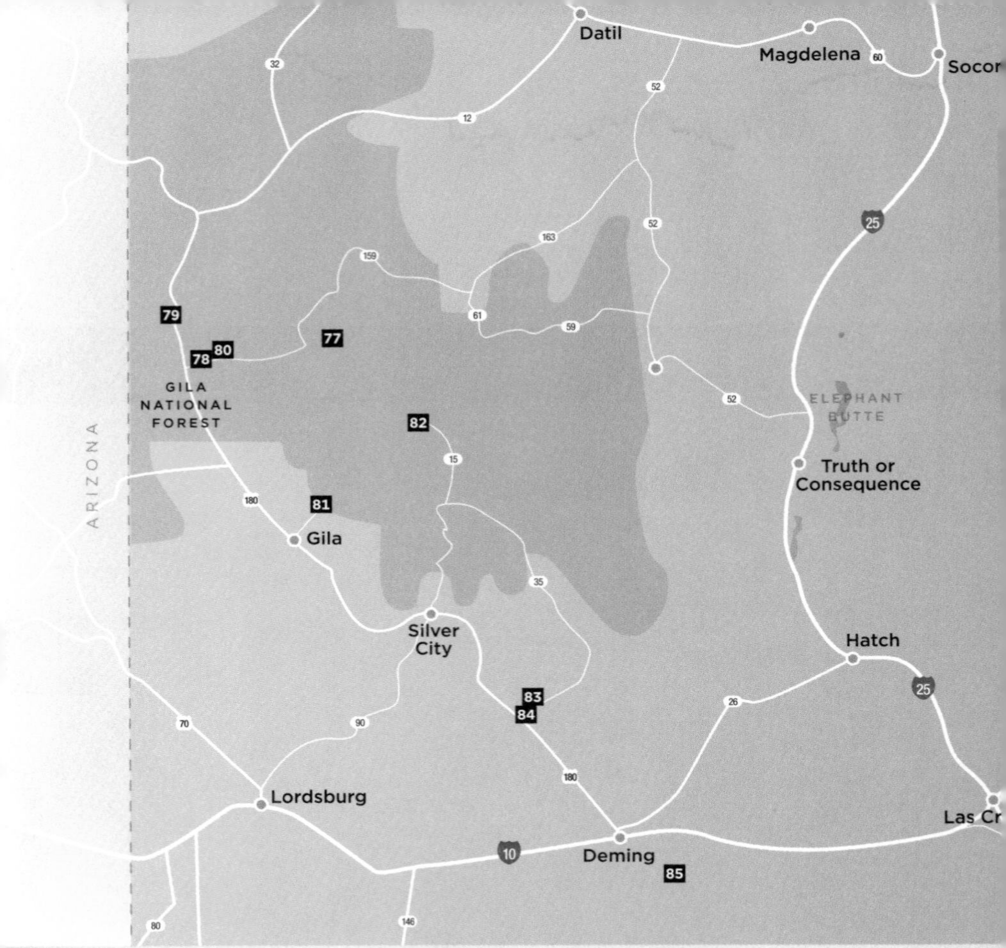
Datil
Magdelena
Socor
Elephant Butte
Truth or Consequence
Gila National Forest
Arizona
Gila
Silver City
Hatch
Lordsburg
Deming
Las Cr
77
78
79
80
81
82
83
84
85

**77** Snow Lake/Gila National Forest

**78** Catwalk National Recreation Area

**79** Cosmic Campground International Dark Sky Sanctuary

**80** Mogollon Ghost Town

**81** Gila Riparian Preserve

**82** Gila Cliff Dwellings National Monument

**83** City of Rocks State Park

**84** Faywood Hot Springs

**85** Rockhound State Park

W elcome to the remnants of the Wild West. Surrounded by small towns and Chihuahuan Desert, the 3.3 million-acre Gila National Forest is the centerpiece of this sector of New Mexico. It is one of the most remote, pristine, and least developed national forests in the Southwest. The northern portion of the Gila area is far off the beaten path and has the least amenities. The rolling plains, high-altitude mesas, and river valleys attract plentiful wildlife and make for an exciting weekend of naturalist adventures. The small town of Reserve provides an opportunity to refill the gas tank and get a hot meal or cup of coffee. The western portion of the Gila centers around the high mountains, catwalks, ghost towns, and dark skies for stargazing. The towns of Glenwood, Gila, and Cliff cater to outdoor enthusiasts, adding art studios and coffee roasters into the mix. The southern portion, closest to Silver City, is the most developed while still retaining a rough-around-the-edges, quirky New Mexico style. Guided tours of cliff dwellings, outfitters for horse-back riding, large lakes to play in, and hot springs to soak in after a long hike can fill many days of rugged adventuring for a family. While small, Silver City's hotels, breweries, organic markets, restaurants, and artistic flare are on par with any attractive mountain town.

## Gila North

### 77. Snow Lake/Gila National Forest

**Nearest Town:** Reserve

**Best Season to Visit:** Spring–Fall

**Visitor Information:** The water level of the lake varies greatly from year to year. Lake has bathrooms and a boat launch.

**Getting There:** Head south out of Reserve on Main Street/NM 159. This leaves town and enters the forest, eventually turning from a curvy, pothole-ridden paved road to a washboard gravel road. Drive FR 141 to CR 28, following the signs for Snow Lake. High-clearance vehicles recommended on these roads.

The boys awoke at dawn in the tent, so we decided to start the day watching the sunrise. We walked to the edge of Snow Lake, a high-altitude reservoir on the edge of the Gila Wilderness, among a field of late summer sunflowers in the early morning quiet. Across the water, the dark shapes of 20 elk emerged out of the ponderosa forest and cautiously inched up to the water for a drink. The boys and I ducked into the tall grass to watch them. We slowly crab-crawled to the edge of the lake to get a closer look. But their sense of hearing was so acute that they bristled at our every move and scampered to the far end of the lake. As the elk settled down again to drink, a wolf howl pierced the silence. We stood and turned toward the sound on the ridge above the lake to see if we could get a glimpse of the wolves. Then another wolf joined, and another, and another. Elks' hooves pounded through the grass as they beelined for the safety of the trees. The wolf pack's somber yet melodic harmony continued to ring into the vast expanse for several minutes and then fell into silence again. We never saw them, but the experience marked this wild place into our memories forever.

This captivating landscape, with its relatively cool summer temperatures and warm winters, supports a unique combination of birds, plants, and animals in this diverse ecosystem. Over 600 miles of trail ply the Gila area. Known as the friendliest wilderness in the country, the Gila National Forest's two wilderness areas offer families the opportunity to really sink into nature and enjoy the beauty and untamed solitude these wild places harbor. It would be hard to cover the largess of the Gila region in one trip, and the remote nature of campgrounds and long driving distances between areas of interest makes it an ideal site for families to return to for new adventures year after year.

Snow Lake and the Dipping Vat Campground on its western shore make a great basecamp for exploration of the surrounding northern portion of the Gila National Forest and Wilderness. The lake is large enough for all types of flat-water paddling.

From the top of the dam, hiking trails drop into the Gilita Creek valley and continue into the wilderness for days.

Day trips in the area include a drive to Bearwallow Mountain and lookout tower, where wolves are also sometimes heard at sunrise and sunset; fish in nearby Willow Creek, along Bursum Road, for native Gila trout; hike from the trailhead at Wolf Hollow through a forested canyon to the peak of Black Mountain and the fire lookout; picnic at the edge of Cooney Prairie, an expansive meadow surrounded by mesas with excellent wildlife viewing potential.

### WILDLIFE

Rocky Mountain elk roam the Gila in large herds with several dozen females and a few large males. In late September and October, you can listen to the males' enchanting bugle and perhaps catch site of them rutting in the open foggy meadows at dawn in their annual mating ritual. Negrito

The valley of Snow Lake in the Gila National Forest fills with wildflowers in late summer

## Mexican Wolves

The Mexican wolf is an embattled endangered species in New Mexico, Arizona, and northern Mexico. Also known as the lobo, it is a subspecies of gray wolf, slightly smaller than its northern cousins, with gray fur, light brown on its back, and often a cinnamon tint. Mexican wolves once numbered in the thousands, inhabiting Mexico and the Southwestern United States, but due to government campaigns to remove the apex predator from the landscape in support of livestock ranching and settlement, this subspecies of wolf went extinct in the wild. By the mid-1970s, only seven wolves remained in captivity.

In 1998, during a short window of political will, the US Fish and Wildlife Service reintroduced Mexican wolves to Arizona and, later that year, to New Mexico in the Gila Wilderness. Biologists spearheading the return of the wolf believe that once this predator returns to healthy populations, it will restore balance to the Southwest's ecosystems by regulating elk, deer, and javelina populations and their grazing of riparian areas. Twenty years later, that balance has

Mexican gray wolf

yet to be restored and the story of the Mexican wolf is one of continued conflict and incremental success. Poaching, genetic issues, and opposition from locals and powerful ranching and trophy hunting interests keep the Mexican wolf from establishing a thriving population on the landscape.

Despite this, their numbers in recent years have grown, reaching 130 individuals as of 2019. Still, they live as a highly managed species within political boundaries drawn on a map. Sightings are extremely rare, but campers may be able to hear the wolves while visiting the Gila National Forest.

Mountain north of Snow Lake has excellent elk viewing at dawn and dusk. The forests are also full of red and Abert's squirrels, cottontails, jackrabbits, black bears, mountain lions, Mexican wolves, coyotes, bobcats, white-nosed coati, mule deer, and black-tailed deer. Though the larger mammals are surprisingly hard to see, plentiful tracks, scat, and other animal markings tell their tales if you learn to read the signs.

### BIRDWATCHING

Bald eagles and ospreys commonly hunt on Snow Lake. Cormorants, great blue herons, American coots, and other waterbirds are also common. Lesser goldfinches can sometimes be seen feeding in flocks of up to several hundred in the meadows. Endangered Mexican spotted owls are rarely seen but sometimes heard. Watch for great horned owls, Lewis's woodpeckers, northern cardinals, flocks of pinyon jays, five species of hummingbirds, wild turkeys, and

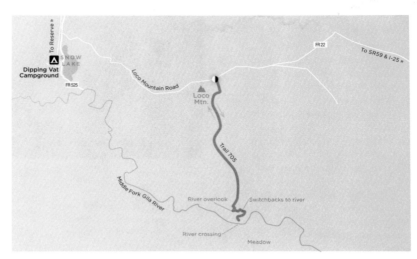

**AEROPLANE MESA TO GILA MIDDLE FORK** 8 miles round trip

many more. Bring your binoculars and birdwatching books!

### HIKE | AEROPLANE MESA TO GILA MIDDLE FORK

**Distance:** 8 miles round trip

**Difficulty:** Moderate

**Getting There:** Four miles east of Dipping Vat Campground on CR 021. The trailhead is located in Aeroplane Mesa Campground.

After a short, steep climb up a hillside, the trail tops out with a stunning view of the Mogollon and Black Range peaks. From there, easily descend Aeroplane Mesa through the expansive meadows and clusters of shady ponderosa pines to reach the cliffs above the river. The meadows are flush with wildflowers after monsoon rains in September. The approximately 900' descent to the middle fork river along switchbacks is the moderate portion of the trail. At the bottom, find the refreshingly cool river with several enticing swimming holes.

The river is surrounded by wet and dry meadows and conifer forests. This hike can be done as a long day hike or an overnight backpack. Several nice camping spots can be found under the trees or in the meadow along the river. From Trotter Meadow, hiking trails continue into the wilderness for many miles of endless exploration on day hikes or continued backpacking. Walk up- or downriver for a mile or two to find active beaver ponds and other wildlife. In the cliffs above the river, a pair of peregrine falcons have been known to nest.

Mineral Creek's enticing cascades and swimming holes

## Gila West

The tall Mogollon peaks, with their rugged valleys that drain to the Chihuahuan Desert below, take center stage in this section of the Gila. A stroll along the catwalks, a visit to a ghost town or two, morning wildlife viewing, and a hike to a natural hot spring will fill a long weekend with family fun. Glenwood has several restaurants and motels. A few gas stations along US 180 provide refueling and snack breaks when a hungry family needs it most. However, the nearest grocery store is in Silver City, so stock up before arriving.

### HIKE | MINERAL CREEK

**Distance:** 4 miles out and back
**Difficulty:** Easy
**Getting There:** From US 180, turn onto Mineral Creek Road at the tiny town of Alma.

Walk along Mineral Creek through a mountain canyon with colorful rock walls, natural arches, and other geologic formations to an old mining site. Water features

**MINERAL CREEK**  4 miles out and back

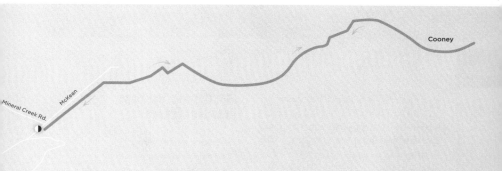

The modern marvel of Catwalk National Recreation Area

and climbable rock formations make this an enticing family hike. My kids appreciated the natural waterslides that dropped into cool swimming holes. Be sure to bring a change of clothes. Families will want to take their time meandering through the canyon and enjoy the water play. Cross the creek several times and plan to get wet. The aspens, cottonwoods, and sycamores are spectacular in early November, making this a great fall hike. Find the Cooney Mine site 2 miles in, where building ruins and rusting equipment are the only remains of the former village. Watch for American dippers, North America's only aquatic songbird, standing on rocks and diving after insects in the creek along the way, as well as canyon frogs and Gila trout in pools.

## 78. Catwalk National Recreation Area

www.fs.usda.gov/recarea/gila

**Nearest Town:** Glenwood

**Best Season to Visit:** Year-round

**Visitor Information:** Day-use area open from sunrise to sunset.

**Getting There:** From Glenwood, travel north on NM 180. Turn right on NM 174 for 5 miles to the Catwalk and Whitewater picnic grounds.

♿ partially accessible

The name for the area, the Catwalk, refers to the mile-long man-made structure in Whitewater Creek canyon. Kids (and adults) will find it thrilling to wind through the center of the canyon while perched a dozen feet above the creek. The bridges and pathways follow the contours of Whitewater Creek as it cuts through the canyon, providing dramatic views of the canyon walls. The first portion of the trail is relatively easy and leads to hidden pools and waterfalls, which my kids were delighted to splash around in. Beyond the developed trail, more rugged paths used to lead into the Gila Wilderness. Now, huge boulders brought down the mountain by the immense power of floods block passage farther into the canyon. After our hike, we picnicked at tables at the trailhead where the cool, rushing creek is lined with shady sycamore trees.

The catwalk structure was originally built in the 1890s as a plank-board walkway placed atop a steel pipe used to bring water to the ore processing plant, ruins of which can still be seen near the parking area. Although most of the pipe is now gone, much of the current trail follows this original route. The structure was completely wiped out by a catastrophic flood in 2013. The catwalk has since been completely rebuilt by the Forest Service, raised high above the streambed to protect it from future floods. It is now a modern wonder rather than a historical one.

## BIRDWATCHING

Watch for American dippers, golden eagles, violet-green swallows, white-throated swifts, several warbler species, orioles, canyon and rock wrens, painted redstarts, and western tanagers.

## WILDLIFE

Scan the cliffs for Rocky Mountain bighorn sheep. Visitors report frequent encounters with them on the trail and picnic area in early mornings. New Mexico Game and Fish reintroduced the endangered Gila trout to this creek in 2018. Raised in a fish hatchery, they are larger than wild trout and easily spotted in the creek.

# 79. Cosmic Campground International Dark Sky Sanctuary

*Gila National Forest Glenwood Ranger District*

(575) 539-2481

www.fs.usda.gov/recarea/gila/recarea/?recid=82479

www.sites.google.com/site/cosmiccampgroundinformation/friends-of-cosmic-campground

**Nearest Town:** Glenwood

**Best Season to Visit:** Year-round

**Visitor Information:** Check Friends of Cosmic Campground website for star parties and events.

**Getting There:** Located 13 miles north of Glenwood on US 180.

&#9855; accessible

This campground is renowned for the exceptional quality of starry nights with a 360-degree, unobstructed view of the night sky. With minimal shade and little to do or see in the direct area, consider this a great place to cook up dinner and camp after a day at the Catwalks.

Cosmic Campground is the first International Dark Sky Sanctuary in North America and one of only 10 certified sanctuaries in the world. The nearest significant source of artificial light is more than 40 miles away, across the state line in Arizona. The campground has several developed and dispersed camping spots, a vault toilet, and observation/telescope pads. Night vision is necessary to enjoy the night sky. White light from either your flashlight or your cell phone dims your night vision and the wonders of the natural night sky for 20–30 minutes. Special rules apply in the campground to preserve the dark skies: using red filters over flashlights, no campfires when others are present, and arriving before dark so headlights don't distort yours and others' night vision.

Friends of the Cosmic Campground often hosts "star parties" here where amateur astronomers gather to gaze at the night sky together. These often involve guided star tours, lectures, astrophotography, and telescopes to see night sky features up close. Check their website for details and events.

## HIKE | SAN FRANCISCO HOT SPRINGS

**Distance:** 2.5 miles out and back

**Difficulty:** Moderate

**Getting There:** Take NM 180 south of Glenwood for 11 miles. Turn right on County Road 25, which takes you to the trailhead.

A scenic hike to a river and warm water springs to play in never fails to entice kids. The San Francisco Hot Springs group is one of the better known and more easily visited hot springs in the Gila National Forest. It consists of three separate groups of springs that are spread out along a quarter mile of the river floodplain.

The actual presence of the various springs will vary from year to year, depending upon the number and magnitude of flood events. The Upper Group of hot springs occur on private property. The Middle and Lower Group of springs are on National Forest land, immediately downstream from the Upper Group, and are accessible from the trail. The temperature of the springs varies depending on the flow of the river but ranges from 100°F to 120°F. The Middle Group of hot springs is located against a rock cliff on the west side of the river, directly across from where the San Francisco Hot Spring Trail comes down to the river. The Lower Group of hot springs is located on the opposite side of the river about 450' south of the Middle Group, right where the canyon and river make a sharp turn to the west.

The Milky Way rises over Cosmic Campground

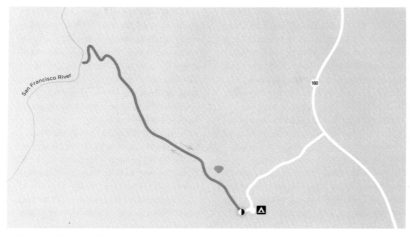

**SAN FRANCISCO HOT SPRINGS** 2.5 miles out and back

Even if the springs are not at their best, the scenery is gorgeous in the rugged and pristine box canyon of the San Francisco River and the bird and animal life is abundant and diverse. Bring your binoculars to birdwatch while you soak, and the kids play. Camping and vault toilets are available at the trailhead.

## 80. Mogollon Ghost Town

**Nearest Town:** Glenwood

**Best Season to Visit:** May–October

**Visitor Information:** Businesses are open on Fridays, Saturdays, and Sundays.

**Getting There:** From US 180, take Route 159 (a.k.a. Bursum Road) about 12 miles east. The winding mountain road turns to a narrow single lane unfit for RVs or trailers. A high-clearance vehicle is recommended.

Once a bustling, raucous mining town, Mogollon is one of the best "ghost towns" in the state of New Mexico. Getting to the ghost town is part of the fun. Bursum Road ascends more than 2,000' and becomes

steep and narrow in many places before reaching Mogollon. Watch for abundant wildlife, including small herds of javelinas and glimpses of the white-nosed coati, a relative of the raccoon, that inhabits parts of the Southwest.

We strolled among the almost 100 historic buildings, some of which are still inhabited by a few residents. My 7th grader was taken with the palpable history of the place. Behind remodeled homes, the original mining cabins covered in ivy still stand, albeit leaning under the force of gravity. We wondered about the passages behind the now-barricaded entrances to underground mines lining the mountain behind the cabins. We imagined the rugged and often short (according to gravestones in the cemetery) lives these miners led. Taking in the long view from the hike to the cemetery, we wondered where 6,000 souls (at the town's peak population) fit in this narrow canyon. How did they feed and clothe themselves and get medical care?

Mogollon was founded by James Cooney, a soldier stationed at Fort Bayard, some 80 miles to the southeast. He discovered rich gold and silver deposits in nearby Mineral Creek canyon as he was scouting for the US cavalry and returned later to stake his claim. He was promptly chased out by the residing Apaches. Cooney returned only to be killed in conflict with the Apaches in 1880. James Cooney's brother, Michael, inherited the claim and continued his brother's mining operations. Even though Apache raids continued, it didn't stop a flood of prospectors.

Several large mining operations were established near Mogollon, which vacillated between 3,000 to 6,000 miners during the 1890s. Miners lasted only a few years working here, as most developed black lung, a condition from inhaling toxic dust in the mines.

Due to the isolation and the rugged terrain surrounding the community, Mogollon had a reputation as one of the wildest mining towns in the West. There was little in the way of law enforcement. Gamblers, miners, and robbers considered the community a safe haven. There were five saloons, two restaurants, four merchandise stores, two hotels, and numerous brothels (located in two infamous red-light districts).

The stage provided daily service between Mogollon and Silver City, hauling passengers, commodities, and gold and silver bullion between the two. The 80-mile journey took 15 hours and was often a harrowing ride. Between 1872 and 1873, the stagecoach was robbed 23 times by the same guy. They eventually apprehended him.

From its earliest days, Mogollon was plagued with fire and flood that repeatedly wiped out the town and occasionally still threatens it today—the latest flood, in 2013, stranded tourists in town. The last mine here closed in 1952. Many of the old buildings have survived because of a handful of residents who serve as caretakers. The numerous buildings are primarily used as residences and summer homes. The town was added to the National Register of Historic Places in 1987. Visitors to Mogollon will find an art gallery, mining museum, antique store, and small cafe sometimes open for business, along with seasonal weekend accommodation.

Follow the old road for a steep 1-mile hike or four-wheel drive to the cemetery. Remnants of mining operations are visible along the way, as well as long views of the town.

It's not exactly clear who to call to find out if they are open, but that's part of the fun of visiting a ghost town—you never know exactly what you might find. As you'd expect, the hotel (which is only for adults) is reportedly haunted.

*Silver Creek Inn*
reservations@silvercreekinn.com
www.silvercreekinn.com

## LOCAL ATTRACTIONS, BUSINESSES

*Alma Post and Cafe*: Combination convenience store, gas station, and restaurant. (575) 539-2233, www.facebook.com/AlmaGrillNM/

*Glenwood Fish Hatchery*: Visitors welcome during business hours. (575) 539-2461, www.wildlife.state.nm.us/fishing/fish-hatcheries/

*Buffalo Mountain Coffee Roasting Company*: Selling small-batch, locally roasted coffee at local stores and restaurants. Check their website for future cupping and tasting events at their new roasting facilities in Glenwood. (505) 807-1546, www.buffalomountaincoffee.com

# Gila/Cliff

Nestled within the beautiful Gila Valley, the two small agricultural towns of Gila and Cliff are situated on opposite sides of the Gila River. The river streams out of the rugged Mogollon Mountains and vast Gila National Forest and Wilderness. Both communities share a rich ranching and farming heritage that began with the arrival of colonizer settlement in the area during the mid-1800s. The area has excellent birdwatching, fishing, and stargazing. A wide range of hiking trails are readily accessed in the area, from easy to strenuous multiday treks. Several guesthouses and ranches offer accommodations in the area. Opportunities for camping on public lands also abound.

## FISHING

Bill Evans Lake is a popular fishing spot with locals and travelers alike. It once held the New Mexico record for a 15-pound largemouth bass. New Mexico Fish and Game stocks the lake with rainbow trout, smallmouth and largemouth bass, sunfish, and catfish. Dispersed camping and flat-water paddling are also popular at this lake. The Gila River provides miles of fishable stream for small- and largemouth bass, trout, and channel and flathead catfish.

## HIKE | TURKEY CREEK HOT SPRINGS

**Distance:** 8 miles round trip

**Difficulty:** Moderate

**Getting There:** From NM 180, turn right onto NM 211. Drive north 4 miles to the town of Gila. Continue north on NM 153 for 4 more miles where the pavement ends and FR 155 (a.k.a. Turkey Creek Road) begins. Continue northeast on FR 155 for 6 miles. The trailhead for Gila River Trail begins where the road ends on the east bank of the Gila River. Nine miles of FR 155 is a rough, winding, gravel road. High-clearance vehicles are strongly recommended.

Known as the best hot springs in the Gila area, the series of clear pools in a forested canyon are just far enough into the wilderness to feel like you deserve a good soak when you arrive. Families with kids will enjoy this as an overnight backpacking trip. Kids will be enchanted playing on the slick rock waterslides that plunge into a deep, warm pool with several swimming holes below.

Find good camp spots along a flat area near the junction with Skeleton Canyon Trail. This is a good place to leave your packs, since from the junction, the hot springs trail veers to the right for another mile and requires some bushwhacking, boulder hopping, and an infamous squeeze under a rockfall to reach the destination. But the effort is worth it, as for a quarter mile along Turkey Creek, water bubbles out of the ground at 165°F, generously creating dozens of soaking pools.

## TURKEY CREEK HOT SPRINGS
8 miles round trip

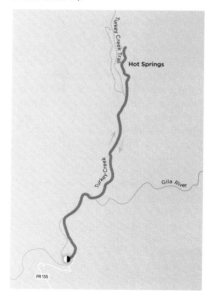

Bring a good trail map and description to make it to the hot springs. The Gila River can flood from spring runoff and summer monsoon storms. This hike should be attempted in the right season after talking with locals about current conditions. While remote and in the wilderness, the hot springs are a popular destination, and you will likely share it with other hikers or campers.

## 81. Gila Riparian Preserve

**Nearest Town:** Gila/Cliff

**Best Season to Visit:** Year-round; spring and fall for birdwatching.

**Visitor Information:** Bathrooms and dispersed camping available along the river.

**Getting There:** From Cliff, take NM 211 for about 1.5 miles. Follow the left fork in the road (NM 293) and continue up the valley about 7 miles until the road dead-ends in a national forest campground and Mogollon Box Day Use Area. The preserve begins on the north side of the green fence.

We arrived here on a warm fall afternoon. The leaves were beginning to turn various shades of yellow and gold. Past a metal gate, an old road leads hikers through the preserve to the Gila River Gaging Station. We didn't get that far, however, as my kids were immediately attracted to the sandy shores, flowing water, and endless fort building possibilities under the huge cottonwood trees. We found a good spot, laid out a blanket, broke out the binoculars and bird field guides, and whittled away the afternoon spotting colorful birds and playing freely under the cottonwoods.

Owned and managed by the Nature Conservancy, the Gila Riparian Preserve protects more than 1,200 acres of the Southwest's fragile riparian habitat and woodlands surrounding the Gila River, the last of the Southwest's major free-flowing rivers. The Lichty Ecological Research Center, located on the preserve, is a research hub where scientists study the Gila and Mimbres Rivers' flows, ecological functions, and species. The Gila River supports one of the highest concentrations of breeding birds in North America and habitat for neotropical migratory songbirds, including the federally endangered southwestern willow flycatcher. Over 300 species of bird have been recorded. A host of other rare animal species also use the preserve's habitats. Beyond the Gila River Gaging Station, hikers can continue into the rugged and challenging Mogollon Box Canyon.

### BIRDWATCHING

The Preserve and Gila/Cliff area in general host a wide array of habitat, from riverine forested floodplain to mesquite- and cactus-covered mesas, to juniper- and pinon-covered foothills, to fir- and spruce-covered mountains up to 11,000' in elevation. Expect to find an extremely broad range of species at all times of the year. Over 300 different species of birds have been recorded in this area, including numerous rare and uncommon species, such as sandhill cranes, bald eagles, willow flycatchers, common black hawks, and several species of hummingbirds (including black-chinned, broadtail, and rufous, as well as the large elegant and tiny calliope). On the preserve in early morning or late evening, watch for cordilleran and vermillion flycatchers, yellow-breasted chats, western wood pewees, pyrrhuloxias, and Bell's and solitary vireos.

### LOCAL ATTRACTIONS, BUSINESSES

*Leopold Vista Overlook and Picnic Area*: Offers vast panoramic views of the Mogollon Mountains and the Gila Wilderness. Off US 180 near Gila/Cliff.

The Gila Cliff Dwellings perched high on a cliff above the Gila River

*Art Gallery at Casitas de Gila Guesthouses*:
Features paintings, pottery, jewelry, and
more by local artists. Call ahead to
schedule a visit. (575) 535-4455, www
.galleryatthecasitas.com

## Gila South

The southern portion of the Gila area is the
most developed and visited section of the
national forest. NM 15 (a.k.a. Trail of the
Mountain Spirits Scenic Byway) leaves
from Silver City and passes through forested hillsides, deeply cut canyons, and
intermittent streams to reach the Gila Cliff
Dwellings National Monument.

### BIRDWATCHING

Cherry Creek Campground, and less than a
mile later the McMillan Campground, are
both good spots for many high-elevation
conifer forest birds, including some special-
ties of the Southwest. In nesting season,
look for spotted owls, white-throated
swifts, acorn woodpeckers, greater pewees,
cordilleran flycatchers, plumbeous vireos,
Hutton's vireos, Steller's jays, Mexican jays,
mountain chickadees, bridled titmice,
pygmy nuthatches, olive warblers, Virginia's
warblers, Grace's warblers, black-throated
gray warblers, red-faced warblers, painted
redstarts, dark-eyed juncos, hepatic tanagers, and pine siskins.

Up the road at Lake Roberts, you may
find waterfowl, such as pied-billed grebes,
double-crested cormorants, migrant
ospreys, black phoebes, western scrub-jays,
bushtits, western bluebirds, and spotted
towhees.

## 82. Gila Cliff Dwellings National Monument

(575) 536-9461

www.nps.gov/gicl

**Nearest Town:** Gila Hot Springs

**Best Season to Visit:** Year-round

**Visitor Information:** The visitor center and the dwellings are open to the public daily, except for major holidays. Check the park's website for current hours. No cell phone service or trash receptacles in the monument. Come prepared with everything you need for the day and plan to pack everything out.

**Getting There:** Located 44 miles from Silver City on NM 15. The two-lane road is slow and winding and takes about two hours to travel. Accessible to low-clearance cars.

The dwellings are family friendly and kids will relish the opportunity to climb ladders and walk freely through the ancient rooms. On our visit, we stopped first at the visitor center museum and park store, where we picked up their Junior Ranger packets, watched the educational movie, and used bathrooms with potable water and flush toilets. A short drive takes visitors to the dwellings' trailhead, where there's a small natural history museum and interpretive displays from the area. Take the 1-mile loop trail from the parking area along a lush river canyon and up several sets of rustic stairs to the dwellings. Ask your kids to imagine what life was like high in these cliffs hundreds of years ago. What did they eat? Where did their kids play? Ranger tours in the dwellings will then add details to their imagining.

Deep in the mountains of the Gila National Forest, surrounded by rugged wilderness, the Gila Cliff Dwellings preserves five connected cliff alcoves inhabited by the Mogollon people between 1275 and 1300 AD. The Tularosa Mogollon people planted the mesa above and riverside fields below the dwellings with squash, corn, and beans.

They ground cornmeal with metate and mano, wove cotton cloth, traded with other communities and cultures, hunted wild game, and gathered wild edible plants. They were skilled potters, producing handsome brown bowls with black interiors and black-on-white decorated vessels. Archaeologists suggest that about 8 to 10 families lived in the cliff dwellings for roughly one generation. About 42 rooms were constructed from layers of local flat stone and wood.

The Mogollon culture is part of what anthropologists define as Oasis-American culture. In contrast to nomadic hunter-gathering cultures of the time, the presence of reliable water sources in an otherwise arid land allowed them to develop societies centered around agriculture. In addition to the Ancient Puebloan Anasazi culture that dominated farther north in the Southwest, the Mogollon were dominant in what is now southern New Mexico, southern Arizona, and northern Mexico. It is believed that dwindling resources caused these cliff dwellers to depart their homes and abandon their fields by about 1300. Or perhaps they were ready for a new location and embarked on an adventure to seek their next place to call home. This is a good place to talk about sustainable use of natural resources with your children and how that relates to our lives today.

### HIKE | LIGHTFEATHER HOT SPRINGS

**Distance:** 0.5 miles one-way

**Difficulty:** Easy

**Getting There:** From the visitor center, cross the road to find the trailhead.

This is the most accessible undeveloped hot springs in the Gila. This hike enters the wilderness area, crosses the river a couple of times, and takes you to a natural hot spring between towering cliffs of the lower portion of the Middle Fork River. The water exits

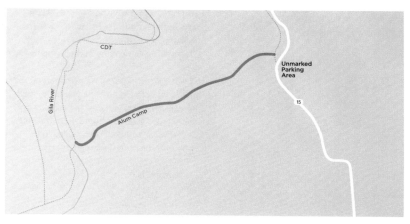

**ALUM CAMP TRAIL** 3.6 miles round trip

the cliffs at a scalding 130°F but cools to a pleasant warm temperature in small pools at the river's edge. Kids will enjoy moving the rocks around to create pools with just the right temperature. Watch for dragon-flies flitting around as you soak. Leaf colors are vibrant along this trail in the fall.

### HIKE | ALUM CAMP TRAIL

**Distance:** 3.6 miles round trip

**Difficulty:** Moderate

**Getting There:** Alum Camp Trailhead is located on NM 15 between mile posts 35 and 36. Look for a large gravel pullout on the crest of a hill to the west. The Alum Camp trailhead is marked only by a small metal wilderness boundary sign.

This short but fun hike begins with expan-sive views on the south rim of the Gila River Valley. My kids were delighted to find horny toads and other lizards in abundance along the way. The trail descends along long switchbacks down a piñon-juni-per-dotted hillside, then gradually descends to the sycamore-lined riverbank. Ask your kids to examine the multicolored bark of

the ancient sycamores. If the water is low and you don't want to climb back up the hill, turn right at the Gila River Trail 724 junction and follow the river back to the bridge between Forks and Grapevine Campgrounds for a 4.3-mile trek.

### HIKE | JORDAN HOT SPRINGS

**Distance:** 6 miles one-way

**Difficulty:** Moderate

**Getting There:** The TJ Corral trailhead is 1 mile from the Gila Visitor Center on the road to the Gila Cliff Dwellings National Monument.

A rugged hike into a remote setting with semideveloped natural pools makes this one of the most popular thermal features in the Gila Wilderness. Try this route as an overnight backpack with older kids and teenagers, who will find the pools warm and inviting after a long hike, as will their parents. The surrounding canyon, with towering cliffs and lush plant life, is majes-tic. The quickest route is to take Little Bear Canyon Trail 729 until you hit the Middle Fork River. Cross the river and continue on Middle Fork Trail 157 to the hot springs.

**JORDAN HOT SPRINGS** 6 miles one-way

There are several good campsites across the river and upstream from the hot springs. Camping is prohibited within 400 yards of the springs.

## CAMPING

Upper and Lower Scorpion Campgrounds are located on the road to the cliff dwellings. Small RVs can park overnight in the parking lots; all sites are otherwise walk-in tent sites. Two free Forest Service campgrounds—Forks and Grapevine—are located along the Gila River off NM 15 before the town of Gila Hot Springs.

In the town of Gila Hot Springs, find an RV park with drive-through sites along the west side of the road across from Doc Campbell's Post, a country store with a few amenities and free Wi-Fi during open hours.

The Gila Hot Springs Campground is a privately owned campground on the edge of the Gila River with 12 shaded campsites and three natural hot pools. Flower gardens

and the flowing river add to the relaxing atmosphere of this lovely place. Kids are welcome, though rowdy behavior is not. They will enjoy soaking and playing by the river.

After dark, clothing is optional if all the guests in a pool agree. The pools are open for campers all night; day-use soakers are restricted to daylight hours. Reservations can be made online. Follow signs to the right off NM 15, passing a goat farm on the way. (575) 536-9944, www.gilahotsprings campground.com.

## POINT OF INTEREST: LAKE ROBERTS

This 72-acre reservoir sits at 6,000', surrounded by ponderosa and oak forest. Managed by the New Mexico Department of Game and Fish and stocked with rainbow trout in the spring and fall, this lake is a favorite among anglers. A boat ramp and picnic area are the only amenities on the lake. Two campgrounds sit on the hill overlooking the lake, with tent and RV sites and restrooms.

## LOCAL ATTRACTIONS, BUSINESSES

*Wilderness Lodge and Hot Springs*: A lodge and adventure basecamp for large groups. (575) 536-9749, www.gilahot.com

### Special Considerations in the Wilderness

Stay clear of narrow canyons during flash flood weather; river crossings may be dangerous during high water runoff in the spring or during summer thunderstorms. Keep your head and nose out of hot springs water. A warm-water amoeba, *Naegleria fowleri*, can enter the brain through nasal passages and cause a rare type of meningitis. Always filter water from creeks or springs before drinking.

*Doc Campbell's Post*: The only store in the area. (575) 536-9551

## 83. City of Rocks State Park

(575) 536-2800

www.emnrd.state.nm.us/SPD/cityofrocks
statepark.html

**Nearest Town:** Deming/Silver City

**Best Season to Visit:** Fall–spring

**Visitor Information:** Open year-round. Entrance and camping fees apply.

**Getting There:** The park lies in the Mimbres River Valley, halfway between Deming and Silver City along US 180, then 3 miles northeast on NM 61 and 1 mile down a side road.

&#9855; accessible

In the middle of the Chihuahuan Desert region of southwestern New Mexico, large, sculptured volcanic rock columns and pinnacles rise as high as 40' and cover a square mile. This unusual scene is known as City of Rocks, where the rock formations are separated by paths or lanes resembling city streets. These rocks were formed about 34.9 million years ago when a very large volcano—Emory Caldera, centered near Hillsboro Peak at the southern end of the Black Range—erupted. Erosion over millions of years slowly formed the sculptured columns seen today, creating a stunning, otherworldly landscape. Little vegetation grows around the boulders, just the occasional Emory oak tree; between most boulders are either bare, sandy chambers or narrow, slot-like passages.

With campsites, hiking trails, excellent mountain biking, wildlife viewing, birdwatching, dark sky stargazing, picnic areas, and a desert botanical garden, the park offers adventure enough for a weekend. Kids will most enjoy exploring the tall rocks that can be climbed and others with sheer sides that form narrow mazes. The new

visitor center includes a large display area and modern restrooms with hot showers.

### STAR PARTIES

City of Rocks State Park has its own observatory with a 14" telescope operated by solar power. The park, along with the National Public Observatory, hosts one star party per month in the Orion Campground. During the two-hour star parties, visitors will get a laser-guided presentation of the night sky, use an iPad to identify constellations, and will get to look through the telescopes.

## 84. Faywood Hot Springs

(575) 536-9663

www.faywoodhotsprings.com

**Nearest Town:** Deming

**Best Season to Visit:** Year-round

**Visitor Information:** Cabins, guesthouses, RV hookups, and tent camping are all available on-site. The visitor center has a hot drink bar with snacks for sale, but bring your own food if you plan to stay overnight. Some pools are clothing optional.

**Getting There:** From Deming, take US 180 west for 24 miles. Turn right (north) onto NM 61 and find the hot springs entrance after about 2.4 miles.

Faywood Hot Springs—a rustic, natural geothermal resort in southwestern New Mexico—has many outdoor public and private soaking pools for those looking to relax in healing mineral water baths. Children are welcome at the hot springs but must be accompanied by an adult at all times. Likely due to its remote location, we had a public pool to ourselves when we visited, affording our kids the freedom to splash and play water games.

Hiking in the Florida Mountains in Rockhound State Park

## 85. Rockhound State Park

(575) 546-6182

www.emnrd.state.nm.us/SPD/rockhound
statepark.html

**Nearest Town:** Deming

**Best Season to Visit:** Fall–spring

**Visitor Information:** Open year-round.
Admission and camping fees apply. The gate
to the park is closed sunset to 7 a.m.

**Getting There:** From Deming, take NM 549 east
for 4.3 miles. Turn right onto NM 142/Stirrup
Road SE. Veer left onto NM 198 to enter the
park.

&#9855; accessible

Nestled at the base of the Little Florida
Mountains with commanding views of
expansive desert, Rockhound State Park is
known for its mineral specimens. Unlike
most national and state parks where
removing natural objects is forbidden, here
visitors are encouraged to prospect and col-
lect minerals, subject only to a 15-pound
weight limit. Gray perlite, thunder eggs,
geodes, jasper, onyx, agate, crystalline rhyo-
lite, Apache tears (obsidian), and quartz
crystals are among the more common rocks
and minerals found in the park.

On our arrival at the park, my kids were
most excited about prospecting for thunder
eggs. Thunder eggs are rough spheres, most
about the size of a baseball. They usually
look like ordinary rocks on the outside, but
slicing them in half and polishing them
may reveal intricate patterns and colors.

Kids may wonder where they got their
name, and the story won't disappoint. The
name "thunder egg" is believed to come

from Indigenous peoples who found these
rocks near Mount Jefferson and Mount
Hood in Oregon and thought that when the
gods or spirits who inhabited the mountains became angry with one another they
would hurl the rocks at each other with
accompanying thunder and lightning.

A 1.1-mile loop path runs over the lower
slopes starting at either side of the campground. The main location to find minerals
is a shallow ravine toward the south edge of
the park reached by walking a couple hundred yards along the south end of the path,
then scrambling up the hill a little. Rock
hounds should come equipped with a large
hammer, several chisels, and a spade and be
prepared to spend several hours on the hillside.

The park has a nice campground with
good facilities, spacious sites, and
far-reaching views. Behind the campsite,
steep, rocky, cacti-covered hills rise several
hundred feet above the desert.

### WILDLIFE

Despite the dry, seemingly inhospitable
environment, life abounds. The area is
home to many lizards and snakes, deer,
pronghorn, coyotes, prairie dogs, rabbits,
badgers, and many birds. Mountain lions
and desert bighorn sheep may be seen at
the higher elevations of the Florida Mountains.

After winter rains, the Mexican poppies
grow in spring around the park in spectacular color.

# Resources

Alley, Sarah Bennett. *Mountain Biking New Mexico*. Guilford, CT: Falcon Guides, 2001.

Catron, Jean-Luc, et al. *A Field Guide to the Plants and Animals of the Middle Rio Grande Bosque*. Albuquerque: University of New Mexico Press, 2008.

D'Antonio, Bob. *Mountain Biking Northern New Mexico: A Guide to the Taos, Santa Fe, and Albuquerque Area's Greatest Off-Road Bicycle Rides*. Guilford, CT: Falcon Guides, 2004.

Foley, Jay. *Taos Rock Climbs & Boulders of Northern New Mexico*. Boulder, CO: Sharp End Publishing, 2005.

Hoard, Dorothy. *A Guide to Bandelier National Monument*. Los Alamos, NM: Los Alamos Historical Society, 2009.

Jackson, Dennis R. *Rock Climbing New Mexico*. Guilford, CT: Falcon Guides, 2006.

Julyan, Bob. *Best Hikes with Children New Mexico*. Seattle, WA: Mountaineers Books, 2003.

Julyan, Bob. *Wild Guide: Passport to New Mexico Wilderness*. Albuquerque: New Mexico Wilderness Alliance, 2016.

Julyan, Robert, and Mary Stuever, eds. *Field Guide to the Sandia Mountains*. Albuquerque: University of New Mexico Press, 2005.

Littlefield, Larry J., and Pearl M. Burns. *Wildflowers of the Northern and Central Mountains of New Mexico: Sangre de Cristo, Jemez, Sandia, and Manzano*. Albuquerque: University of New Mexico Press, 2015.

Martin, Craig, Teralene Foxx, and Dorothy Hoard. *Plants of the Jemez Mountains: Volume 1–3*. Los Alamos, NM: All Seasons Publishing, 2018.

Selby, Christina. *Best Wildflower Hikes New Mexico*. Guilford, CT: Falcon Guides, 2020.

Tekiela, Stan. *Birds of New Mexico*. Cambridge, MN: Adventure Publications, 2003.

Tekiela, Stan. *Birds of the Southwest*. Cambridge, MN: Adventure Quick Guides, 2014.

The author and her family on Hermit's Peak

# About the Author

Christina Selby is an independent conservation photographer, writer, and naturalist. She visited Santa Fe 16 years ago at the end of a six-month cross-country road trip and never left. Her work has led her to search for lost monkeys in the Amazon, follow honeybees through the Himalayas, kayak the Sea of Cortez, track elusive Mexican wolves in the Southwest, and chase wildflower blooms across the stunning landscapes of the Southern Rockies. Her favorite adventures, though, are those spent with her two boys, husband, and Great Pyrenees, Glacier, in the wilds of New Mexico. In 2020, Falcon Guides published her *Best Wildflower Hikes New Mexico*, detailing the wildflowers found on 42 hikes across the state. Her work has been published in *New Mexico Magazine*, *bioGraphic*, *Scientific American*, *National Geographic Online*, *Outdoor Photographer*, *High Country News*, and Mongabay, among other publications.

SOUTHWEST ADVENTURE SERIES
*Ashley M. Biggers*, Series Editor

The Southwest Adventure Series provides practical how-to guidebooks for readers seeking authentic outdoor and cultural excursions that highlight the unique landscapes of the American Southwest. Books in the series feature the best ecotourism adventures, world-class outdoor recreation sites, back-road points of interest, and culturally significant archaeological sites, as well as lead readers to the best sustainable accommodations and farm-to-table restaurants in Arizona, Colorado, Nevada, New Mexico, Utah, and Southern California.

Also available in the Southwest Adventure Series:

*Arizona's Scenic Roads and Hikes: Unforgettable Journeys in the Grand Canyon State* by Roger Naylor

*Arizona State Parks: A Guide to Amazing Places in the Grand Canyon State* by Roger Naylor

*Eco-Travel New Mexico: 86 Natural Destinations, Green Hotels, and Sustainable Adventures* by Ashley M. Biggers

*Skiing New Mexico: A Guide to Snow Sports in the Land of Enchantment* by Daniel Gibson